CHILDREN'S ENCYCLOPEDIA OF
Earth

CHILDREN'S ENCYCLOPEDIA OF
Earth

MICHAEL ALLABY

RED
LEMON
PRESS

This edition published in 2015 by
Red Lemon Press
(an imprint of Weldon Owen)
Deepdene Lodge
Deepdene Avenue
Dorking RH5 4AT

Website: www.weldonowen.co.uk

Conceived and produced by Weldon Owen Pty Ltd
61 Victoria Street, McMahons Point
Sydney, NSW 2060, Australia

ISBN: 978-1-78342-060-5

Printed in Latvia by Livonia

A Weldon Owen production

10 9 8 7 6 5 4 3 2 1

Previous page: Molten lava meets the sea with clouds of steam
on the island of Kilauea, Hawaii, USA.

Right: From a helicopter, the cliffs of one of the 115 islands of
the Seychelles can be seen rising from turquoise-blue waters.

Contents

How to use this book 8

Our Place in Space. 10

The Universe. 12
The Solar System 14
Planet Earth 16
    Earth's formation. 18
    Earth's Sun 20
    Earth's Moon. 22

Earth's History. 24

Life on Earth. 26
    Plants through time. .28
    Explosion of life 30
    Teeming oceans 32
    Age of fish 34
    End of an era 36
    Rise of reptiles. 38
    Dinosaurs rule. 40
    Age of mammals 42
    Home to humans 44

Inside Earth 46

Journey to the Centre. 48
Restless Earth 50
Continents on the Move. 52
Folds and Faults 54
Rocks 56
    Igneous rock 58
    Sedimentary rock 60
    Metamorphic rock. 62
    Rocks in the landscape 64
    Using rocks 66

Minerals 68
    Ornamental minerals and crystals 70
    Precious and semiprecious minerals. 72
    Metals 74
Fossils 76
    Plants and invertebrates 78
    Vertebrates 80
    Reconstructing fossils 82

Dynamic Earth. 84

Volcanoes 86
    Hot-spot volcanoes .88
    Kilauea 90
    Volcanoes around the world 92
    Volcanic landscapes. .94
    Craters and calderas .96
Earthquakes 98
    Tsunamis. 100
    Earthquakes around the world 102
Geysers and Hot Springs. 104
Glaciers and Ice Sheets .106
Avalanches and Landslides 108
Weathering and Erosion 110
    Eroded landscapes .112

Oceans. 114

World Oceans. 116
    Pacific Ocean 118
    Atlantic Ocean 120
    Indian Ocean. 122
    Arctic Ocean 124
    Southern Ocean 126
The Spreading Seas. 128

Currents 130
Waves and Tides. 132
Ocean Zones and Habitats 134
    Coral reefs 136
    Along the coast 138
    Into the deep 140
    The ocean floor. 142

Land. 146

Mapping Earth 148
Continents 150
Islands 156
    Atolls 158
Ecosystems 160
    Tropical forests 162
    Temperate and coniferous forests 166
    Grasslands 168
    Tundra 170
    Deserts 172
    Mountains 176
    Rivers 180
    Estuaries 182
    Wetlands. 184
    Arctic regions 186
    Antarctic regions. 188
    Agricultural areas 190
    Urban areas 192
Biodiversity 194
Global Environment 196

Weather. 198

World Weather. 200
Climate Zones. 202
The Weather Engine 204
    World winds 206
    The water cycle. 208
    Clouds 210
    Kinds of clouds 212
    Winds 214
    Rain, hail and snow. 216
    Storms 218
    Tornadoes 220
    Hurricanes. 221
    Lightning 222
Global Freezing. 224
Global Warming 226
    Effects of global warming 228

Earth's Resources. 230

Earth's Riches 232
    Oil and gas 234
    Coal 236
    Solar and wind energy 238
    Power from water. 240

Fact File 242
Glossary 248
Index 250
Credits 256

How to use this book

This book is divided into eight chapters. The first chapter locates Earth in the Solar System and the Universe. The second chapter guides us through Earth's history. The third and fourth chapters delve deep beneath Earth's surface to discover what it is made of and witness it in action. The fifth chapter explores the oceans; the sixth travels over the land. The seventh chapter looks above at the weather. The final chapter reviews Earth's resources and energy sources. An extensive fact file and glossary can be found at the end of the book.

ABBREVIATIONS

mm	millimetres	in	inches
cm	centimetres	ft	feet
m	metres	mi	miles
km	kilometres	sq. mi	square miles
sq. km	square	t	tonnes
	kilometres	kg	kilograms
°	degrees (temperature)	g	grams
°N	degrees north	mya	million years ago
°S	degrees south	bya	billion years ago

Colour coding
Each chapter is colour coded.

Section name
This shows the topic being discussed in the page or section.

Maps
Some maps look at geographical features; others highlight aspects of the section's subject.

Introductory text
This text introduces the topic of the page or section.

Full-page feature
Some pages have a full-page feature. These show aspects of the topic in more detail.

Inset box
Labelled illustrations or diagrams present related topics.

PACIFIC FACTS

Area	155.6 million square km (60.1 mil. sq. miles)
Average depth	4,001 m (13,127 feet)
Maximum depth	10,920 m (35,826 feet)
Maximum width	18,000 km (11,185 miles)
Maximum length	13,900 km (8,637 miles)
Coastline length	135,663 km (84,301 miles)

WORLD RECORDS

WORLD'S SMALLEST COUNTRY
Vatican City, 0.44 square km
(0.17 sq. mile)

WORLD'S TALLEST STALAGMITE
Kráshnohorská Cave, Slovakia,
32 m (105 feet)

FAST FACT

You cannot travel to Earth's centre. The pressure would squeeze you and the heat would cook you before you reached the mantle. The deepest you can go is 2,080 m (6,824 feet) into Voronya Cave, Georgia.

GEOLOGICAL TIMELINE

A number of spreads in the Earth's History chapter are accompanied by a geological timeline. This is divided into two parts – larger eras and smaller periods. In each spread, one period of time is highlighted.

FACT BOXES

Three kinds of fact boxes appear in this book: Ocean Facts in the Oceans chapter; World Records in the Land chapter; and Fast Facts throughout.

PALEOZOIC: AGE OF ANCIENT LIFE				
CAMBRIAN	ORDOVICIAN	SILURIAN	DEVONIAN	CARBONIFEROUS
542	488	444	416	359

Subsections
Within each chapter
are sections, and some
sections have their
own subsections.

Arrows
Arrows pinpoint
each illustrated
object.

Feature box
Interesting aspects
of the topic appear
in feature boxes.

Running head
The right-hand
running head shows
different sections
within the chapter.

Object information
Each object is named.
Some objects have
additional information.

Distribution map
This is explained in
detail at the bottom
of this page.

Photo and caption
Captioned photos
show scenes or images
relating to the theme
of the page.

Habitat Watch
This is explained in
detail at the bottom
of this page.

Main image
This illustrates the
theme of the page,
and is accompanied
by a caption.

Labelled diagram
Detailed, labelled
diagrams supply
more information.

DISTRIBUTION MAP

Each ecosystem discussed in
the Land chapter is located
on a world map. The featured
ecosystem is coloured yellow. If
a second ecosystem is shown, it is
coloured blue. Green indicates
where the ecosystems overlap.

☐ Temperate forests   ☐ Coniferous forests   ☐ Temperate and coniferous forests

HABITAT WATCH

Most habitats and ecosystems
on Earth are fragile – they are
sensitive to changes, which may
be caused by humans. Habitat
Watch boxes highlight habitats,
or animals within them, that are
particularly vulnerable.

HABITAT WATCH

Crown-of-thorns starfish, seen here
feeding on coral polyps, attack reefs
throughout the world. They have
caused considerable damage
to Australia's Great Barrier
Reef. Reefs also suffer
from bleaching, caused
by the loss of their algae due
to pollution.

	MESOZOIC: AGE OF REPTILES			CENOZOIC: AGE OF MAMMALS	
AN	TRIASSIC	JURASSIC	CRETACEOUS	PALEOGENE	NEOGENE
	251	200	146	65.5	23	0

Our Place in Space

The Universe

Earth and the other planets, the Sun and the other stars, galaxies, the space around them, and the energy that comes from them are all part of what we call the Universe. About 14 billion years ago, all matter and energy, even space itself, was packed into a single point. Then there was a tremendous explosion – the Big Bang – and the basic materials of the Universe, the gases hydrogen and helium, came to be. These gases collected into large bodies called galaxies. As stars within the galaxies exploded, other elements formed, including carbon, the building block of life on Earth.

Earth and the Solar System formed from a cloud of gas and dust 4.6 million years ago. The Orion Nebula may one day collapse to form a solar system much like ours.

LIFE IN THE UNIVERSE

We have learned everything we know about the Universe with the help of robots called satellites and space probes. Since the 1960s they have roamed the Solar System to explore where no one has ever travelled. So far, no probe has found evidence of life beyond Earth.

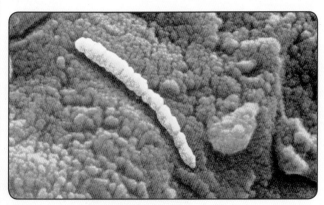

When a meteorite from Mars was viewed under a microscope, this tubelike structure was found. Some think this may be a tiny Martian fossil.

HOW WOULD LIFE LOOK?
The earliest living things on Earth were simple cells. Perhaps other life in the Universe is as simple as this creature?

1 EARTH
Our home is a small, watery, blue planet that orbits about eight light-minutes from the warmth and light of an ordinary yellow star, the Sun. So far, Earth is the only place in the Universe where we know life exists.

OUR PLACE IN SPACE

Earth is just one of eight planets in the Solar System. Our Solar System is part of the Milky Way galaxy, just one galaxy in a cluster of galaxies called the Local Group. These clusters of galaxies gather into superclusters of billions of galaxies.

THE BLUE MARBLE
Astronauts who visited the Moon saw the distant Earth as a blue marble floating in the blackness of space, above the grey, lifeless landscape of the Moon.

5 THE KNOWN UNIVERSE
To reach the most distant
objects in the known Universe,
even travelling at the speed of light,
it would take nearly 14 billion years.
Along the way we would pass chains
and clusters of billions of other galaxies.

4 THE LOCAL GROUP
A beam of light would take 2.5 million
years to reach the closest large galaxy
to ours, the Andromeda galaxy. This is
one of our neighbours in a small family
of galaxies called the Local Group.

3 THE MILKY WAY GALAXY
Even zipping at the speed of light
(300,000 km per second/186,000
miles/s) – the fastest that
anything can travel – a
light beam would still
take 100,000 years
to travel across
our galaxy.

2 THE SOLAR SYSTEM
Zoom out, and Earth is
just one planet in a system
of worlds, which includes
seven other major planets
and several dwarf planets.
It takes about six hours for
light to travel from the Sun
to the dwarf planet Pluto,
on the outer edges of
the Solar System.

The Solar System

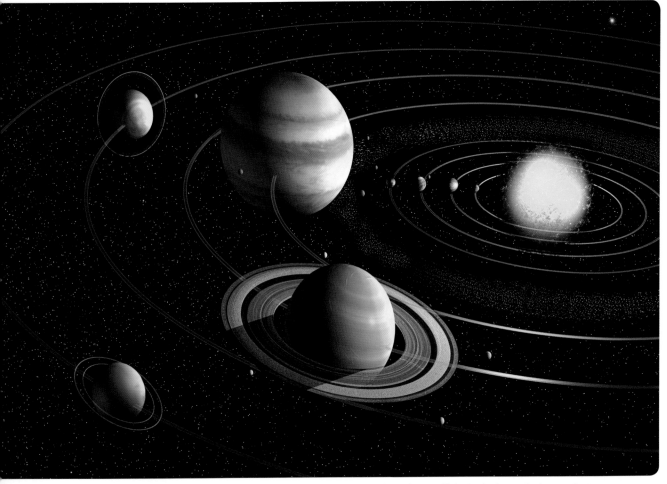

The major planets travel around the Sun in ringlike paths called orbits. The inner planets do not take very long to orbit the Sun, but it may take the outer planets many years.

Earth belongs to a cosmic family called the Solar System. The Sun controls this collection of eight major planets, dozens of moons and countless asteroids and comets. The major planets fall into two groups. The inner, rocky planets are Mercury, Venus, Earth and Mars. The outer gas giants are Jupiter, Saturn, Uranus and Neptune. Tiny Pluto was called a planet when it was discovered in 1930, but in 2006 it was reclassified as a dwarf planet. It is just one member of the Kuiper Belt, a vast collection of small, icy worlds at the edge of the Solar System. The other two dwarf planets are Ceres and Eris, but there are many more objects waiting to be classified.

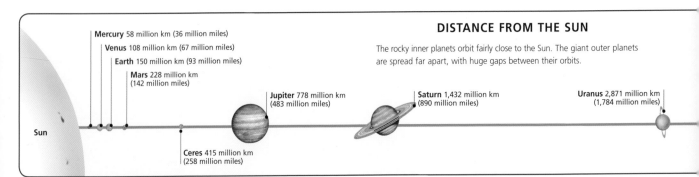

DISTANCE FROM THE SUN

The rocky inner planets orbit fairly close to the Sun. The giant outer planets are spread far apart, with huge gaps between their orbits.

Mercury 58 million km (36 million miles)
Venus 108 million km (67 million miles)
Earth 150 million km (93 million miles)
Mars 228 million km (142 million miles)
Jupiter 778 million km (483 million miles)
Saturn 1,432 million km (890 million miles)
Uranus 2,871 million km (1,784 million miles)
Ceres 415 million km (258 million miles)

Sun

THE INNER PLANETS

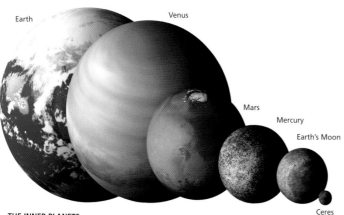

The four planets closest to the Sun make up the inner Solar System. They consist mostly of rock and are much smaller than the four gas giants.

Earth
Venus
Mars
Mercury
Earth's Moon
Ceres

THE OUTER PLANETS

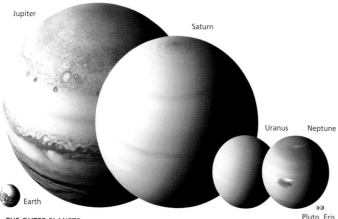

The four planets of the outer Solar System are called gas giants because they are largely made up of the gases hydrogen and helium.

Jupiter
Saturn
Uranus
Neptune
Earth
Pluto Eris

Asteroid belt Asteroids are made of rock and metal. Many thousands of them orbit between Mars and Jupiter in the asteroid belt.

Comet Hale Bopp A comet is a body of ice and dust that orbits the Sun. As it nears, the ice warms up and the comet forms long gas and dust tails.

THE PLANETS

The eight major planets in the Solar System are very different in their size and structure. Together, the mass of all the planets would make 447 Earths, which is just 0.13 per cent of the mass of the Sun.

 MERCURY
Mercury's surface is covered with craters and basins. It has a large central core.

 VENUS
Venus is covered with white sulfuric clouds, under which lie volcanoes and mountains.

 EARTH
Earth has a solid core of iron and nickel, a liquid outer core and a lighter mantle and crust.

 MARS
Mars is a freezing planet with ancient craters and volcanoes. Water is frozen at the poles.

 JUPITER
Jupiter is a giant ball of gas, mainly hydrogen and helium, and does not have a solid surface.

 SATURN
Saturn is a gas giant topped with cloud belts and swirling storms of ammonia and ice crystals.

 URANUS
Uranus has a gassy surface, below which is a slushy mix of water and gases and a rocky core.

 NEPTUNE
Neptune is coloured blue by the methane in its surface, below which is slush and a rocky core.

Neptune 4,498 million km (2,795 million miles)

Pluto 5,914 million km (3,675 million miles)

Eris 10,122 million km (6,290 million miles)

Planet Earth

Earth's landforms can be photographed from satellites in space. This view shows part of Europe and Africa, with the boot-shaped Italy extending into the Mediterranean Sea.

Earth is the only place we know of in the entire Universe with the right conditions for life to thrive. Liquid water is vital for all life and Earth is at the right distance from the Sun for water to exist on the surface. If Earth were closer to the Sun, our rivers and oceans would boil and evaporate. If further away from the Sun, Earth would be a frozen world of ice. Beneath the rocky surface, Earth has a hot, molten interior. Liquid rock erupts to the surface from volcanoes and weaknesses in Earth's crust. This continuously renews the surface, creating new mountains and raising minerals from deep within the planet.

OUR ATMOSPHERE

Earth's atmosphere is a layer of gases that surrounds the planet.
It is divided into several regions. The troposphere contains most
of the water vapour that we see as clouds. Above that is the
stratosphere, where the ozone layer protects us from harmful
radiation. Beyond the upper boundary of the atmosphere lies
the cold darkness of space.

Exosphere
More than
500 km (310 miles)

Thermosphere
80–500 km (50–310 miles)

Mesosphere
50–80 km (30–50 miles)

Stratosphere
15–50 km (9–30 miles)

Troposphere (Sea level)
0–15 km (0–9 miles)

THIN LAYER
Compared with the
size of Earth, the
atmosphere looks
as thin as a coat
of varnish.

PLANET OF EXTREMES

The surface of Earth offers an incredible
variety of environments. Life of some kind
can exist in almost all of them.

Polar regions The frigid poles receive much
less sunlight than the rest of the planet.

Deserts Rainfall is so low in these harsh
regions that little vegetation can grow.

Tropics The regions near the equator are warm
all year round, with plentiful rainfall.

Mountains Plant life changes higher up
a mountain as the temperature drops.

COMPARING EARTH

Earth is a very active world.
Activity above and below
the surface is continuously
forming new mountains
and trenches. These surface
features are slowly worn away
by water in rivers, rain, ice
and the pounding ocean
waves. Our closest neighbour
planets, Venus and Mars, do
not have liquid water on their
surfaces. Their mountains
and trenches have not eroded
as much and are larger than
anything on Earth.

Olympus Mons Mars
(26 km / 16 miles)

Maxwell Montes Venus
(10.8 km / 6¾ miles)

Mount Everest Earth
(8.85 km / 5½ miles)

Diana Chasma Venus
(–2.9 km / –1¾ miles)

Mariana Trench Earth
(–11 km / –7 miles)

Earth's formation

About 4.6 billion years ago, a massive, rotating cloud of hot gas and dust condensed to form the Solar System. The planets first appeared around a young star, the Sun, as grains of dust that clumped together, forming larger and larger bodies. Evidence suggests at least two planets formed about 150 million km (93 million miles) from the Sun: the young Earth and a small planet called Theia. The two worlds smashed together and debris from both planets formed the Moon. Earth suffered countless collisions with smaller objects, slowly gaining extra mass. Initially the planet was completely molten, but as Earth grew it cooled and formed a solid crust. Enough gravity was generated to retain a gaseous atmosphere that includes water vapour.

ROCKS FROM SPACE

Not all material from the early Solar System became the Sun and the planets. Millions of small, rocky bodies called asteroids circle the Sun, mainly between the orbits of Mars and Jupiter. Some are mere pebbles; others are the size of mountains. Objects that burn up in the atmosphere are called meteors. Objects that reach the surface are called meteorites.

From the air, the scar of Meteor Crater in Arizona, USA, is clearly seen. It was caused by a large meteorite about 50,000 years ago.

A SHORT HISTORY OF EARTH

In the beginning
Dust and debris from the massive cloud around the young Sun collect together to form the inner planets. Because of gravity these little worlds collide, forming larger and larger objects, eventually becoming planets.

Heating up
Earth is struck, and debris from the impact forms the Moon. Many bombardments, plus heat from within Earth, create a superheated, molten planet. Heavy elements sink to the centre while lighter ones rise.

Cooling off
Earth cools and forms a solid, rocky crust. The atmosphere forms. Gases ejected from volcanoes and other sources from deep within the planet add to the atmosphere.

Settling down
There are fewer impacts from space. Earth's interior divides into a core and mantle. Water vapour in the sky condenses and rain falls on the planet, creating oceans. The stage for life is set.

FORMING THE SOLAR SYSTEM

1 A gigantic cloud of gas and dust collapses. The cloud begins to rotate and develops into a flattened disk.

2 After millions of years, most of the material gathers in the centre, forming what eventually becomes the Sun. Out along the disk, matter clumps together in bands.

3 Collections of dust form rocky bodies several miles across, which collide and join with each other to become the inner planets.

4 Eight planets, including Earth, remain in orbits around the Sun.

Earth underwent a period of intense bombardment early in its history. Each impact added more mass to the young planet.

Earth's Sun

The Sun is the centre of the Solar System. This enormous star gives us all the light and heat we need to grow food and keep warm. But it is not the largest star in the Universe – in fact, it is quite a small one. It seems very big and bright to us because it is only 150 million km (93 million miles) away from Earth. Light from the Sun takes only eight minutes to reach us; light from the next brightest star takes eight years! Scientists believe the Sun was formed about 4.6 billion years ago, perhaps when a nearby star exploded and caused a huge cloud of dust and gas to collapse in on itself. The hot, central part of the cloud became the Sun, while some smaller pieces formed around it and became the planets.

SUN FACTS

ORIGIN OF NAME
From Old English word *sunne*

DISCOVERED
Known since antiquity

AGE OF THE SUN
4.6 billion years

GRAVITY
28 (Earth = 1)

VOLUME
1,304,000 (Earth = 1)

DIAMETER
1,392,530 km (865,278 miles)

CORE TEMPERATURE
15 million°C (27 million°F)

Photosphere

Convective zone

Radiative zone

Core

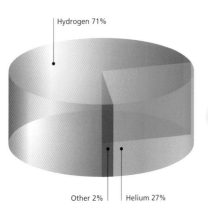

Hydrogen 71%

Other 2%   Helium 27%

INSIDE THE SUN
The Sun is made up of gases, mostly hydrogen, and is powered by a process called nuclear fusion. Energy is produced in the superhot core.

Sunspots

Prominence

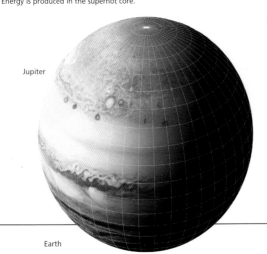

Jupiter

Jupiter

Earth

HOW BIG IS THE SUN?

The Sun is 900 times bigger than Jupiter, the largest planet. Jupiter itself is 1,112 times larger than Earth.

North pole

Sunspots

Sunspots

South pole

STUDYING THE SUN

In 1995 an observatory called SOHO was launched to study the Sun at a distance of 1.5 million km (930,000 miles) from Earth, where it had an uninterrupted view of the Sun.

Images from SOHO provide information about the inner workings of the Sun.

ENERGY BURST
Solar flares are huge eruptions that occur at the Sun's surface. They release a massive amount of energy far into space.

RIBBONS OF LIGHT
When particles from solar flares hit Earth's polar regions, they cause colourful ribbons of light called auroras, or northern and southern lights.

A penumbra of brighter, hotter gas surrounds the umbra in larger spots.

The umbra is the dark, cool core of the sunspot.

INSIDE A SUNSPOT
Sunspots are dark patches that extend deep into the surface of the Sun. They occur where gases stop boiling and the surface cools down. Sunspots are often much larger than Earth.

Sunspots extend deep into the top layer of the Sun.

Earth's Moon

The Moon is Earth's only natural satellite. It formed soon after Earth did, from the debris that flew out when another object struck Earth. As the Moon formed, it was constantly bombarded by meteorites, which punched deep craters into its surface and created broad basins. Dark lava flowed from under the surface to fill the basins. Early astronomers thought these dark areas were the dried-up beds of oceans, so they called them maria, which means 'seas' in Latin. Astronomer Neil Armstrong became the first human to walk on the Moon in 1969. From then until 1972 the Apollo program landed another 11 people on the Moon for stays of a few days.

MOON FACTS

ORIGIN OF NAME
Mona, the Anglo-Saxon Word for 'Moon'

DISTANCE FROM EARTH
384,401 km (238,856 miles)

DIAMETER
3,476 km (2,160 miles)

MASS
1.2% X Earth's mass

ATMOSPHERE
None

LENGTH OF DAY (IN EARTH DAYS)
Rotation time and solar day: both 29.5

Rocky crust

Rocky mantle

Molten zone

Core

Montes Jura

SINUS IRIDUM (Bay of Rainbows)

MARE IMBRIUM (Sea of Showers)

Plato

Cassini

Aristillus

Euler   Archimedes

Timocharis

APOLLO 15 LANDING SITE

Montes Apenninus

OCEANUS PROCELLARUM (Ocean of Storms)

Eratosthenes

Kepler

Copernicus

APOLLO 12 LANDING SITE

APOLLO 14 LANDING SITE

Letronne

MARE COGNITUM (Sea of Knowledge)

Ptolemaeus

Gassendi

Alphonsus   Albate

MARE HUMORUM (Sea of Moisture)

MARE NUBIUM (Sea of Clouds)

Arzachel

Purbach

Pitatus

Deslandres

Tycho

FORMING A CRATER
The Moon's craters were formed when asteroids, meteorites or comets smashed into its surface at high speed.

The object hits the surface and a wide cavity is formed.

Material from the surface is thrown outwards and sometimes forms other craters where it lands.

PHASES OF THE MOON
As the Moon revolves around us, we see different parts of it lit by the Sun. When the Moon lies between us and the Sun, the side of the Moon facing us is dark – the New Moon. When it is opposite the Sun, the Moon appears fully lit – the Full Moon.

New Moon

Waxing Quarter

First Quarter

Waxing Gibbous

Full Moon

GORIS
...
◦ Aristoteles
doxus   Hercules ◦   ◦ Atlas
asus

RE SERENITATIS
a of serenity)

◦ Posidonius

Cleomedes ◦

Macrobius ◦
APOLLO 17
LANDING SITE

MARE
CRISIUM
(Sea of Crises)

MARE
TRANQUILLITATIS
(Sea of Tranquillity)

APOLLO 11
LANDING SITE

MARE
FECUNDITATIS
(Sea of fertility)

APOLLO 16
DING SITE

neophilus

MARE
NECTARIS
(Sea of Nectar)

rina ◦

Fracastorius ◦

◦ Piccolomini

Earth

The Moon

HOW BIG IS THE MOON?
The Moon is 27 per cent the size of Earth.

MAPPING THE MOON

The nearside hemisphere (left) is the side of
the Moon that always faces Earth. The farside
hemisphere (below) was revealed only when
probes visited. The Moon has a small hot core,
a thick mantle and a cratered crust.

Birkhoff ◦

D'Alembert ◦

Landau ◦
Kovalevskaya ◦

MARE
MOSCOVIENSE
(Sea of Moscow)   Fitzgerald ◦   ◦ Cockcroft

◦ Mach

Mendeleev ◦   ◦ Anderson   Hertzsprung ◦

◦ Schuster

Chaplygin ◦   Korolev ◦

Keeler ◦   ◦ Heaviside
Tsiolkovskiy
◦ Aitken   Galois ◦

Gagarin ◦
MARE
INGENII
(Sea of Cleverness)   ◦ Van de Graaff
Pavlov ◦   ◦ Leeuwenhoek
Roche ◦
Leibnitz ◦   ◦ Apollo
Oppenheimer ◦

◦ Planck

MARE
ORIENTALE
(Eastern Sea)

Some craters have rays of
shattered rock flung across
the landscape.

New Moon

Waning Quarter

Last Quarter

Waning Gibbous

EXPLORING THE MOON

As our nearest neighbour in space, the Moon has
been studied more than any other object in the
Solar System.

1959–76
Luna program

1961
Ranger program

1966
Luna 9/
Surveyor 1

1968
Surveyor 7

1969–72
Apollo program

1994
Clementine

Earth's History

Life on Earth

Simple bacteria appeared about 3.8 billion years ago but, for billions of years after that, life did not produce anything more complex than jellyfish and seaweeds. About 550 million years ago, there was a dramatic increase in the number and kinds of animals, known as the 'Cambrian explosion'. Starting from that time, Earth's history is divided into three long eras, containing eleven shorter periods. These divisions mark changes in the environment and the kinds of plants and animals that lived at different times. During Earth's long history, there have been five mass extinctions, when much of life on our planet was destroyed.

A HISTORY OF LIFE ON EARTH

Over the past 3.8 billion years, many different species of plants and animals have evolved, thrived and become extinct as conditions on our planet changed. Humans are latecomers to planet Earth.

First life: single-celled bacteria

4 bya

Atmosphere forms

Earth forms

4.6 bya

3.5 bya

3 bya

2.5 bya

2 bya

1.5 bya

1 bya

Jellyfish

Seaweeds

542 mya

Cambrian explosion: trilobites and other hard-shelled marine animals

CAMBRIAN

Mammal-like reptiles

PERMIAN

CARBONIFEROUS

299 mya

First reptiles, first winged insects, first conifer plants

359

251 mya

TRIASSIC

200 mya

First dinosaurs, first mammals

JURASSIC

146 mya

First birds

First flowering plants

KEY
- Archean era
- Proterozoic era
- Paleozoic era
- Mesozoic era
- Cenozoic era
- — Mass extinction
- bya   billion years ago
- mya   million years ago

Scientists believe that Earth formed 4.6 billion years ago. The oldest rocks, in the Isua region of Greenland, are 3.8 billion years old.

LIVING FOSSILS

Stromatolites are built up over centuries by countless blue-green bacteria that cement grains of mud together. Their shape looks a bit like a stone cauliflower. The living structure grows upward and outward, layer upon layer. Fossil stromatolites, 3.5 billion years old, are some of the oldest evidence of life on Earth.

Growth zone

Older layers

Base

Living stromatolites are found today in a handful of sheltered bays. These 4,000-year-old specimens grow at Hamelin Pool in Shark Bay, Western Australia.

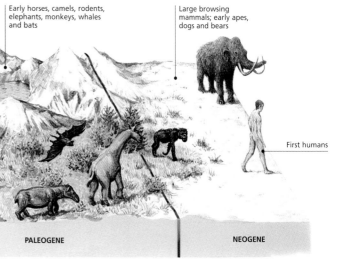

First jawless fish

First corals

ORDOVICIAN

488 mya

444 mya

First jawed fish

First land plants

DEVONIAN

SILURIAN

416 mya

First land animals

First insects and amphibians, first seed plants and trees

First large mammals, first primates

Early horses, camels, rodents, elephants, monkeys, whales and bats

Large browsing mammals; early apes, dogs and bears

First humans

CRETACEOUS

PALEOGENE

NEOGENE

First small mammals and marsupials

65.5 mya

23 mya

Present

Plants through time

CARBONIFEROUS: 359–299 MILLION YEARS AGO (MYA)
Giant horsetails, club mosses, and ferns grew.

Earth is 4.6 billion years old, but for more than 1
billion years only non-living things, such as rocks and
water, could exist because of the poisonous gases in the atmosphere
and the fierce heat of the Sun. The first true plants grew in the oceans
about 550 million years ago, and the first land plants appeared about
400 million years ago. These primitive land plants grew near lakes.
They were the ancestors of the spore-bearing plants – the giant club
mosses, horsetails and ferns that formed huge forests during
the Carboniferous. Seed-bearing plants, such as conifers,
appeared 350 million years ago, and flowering
plants appeared only 135 million years ago.

PERMIAN: 299–251 MYA
Seed-bearing gingkoes and conifers thrived.

TRIASSIC: 251–200 MYA
Cycads flourished.

Permian
Gingko is the only
survivor of a group of
plants that appeared
in the Permian.

Triassic
Cycad

Carboniferous
The modern horsetail
is essentially the same
as those that existed
in the Carboniferous.

TREE FERNS
Ferns are land plants with woody stems
that reproduce by tiny cells called spores.
Tall tree ferns appeared and thrived
during the Carboniferous. Today they
are restricted to moist forests.

SWAMPY CARBONIFEROUS
Giant club mosses (1), giant horsetails (2) and cordaitales (3) grew as tall as houses.

COOLER PERMIAN
Ginkgoes (4) and conifers (5) shared the world with other early plants.

DRIER TRIASSIC
Cycads (6) flourished.

COOLER AND WETTER JURASSIC
New species of conifers, such as swamp cypress (7) and monkey puzzle (8), appeared in the lush, ferny undergrowth (9).

FLOWERING CRETACEOUS
Flowering plants, such as bulrushes (10), magnolia bushes (11) and willow trees (12) appeared.

PALEOGENE
Flowering plants began to rule the plant kingdom.

Paleogene to modern day
The strawberry is just one of more than 235,000 species of flowering plants that exist today.

Cretaceous
Magnolia

JURASSIC: 200–146 MYA
New species of conifers appeared.

Jurassic
Conifer

CRETACEOUS: 146–65.5 MYA
Flowering plants, including trees, appeared.

PALEOGENE: 65.5–23 MYA
Flowering plants dominated.

Explosion of life

Before the 'Cambrian explosion' about 550 million years ago, only blind, soft-bodied creatures swam in the oceans. After the 'explosion', the oceans teemed with more complex animals with eyes, shells and spines. Primitive sponges built the first reefs. But, while the seas were full of life, dry land remained empty and lifeless. Many Cambrian animals were arthropods, with hard, jointed cases covering the outside of their bodies. Some were predators that hunted down and ate other animals. Living arthropods include insects, spiders and crabs. The ancestors of backboned animals also appeared at this time as tiny, wormlike, jawless fish.

ANCIENT TRILOBITES

Trilobites were a successful group of marine arthropods and were among the first animals to evolve eyes. Their bodies were covered with a hard shell that was divided into a shieldlike head, a thorax or abdomen and a tail. They existed for about 300 million years.

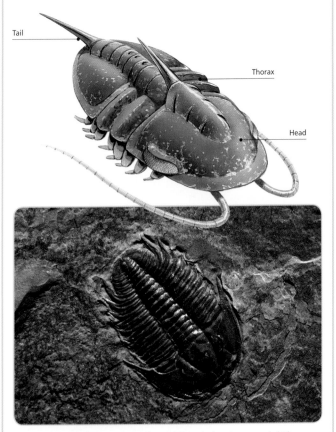

Tail

Thorax

Head

Trilobite fossils are common, and more than 15,000 species have been recorded. They became extinct at the end of the Permian.

THE CAMBRIAN SEAS

Bizarre creatures filled the Cambrian seas. The fearsome *Anomalocaris* preyed on smaller animals. On the seabed crawled trilobites, armour-plated *Wiwaxia* and the spiny *Hallucigenia*. Sponges filtered the water for edible particles. One special creature was *Pikaia*, the earliest vertebrate, or animal with a backbone. About 490 million years ago, glaciers may have lowered temperatures and oxygen in the water, and many of these ancient creatures became extinct.

PALEOZOIC: AGE OF ANCIENT LIFE				
CAMBRIAN	ORDOVICIAN	SILURIAN	DEVONIAN	CARBONIFEROUS
542	488	444	416	359

CAMBRIAN CREATURES

1 *Vauxia*, a soft-branching sponge

2 *Anomalocaris*, an arthropod relative

3 *Marella*, a primitive crustacean

4 *Pikaia*, the earliest relative of
   vertebrate animals

5 Archaeocyathid, a reef-forming
   sponge relative

6 *Wiwaxia*, an early relative of snails

7 Trilobite, a bottom-dwelling arthropod

8 *Hallucigenia*, a 14-legged creature

9 *Halkieria*, an armour-plated, shelled
   creature

10 Green algae, early relatives of
   land plants

	MESOZOIC: AGE OF REPTILES			CENOZOIC: AGE OF MAMMALS	
‹MIAN	TRIASSIC	JURASSIC	CRETACEOUS	PALEOGENE	NEOGENE
	251	200	146	65.5	23	0

Teeming oceans

While some animal groups died out when the climate changed at the end of the Cambrian, life in the oceans flourished during the next period, the Ordovician. Coral reefs appeared, and provided habitats for snails, trilobites, sea lilies and other animals. Cephalopods – the same group as modern squid and octopus – became common and some evolved into giant marine predators. For protection, the small jawless fish developed hard, bony plates. Much of Earth's water was frozen into great ice sheets. About 450 million years ago, giant glaciers began to cover the land. This reduced the temperature of the oceans and lowered the sea level. Once again, many animals became extinct, including most – but not all – of the trilobites.

THE FIRST CORAL

Coral polyps are soft animals with tentacles, related to jellyfish. Many secrete a hard outer skeleton made of calcium carbonate. Over the generations, these skeletons build up to become coral reefs. Rugose and tabulate corals were common in the Ordovician.

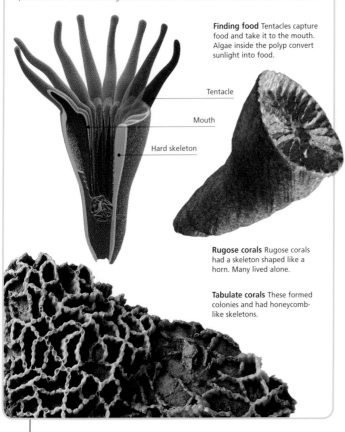

Finding food Tentacles capture food and take it to the mouth. Algae inside the polyp convert sunlight into food.

Tentacle

Mouth

Hard skeleton

Rugose corals Rugose corals had a skeleton shaped like a horn. Many lived alone.

Tabulate corals These formed colonies and had honeycomb-like skeletons.

HUNTERS OF THE DEEP

Life in the seas became more complex during the Ordovician. The top predators were cephalopods, like *Cameroceras*, whose conical shell reached 9 m (30 feet) long. Their prey tried to escape by swimming, burrowing or rolling into a tight ball. Flexible sea lilies, called crinoids, grew on the seafloor, along with tabulate and rugose corals. These early reef communities died when the world became cold and icy toward the end of the Ordovician.

PALEOZOIC: AGE OF ANCIENT LIFE				
CAMBRIAN	ORDOVICIAN	SILURIAN	DEVONIAN	CARBONIFEROUS
542	488	444	416	359

ORDOVICIAN CREATURES

1 *Orthograptus*, a floating graptolite (worm-shaped sea star relative)

2 *Opipeuter*, a large-eyed, swimming trilobite

3 *Climacograptus*, a floating graptolite

4 *Sphaeragnostus*, a floating, rolled trilobite

5 *Tentaculites*, a relative of mollusks

6 *Cameroceras*, a straight-shelled nautiloid

7 *Grewingkia*, a solitary rugose coral

8 *Cyclonema bilix*, a bottom-dwelling snail relative

9 *Calapoecia*, a colonial tabulate coral

10 *Sowerbyella*, a brachiopod

11 *Ectenocrinus*, a crinoid

12 *Xenocrinus*, a crinoid

13 *Nemograptus gracilus*, a graptolite

		MESOZOIC: AGE OF REPTILES		CENOZOIC: AGE OF MAMMALS	
...MIAN	TRIASSIC	JURASSIC	CRETACEOUS	PALEOGENE	NEOGENE
	251	200	146	65.5	23 0

Age of fish

In the Silurian period, giant scorpions hunted in the seas while primitive plants grew on land. One group of fish developed the first jaws with teeth. Arthropods, including sea scorpions, took the first steps out of the water to scavenge along the beaches and riverbanks. Fish took over in the Devonian. Early sharks hunted in the rivers and seas. Some armour-plated fish called placoderms grew to gigantic sizes. Others developed fleshy pairs of fins that were supported by sturdy bones. These were called lobe-finned fish. One group of air-breathing lobe-finned fish developed legs. They crawled out of the water into the first forests, which teemed with primitive insects.

FISH WITH LEGS

Vertebrate animals with four legs evolved from one group of fish, called lobe-finned fish, in the Devonian. Their fins changed into arms and legs, allowing them to move on land. Others stayed in the water and were the ancestors of today's lungfish.

Gogo fish *Gogonasus* was a Devonian fish that was closely related to our four-legged ancestors.

Skull It could breathe air through large holes in its skull, but probably did not leave the water.

Eusthenopteron This lobe-finned fish had shoulder and hip joints like those of modern frogs.

WHEN FISH RULED

Dunkleosteus, measuring 9 m (30 feet), was the mightiest predator of the Devonian seas. This bony-plated giant was the first of the jawed fish. A primitive shark called *Stethacanthus* had a flat-topped back fin and a flat head, both covered with tooth-shaped scales. Spiny trilobites called *Huntonia* scavenged for food on the seafloor, among brachiopods, sponges and corals. Most of these marine animals were wiped out at the end of the Devonian.

PALEOZOIC: AGE OF ANCIENT LIFE				
CAMBRIAN	ORDOVICIAN	SILURIAN	DEVONIAN	CARBONIFEROUS
542	488	444	416	359

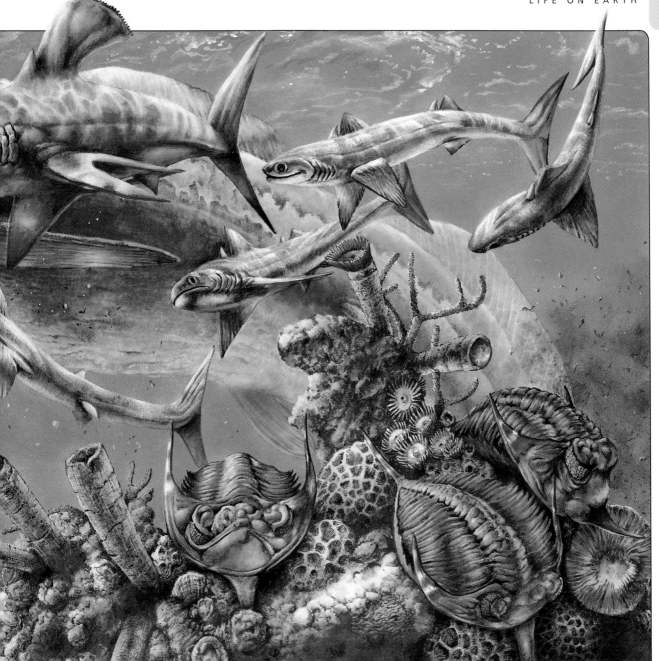

DEVONIAN CREATURES

1 *Dunkleosteus*, an armored jawed fish

2 *Stethacanthus*, a primitive shark

3 *Cladoselache*, a primitive shark with three-pointed teeth

4 *Huntonia*, a trilobite

5 Colonial rugose coral, a reef-forming coral

6 Solitary rugose coral, large, tubular-horned coral

7 *Ctenacanthus*, a primitive shark with two back fins

	MESOZOIC: AGE OF REPTILES			CENOZOIC: AGE OF MAMMALS	
MIAN	TRIASSIC	JURASSIC	CRETACEOUS	PALEOGENE	NEOGENE
	251	200	146	65.5	23 0

End of an era

Swampy forests of huge club mosses and horsetails thrived during the Carboniferous. Much of the coal we use today comes from the remains of those ancient plants. Predatory amphibians lurked under water; giant millipedes scuttled through the undergrowth; and insects took to the air. Land became drier in the Permian and reptiles thrived in this more arid world. The most important reptiles were the mammal-like therapsids, some of which grew to huge sizes. At the end of the Permian, around 251 million years ago, a mass extinction killed more than 90 per cent of marine life and 75 per cent of all vertebrates on land. Coral reefs were wiped out. It took 10 million years for them to recover.

CATASTROPHE!

Earth's greatest mass extinction took place about 251 million years ago. Huge volcanic eruptions in Siberia may have poured poison gases into the atmosphere, or maybe the climate changed drastically and rainfall declined. It took 150 million years to regain the diversity of life in the Permian.

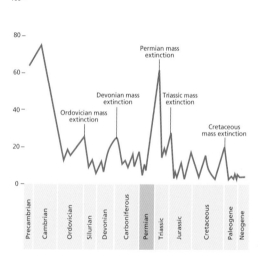

Permian mass extinction

Devonian mass extinction

Ordovician mass extinction

Triassic mass extinction

Cretaceous mass extinction

Precambrian | Cambrian | Ordovician | Silurian | Devonian | Carboniferous | Permian | Triassic | Jurassic | Cretaceous | Paleogene | Neogene

—— Extinction rate (percentage of families that died out)

GONE FOREVER

Large predators, such as *Dinogorgon rubidgei*, did not survive the Permian extinction. Fortunately, some smaller mammal-like reptiles, including our ancestors, did.

FIGHTING FOR SURVIVAL

During the Permian, the atmosphere was thick with volcanic dust. In the oceans, the strange, spiral-toothed shark *Helicoprion* hunted rays and smaller fish. On the bottom of the sea, the last of the trilobites hunted among the brachiopods. Sabre-toothed mammal-like therapsids preyed on bony-plated reptiles in the parched deserts. But for all their size and strength, these creatures were helpless against the catastrophe that made them extinct at the end of the Permian.

PALEOZOIC: AGE OF ANCIENT LIFE				
CAMBRIAN	ORDOVICIAN	SILURIAN	DEVONIAN	CARBONIFEROUS
542	488	444	416	359

PERMIAN CREATURES

1 *Palaeoniscum*, a ray-finned fish

2 *Menapsis armata*, a sharklike ray

3 *Helicoprion*, a shark with whorled teeth

4 *Inostrancevia*, meat-eating therapsid

5 *Araucaria*, a monkey puzzle tree

6 *Scutosaurus*, a bony-plated reptile

7 Crinoid, a sea lily

8 *Phillipsia*, the last trilobite

MESOZOIC: AGE OF REPTILES				CENOZOIC: AGE OF MAMMALS	
MIAN	**TRIASSIC**	**JURASSIC**	**CRETACEOUS**	**PALEOGENE**	**NEOGENE**
	251	200	146	65.5	23 0

Rise of reptiles

By the beginning of the Triassic, 251 million years ago, all the world's landmasses had joined to form one giant continent called Pangaea. The climate over much of Pangaea was hot and dry. New kinds of reptiles evolved, walking on land, swimming in water and flying in the skies. Primitive turtles and crocodiles appeared. One group of reptiles developed legs and hips that allowed them to walk erect on their back legs; they were the first dinosaurs. At about the same time, the first mammals evolved from small therapsids. Towards the end of the Triassic, many large land-dwelling reptiles became extinct and the dinosaurs seized control of planet Earth.

PANGAEA, THE SUPERCONTINENT

Pangaea formed in the Permian when all the landmasses on Earth united in a single supercontinent. It began to break apart in the Jurassic. The land beneath our feet is still moving, and a new supercontinent may form in the distant future.

TRIASSIC PLANTS
Trissiac flora, like cycads, ferns and conifers, were suited to the harsh environment.

Triassic
Pangaea is joined together.

Jurassic
Pangaea splits into two supercontinents.

Cretaceous
These two break up into smaller chunks.

DINOSAURS ARRIVE

The lush riverbanks of the Triassic provided a welcome retreat against the hot, dry conditions of Pangaea. The armoured plant eater *Desmatosuchus* and the terrifying *Postosuchus* were relatives of modern crocodiles. *Paracyclotosaurus*, one of the last giant amphibians, regulated its body temperature by basking in the sun. The first dinosaurs were small, lightly built predators, such as the swift *Coelophysis* that hunted in packs.

PALEOZOIC: AGE OF ANCIENT LIFE				
CAMBRIAN	ORDOVICIAN	SILURIAN	DEVONIAN	CARBONIFEROUS
542	488	444	416	359

TRIASSIC CREATURES

1 *Ornithosuchus*, primitive crocodile relative

2 *Eudimorphodon*, a pterosaur (flying reptile)

3 *Auracarioxylon arazonicum*, a conifer tree

4 *Postosuchus*, an armoured, meat-eating reptile

5 *Coelophysis*, an early meat-eating dinosaur

6 *Placerias*, a tusked mammal-like reptile

7 *Desmatosuchus*, a horned plant-eating reptile

8 *Lariosaurus*, a nothosaur (aquatic reptile)

9 *Palaeocycas*, a primitive cycad plant

10 *Paracyclotosaurus*, a giant amphibian

MESOZOIC: AGE OF REPTILES			CENOZOIC: AGE OF MAMMALS	
MIAN	TRIASSIC	JURASSIC	CRETACEOUS	PALEOGENE	NEOGENE
	251	200	146	65.5	23	0

Dinosaurs rule

Dinosaurs dominated the Jurassic and Cretaceous. The early mammals, our ancestors, were small furry creatures that hid in the shadows. Giant marine reptiles cruised beneath the waves, and pterosaurs soared overhead. Some dinosaurs grew to be the largest animals ever to walk on land. Small meat-eating dinosaurs evolved feathers for warmth and some learned to fly, becoming the first birds. Flowers evolved early in the Cretaceous, along with the insects that pollinated them. Earth's second-largest mass extinction occurred 65.5 million years ago when a huge meteorite struck the planet and 85 per cent of all life was wiped out. Most of the dinosaurs and all the marine reptiles died.

FROM DINOSAUR TO BIRD

Many features found in modern birds, like feathers and wishbones, first appeared in small meat-eating dinosaurs. The oldest known bird, *Archaeopteryx*, had feathered wings and could probably glide efficiently.

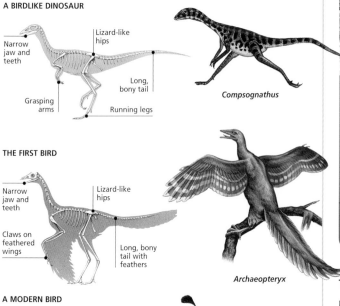

A BIRDLIKE DINOSAUR

Narrow jaw and teeth

Lizard-like hips

Grasping arms

Long, bony tail

Running legs

Compsognathus

THE FIRST BIRD

Narrow jaw and teeth

Lizard-like hips

Claws on feathered wings

Long, bony tail with feathers

Archaeopteryx

A MODERN BIRD

Beak

Feathered tail with no bones

Feathered wings with no claws

California Quail

THE AGE OF DINOSAURS

Dinosaurs reached their peak towards the end of the Cretaceous. Most terrifying were the giant meat eaters *Tyrannosaurus*, shadowed by scavenging *Troodon* looking for leftovers. Some plant eaters, such as *Styracosaurus*, had protective horns or armour. Other reptiles ruled the seas – long-necked *Elasmosaurus* and fish-eating *Plotosaurus*. Soaring overhead were the pterosaur *Quetzalcoatlus*, the largest flying animal ever to have lived, and the smaller *Pteranodon*.

PALEOZOIC: AGE OF ANCIENT LIFE				
CAMBRIAN	ORDOVICIAN	SILURIAN	DEVONIAN	CARBONIFEROUS
542	488	444	416	359

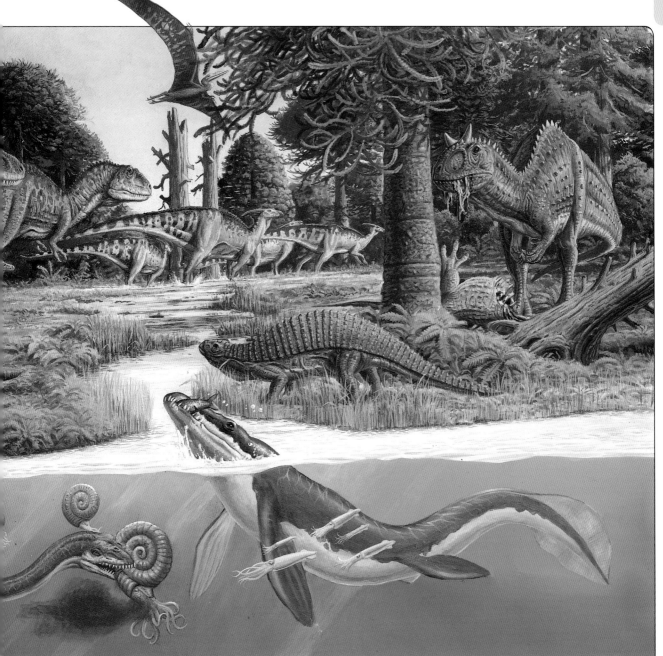

CRETACEOUS CREATURES

1 *Pteranodon*, a pterosaur (flying reptile)

2 *Tyrannosaurus*, a large meat-eating dinosaur

3 *Quetzalcoatlus*, the largest pterosaur

4 *Parasaurolphus*, a duck-billed dinosaur

5 *Carnotaurus*, a meat-eating dinosaur

6 *Nodosaurus*, an armoured plant-eating dinosaur

7 *Belemnites*, a large, coiled ammonite

8 *Plotosaurus*, a fish-eating mosasaur (marine reptile)

9 *Elasmosaurus*, a long-necked plesiosaur (marine reptile)

10 *Hesperornis*, a flightless aquatic bird

11 *Styracosaurus*, a horned plant-eating dinosaur

12 *Troodon*, a small, intelligent, meat-eating dinosaur

	MESOZOIC: AGE OF REPTILES			CENOZOIC: AGE OF MAMMALS	
MIAN	TRIASSIC	JURASSIC	CRETACEOUS	PALEOGENE	NEOGENE
	251	200	146	65.5	23 0

Age of mammals

After the giant dinosaurs died out, mammals began to expand in size and move into new environments during the Paleogene period. This was when whales conquered the oceans and bats took to the air. One group to appear was the primates. The first primates were small tree dwellers with large brains, grasping limbs and complex social behaviour. Today's monkeys, apes and humans are descended from those early primates. For much of the Paleogene, the world was warm and humid. Grasses, which first grew on riverbanks and lake edges, began to spread into drier areas. Dense forests extended to the polar regions. Late in the period, the planet slowly cooled, as Antarctica froze over and the southern ocean currents became colder.

EARLY MAMMALS

The earliest reptile ancestors of mammals had long bodies and did not look much like mammals. They then developed specialised teeth and compact bodies covered with fur. The first true mammals appeared at the end of the Triassic period and developed special bones in the ear that gave them sensitive hearing.

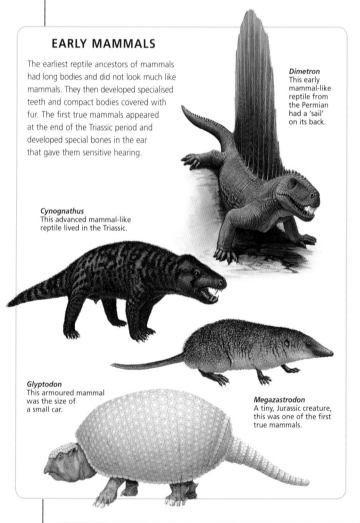

Dimetron
This early mammal-like reptile from the Permian had a 'sail' on its back.

Cynognathus
This advanced mammal-like reptile lived in the Triassic.

Glyptodon
This armoured mammal was the size of a small car.

Megazastrodon
A tiny, Jurassic creature, this was one of the first true mammals.

UNDER ATTACK

This mother *Arsinoitherium* desperately tries to defend her baby against a pack of marauding *Hyaeonodon*. *Arsinoitherium* was a plant eater with giant horns that lived on the plains of northern Africa 35 million years ago. It was a distant cousin of today's elephants, but looked more like a rhinoceros. *Hyaeonodon* were fierce predators with sharp fangs. They had hooves on their toes instead of claws.

PALEOZOIC: AGE OF ANCIENT LIFE				
CAMBRIAN	ORDOVICIAN	SILURIAN	DEVONIAN	CARBONIFEROUS
542	488	444	416	359

GINKGO
Only one species of
ginkgo survives today.
It is sometimes called
a living fossil because
it provides clues to the
plant life of long ago.

This ginkgo leaf fossil was discovered in North Dakota, USA, in rocks from the Paleogene.

MESOZOIC: AGE OF REPTILES				CENOZOIC: AGE OF MAMMALS	
MIAN	TRIASSIC	JURASSIC	CRETACEOUS	PALEOGENE	NEOGENE
251	200	146		65.5	23 0

Home to humans

When the world's climate became cooler and drier between 23 million and 2 million years ago, vast areas of grassy plains replaced the lush tropical forests of southern Africa. Newly formed mountain chains like the Himalaya disrupted global weather patterns. Plant-eating mammals roamed in huge nomadic herds eating the grasses, and developed grinding teeth and stomachs. Many modern mammals can trace their ancestry to smaller animals from this time. Apes left the trees to forage on the ground, and learned to walk upright. This made it easier to see food and predators, and freed their arms to carry their young. The first humans evolved about 2 million years ago. They learned to make stone tools, and they mastered the use of fire. Several forms evolved and died out before our own species, *Homo sapiens*, appeared about 200,000 years ago.

LUCY
Humans evolved from upright-walking apes called australopithecines that lived 4 million years ago. A female australopithecine skeleton, nicknamed 'Lucy', was discovered in Ethiopia in 1974.

STONE AGE BURIAL
These two stone-age humans appear to have been buried together, with their bodies curled around each other. The skull of the right-hand body is crowned with a headdress made from shells. The remains were discovered in Liguria, Italy.

PALEOZOIC: AGE OF ANCIENT LIFE				
CAMBRIAN	ORDOVICIAN	SILURIAN	DEVONIAN	CARBONIFEROUS
542	488	444	416	359

THE NEANDERTHALS

Neanderthals were early humans that lived in caves in Europe about 60,000 years ago. For a time they even coexisted with our own species. Neanderthals were well adapted to harsh conditions during the ice ages, with stocky bodies to help conserve heat and impressive tool-making skills. Despite this, they became extinct about 28,000 years ago.

SIGNS OF LIFE

In addition to fossilised bones, early humans left behind many clues to their habits, such as footprints embedded in rock, their tools, their trash dumps and their artwork. Each discovery allows modern researchers to piece together the lives of the people who came before us.

This fossil shows footprints left by humans who walked there about 3.5 million years ago.

Discovered by four teenagers, Lascaux Cave in France has pictures painted 17,000 years ago.

13,500 BP

NORTH AMERICA

00–800

EUROPE
40,000 BP

43,000 BP

32,000 BP

ASIA

100,000 BP

AFRICA

130,000 BP

30,000 BP

40,000 BP

28,000 BP

SOUTH AMERICA

AUSTRALIA
60,000–40,000 BP

120,000 BP

AD 850–1200
New Zealand

14,700 BP

8300 BP

SPREADING ACROSS THE GLOBE
Modern humans appeared in Africa about 200,000 years ago. They migrated out of Africa into Europe, Asia and Australia. Low sea levels during the last ice age allowed humans to walk from northern Asia across the Bering Strait to the Americas.

KEY
☐ Areas where early modern human remains have been found
➤ Path of migration
BP Before Present

MESOZOIC: AGE OF REPTILES				CENOZOIC: AGE OF MAMMALS	
RMIAN	TRIASSIC	JURASSIC	CRETACEOUS	PALEOGENE	NEOGENE
251	200	146		65.5	23 0

Journey to the Centre

A river of molten, liquid lava flows down a valley. When a volcano erupts, lava forces its way to the surface from the mantle.

About 4.6 billion years ago, Earth was a fiery ball of liquid melted rock. As it slowly cooled, the strength of Earth's own gravity pulled the heaviest elements, such as iron, toward its centre while lighter elements, including oxygen and silicone, floated to the surface. Eventually, Earth separated into four layers. At the centre is a heavy iron core, made up of two distinct parts: a solid inner core and a liquid outer core. Around the core is a lighter mantle layer made mainly of a green gemstone called olivine, which is often carried from the mantle up to the surface by erupting lava. A brittle rocky crust floats on top of the mantle. The ocean floor and the continents on which we live make up Earth's thin, hard crust.

Crust
Earth's thin, brittle crust is broken by long cracks. It varies in thickness from 8 to 70 km (5 to 45 miles).

Mantle
Earth's mantle is hot and solid, but supple enough to move slowly beneath the thin crust and push it around.

Outer core
Earth's outer core is made of liquid iron that moves in big circles.

Inner core
Although it is hot, Earth's inner core is solid because of the incredibly high pressure on the iron and nickel there.

Lithosphere
This is the crust and upper part of the mantle.

Mantle

Convection current

Lithosphere

Crust

EARTH'S HEAT ENGINE

The immense heat of Earth's core tries to escape into space. This sets up convection currents like those in boiling water. Warmer, lighter material rises and pushes against the crust, which sometimes cracks. As this material loses its heat, it sinks and hotter material rises to take its place.

FAST FACT

You cannot travel to Earth's centre. The pressure would squeeze you and the heat would cook you before you reached the mantle. The deepest you can go is 2,080 m (6,824 feet) into Voronya Cave, Georgia.

Restless Earth

At Earth's centre lies a tremendous powerhouse, a blistering hot core. Heat from the core bakes the rock directly above it, in the mantle. As the mantle cooks, hot liquid rocks – called magma – rise like bubbles in boiling water. Cooler parts sink, but they are reheated by the core and soon rise again. This constant cycle forms convection currents. Magma moving in a convection current pushes and tugs at Earth's crust. After Earth formed, these movements cracked the crust and turned it into a giant jigsaw puzzle. The puzzle pieces are called tectonic plates, and they carry the world's oceans and landmasses. When magma oozes up between two plates, the plates separate. But they can travel only so far before they crash into other plates. These collisions cause earthquakes and volcanic eruptions.

Waterfalls and rivers wear mountain ranges down in an endless battle against the forces within Earth, which push the mountains upward.

Geysers are spouts of superheated water that explode from cracks in the ground. They occur only where superheated rocks lie just below the surface.

UNDER THE SURFACE

Convection currents (indicated by red arrows) stretch and squeeze the crust. Where plates separate, ocean ridges and rift valleys appear. Where plates smash into each other, mountains, volcanoes and undersea valleys form.

Undersea collision
When ocean plates collide under the sea, one or both descend. This creates a line of volcanoes alongside a deep trench, like the Mariana Trench.

Hot current

Mid-ocean ridge
Rising and spreading convection currents force plates apart. Basalt erupts along underwater cracks and makes new crust.

Hot-spot volcano
Rising magma breaks through weak spots in the crust and builds hot-spot volcanoes, such as the Hawaiian Islands.

Rivers of lava pour out of deep cracks or vents and build giant volcanoes. Volcanoes are common wherever there are weaknesses in Earth's crust.

Hot springs are common around the edges of Earth's tectonic plates. Underground water is heated as it flows along cracks in the hot rocks.

BELOW THE CRUST

Earth's crust is thin and floats above the mantle. Oceanic crust is made of heavy basalt rock. The thicker continental crust floats higher because it is made of lighter granite rock. So the continents are above sea level, and most of Earth's water lies in the deeper ocean basins.

OCEANIC CRUST
The oceanic crust is made from basalt, a volcanic rock that hardens when magma erupts at mid-ocean ridges.

CONTINENTAL CRUST
The continental crust forms landmasses and is composed of older, lighter rocks, such as granite, gneiss and sandstone.

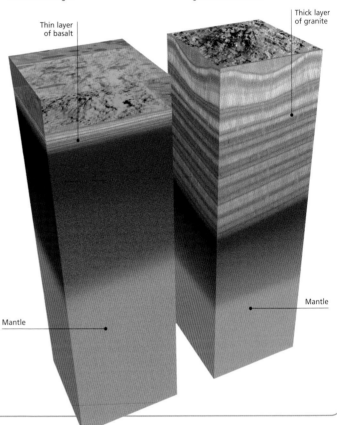

Thin layer of basalt

Thick layer of granite

Mantle

Mantle

Coastal collision
When ocean and continent collide, the heavier oceanic plate is pushed under. Magma rises to the surface, creating volcanoes and mountains.

Sliding plates
Plates sliding sideways alongside one another form long straight fault lines, such as the San Andreas Fault. The jerky movement releases energy as earthquakes.

Continental rift
Rising currents lift and separate continents, and form deep rift valleys. These widen and eventually are flooded by the sea.

Folding crust
When continental crusts collide they cannot push beneath one another. Their edges buckle and fold into giant ranges, such as the Himalaya Mountains.

Continents on the Move

Earth's crust is on the move. Until recently, geologists did not have proof of this, and early theories of continental 'drift' fell on deaf ears. Nevertheless, there were many things that could not be explained unless the continents were once joined, such as finding similar plants and animals on all the southern continents, or the surprising jigsaw fit of South America and Africa. In 1910, a German scientist, Alfred Wegener, noticed that the continents looked like puzzle pieces and suggested they once formed a single continent. In the 1960s, scientists using underwater mapping equipment discovered long ridges under the ocean where Earth's crust had been pulled apart. The idea of continental drift began to be accepted.

A MOVING HISTORY
For millions of years, the movements of Earth's tectonic plates have been shrinking and enlarging seas, and separating and joining continents.

Aleutian Trench

JUAN DE FUCA PLATE

San Andreas Fault

PACIFIC PLATE

Hawaiian Islands

RIVERA MICROPLATE

COC PLA

East Pacific Rise

GALÁP MICROP

NAZ PLA

EASTER MICROPLA

JUAN FERN MICROP

4.6–4.2 billion years ago
Earth grows in size from meteorite and comet strikes. Heavy materials sink to the core.

A LAND APART

While exploring Indonesia in the 1850s, Alfred Wallace saw that the animals in Java, Sumatra and Borneo were different from those in New Guinea and Australia. Although he could not explain it, Wallace discovered the dividing line between the Eurasian and Australian plates. Because there was never a land bridge between the plates for the animals to cross, most species remained separated.

4.2–3.8 billion years ago
As the impacts lessen, Earth cools and forms a solid crust. Water vapour from volcanoes and comets condenses to form oceans.

The coastlines of the Red Sea and the Gulf of Aden started moving apart only about 25 million years ago.

KEY

▨ Earthquake zone
△ Volcanic zone
⊥⊥ Colliding plates
= Separating plates

— Sideways moving plates
···· Uncertain
⇒ Direction of movement

TECTONIC BOUNDARIES

Volcanoes, ocean trenches, mountain ranges and earthquakes mark where Earth's tectonic plates meet. The Pacific Plate's edge, called the 'Ring of Fire', is the most active. Arrows indicate the way each plate moves.

270 million years ago
The landmasses join in the enormous supercontinent, Pangaea, surrounded by a single ocean.

200 million years ago
Pangaea starts to break up, first into the two supercontinents – Laurasia in the north and Gondwana in the south.

Today
The Atlantic Ocean is widening and the Americas are drifting away from Europe and Africa.

50 million years from now
The Atlantic continues to widen and the Pacific closes, bringing North America closer to Asia. Africa collides with Europe, closing the Mediterranean.

Folds and Faults

The immense pressure of plate movements under the surface can snap even the toughest rocks. Cracks between shifting rock layers are called faults. You can see small ones in rock faces and road cuts. Large faults extend for hundreds of miles. The type of fault that forms depends on the way the rocks move. When rocks pull apart, one side slips downward. This is called a normal fault. When rocks push together, one side usually rides up over the other, creating a reverse fault. Sometimes rocks slide past each other in opposite directions or different speeds. This creates a lateral, or transform, fault. All three may occur along a major fault line.

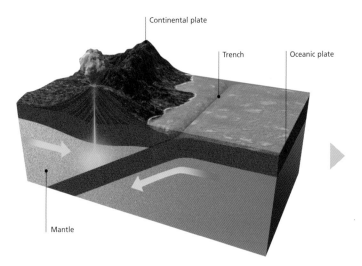

OCEAN MEETS CONTINENT

When an oceanic plate collides with a continental plate, it slides underneath the continent and melts. Rising molten rock pushes through the continental plate and forms volcanoes.

The Torres del Paine, in Chile, are part of the Andes. The mountains grew when the Pacific Plate slid beneath the South American Plate.

OCEAN MEETS OCEAN

When two oceanic plates collide, the denser one slides underneath the other. The sinking plate melts and rising molten rock builds a line of islands called a volcanic arc.

Gunung Semeru is one of hundreds of volcanoes in the Indonesian island arc. They were formed when the Australian Plate melted beneath the Pacific Plate.

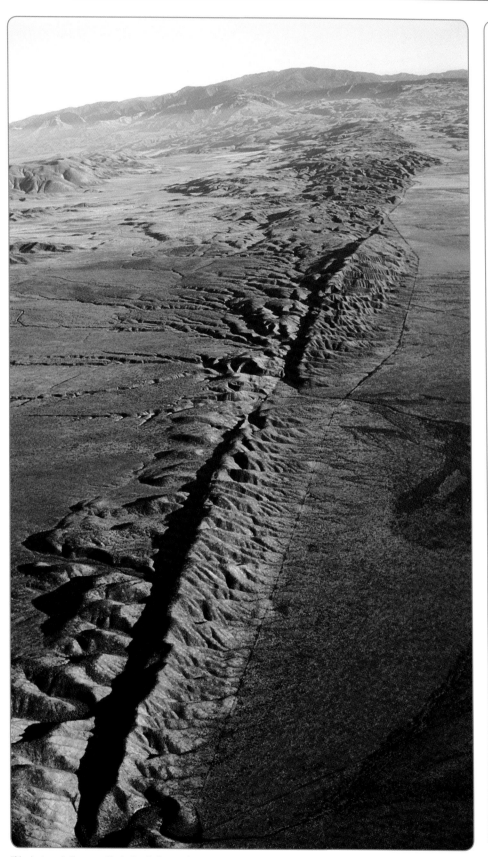

This giant scar in the ground is the San Andreas Fault, in California, USA. On the left side, the Pacific Plate moves slowly northwest; on the right, the North American Plate slides southeast.

KINDS OF FAULTS

Tectonic plates meet one another in different ways – pushing together (converging), sliding side by side or moving away (diverging).

Himalaya Mountains When two continents crash together, they do not sink. Their edges buckle high in the air as mountain ranges.

San Andreas Fault If two plates slide alongside one another, the sliding movement is rough and sudden slips cause big earthquakes.

East African Rift Valley When a continent is pulled apart, deep cracks slowly widen into long rift valleys. Rivers and lakes form in these valleys.

Mid-Atlantic Ridge As continents move apart, basalt lava flows through underwater cracks in the crust. Eventually, an ocean forms with a spreading ridge down its middle.

Rocks

The rocks around you are on a slow-motion roller coaster. Geological forces thrust them up as mountains, throw them into the air as molten rock, break them into bits and pieces and plunge them deep underground. During this turbulent ride, three kinds of rocks appear. When molten rock cools, igneous rocks form. When rocks on Earth's surface are pummelled to pieces by waves, broken up by ice or scoured to bits by other rocks, the fragments settle in layers and become sedimentary rocks. Meanwhile, deep inside Earth, fierce temperatures and intense pressure cook and squeeze rocks, tranforming them into metamorphic rocks.

Molten rock cools and hardens to form igneous rocks.

Heat and pressure underground create metamorphic rocks.

HOW ROCKS FORM

Rocks are made, destroyed and rebuilt in a perpetual 'rock cycle'. Erosion wears down mountains and volcanoes, then rivers carry the sediment to the sea. Sediment on the seafloor is pushed into subduction zones, where it melts and provides lava for volcanoes to complete the cycle.

NAME THAT ROCK

Look at the rocks around you. Do they have big or small crystals? Do they lie in flat, straight beds, or are the layers folded and twisted? These are all clues to the rock's origin.

Conglomerate

Milky quartz

Granite

Quartz — Mica — Feldspar

Banded gneiss

Quartz — Biotite — Feldspar

SEDIMENTARY ROCK
This consists of mineral or rock pieces that have been eroded, transported, then deposited in layers and solidified together.

IGNEOUS ROCK
This has interlocking mineral crystals. The crystals are big if the rock cooled slowly underground, or microscopic if the rock cooled quickly.

METAMORPHIC ROCK
This has folded and wavy bands of minerals that are stretched out from the strong pressure and high temperature that created them.

Rock is broken down by weathering and swept away by erosion.

Rocks, mud and sand are deposited at river deltas and on the seafloor.

Continental crust

Plate movements pull sediments under ground.

River and ocean deposits form layers of sedimentary rock.

Ocean crust

Mantle

Newborn igneous rock is cooled by the ocean as lava flows to the edge of the Kilauea volcano, Hawaii, USA.

This sedimentary rock in Arizona, USA, shows tilted rocks laid below flat ones. These indicate ancient sand dunes.

The Alps formed when the Tethys Sea squeezed against the Eurasian Plate and the rocks changed with pressure.

Igneous rock

Igneous rock, or 'fire rock', comes from cooling magma. As the molten liquid cools, tiny crystals grow, then get bigger. The more time igneous rock has to cool, the bigger the crystals grow. The world's largest crystals have been found in pegmatites. Some are even bigger than a car. Lava that erupts onto Earth's surface and cools quickly has tiny crystals. Igneous rock can be tough and it is often used for buildings and roads.

Gabbro

Pumice

Banded obsidian
Obsidian may be banded if the thick lava flows a bit before cooling.

Ignimbrite

Andesite

Obsidian
Glassy and brittle, obsidian breaks into pieces with razor-sharp edges.

Volcanic tuff
Tuff is made from volcanic ash that has solidified and compressed.

Kimberlite
Kimberlite erupts from deep in Earth's mantle and sometimes brings diamond crystals with it.

Rhyolite
Made of the same materials as granite, rhyolite has smaller crystals because the lava cooled quickly.

Vesicular basalt
This common fine-grained grey rock is cooled lava. Sometimes it is full of gas bubbles.

Obsidian lava
Obsidian lava is high in silica. This makes it flow slowly like thick soup.

LOOKING INSIDE

Basalt When sliced and backlit, basalt shows both short and long crystals surrounded by fine-grained minerals.

Gabbro This has the same composition as basalt, but with much bigger crystals because it cooled slowly underground.

Pegmatite Pegmatite cools very slowly, and so can have large crystals of minerals and gems.

Serpentine Serpentine is a green rock that has been squeezed up along the edges of colliding continents.

VOLCANIC PLUGS

Plugs and dikes are columns of igneous rock that were once part of a volcano. Molten rock that cooled in an old volcano's vent was much harder than the soft ash of the volcano's cone. As the ash eroded away, the volcano's insides were exposed.

Eruption Magma rises to the surface and erupts through the active volcano's main vent to build a steep-sided cone of ash layers and lava.

Gabbro
This dark-coloured rock is made of coarse crystals.

Extinction The volcano eventually becomes extinct and magma cools inside the vent, hardening from the top down into solid igneous rock.

Granite
Granite is made of large crystals that cooled slowly from magma below Earth's surface.

Andesite
Andesite is formed from thick, souplike lava that erupted from volcanoes on the edges of tectonic plates.

Erosion Rivers erode the extinct volcano's sides. They carry away soft ash from the cone and uncover hard lava formations, called plugs and dikes.

Granite
Pretty pink feldspar crystals make this granite look different from white granite.

Pallasite meteorite
Rich in nickel and iron, this meteorite came from the core of an exploded planet.

Sedimentary rock

Sedimentary rock is made from grains of rock or mineral from older rocks that are broken by the forces of weathering and erosion. This loose material is called sediment. Running water, wind and ice carry large amounts of sediment. Large rivers can even move boulders. If their journey in a river is long, rocks can end up quite rounded. Eventually the sediment reaches a lake or ocean where it settles in layers, with fine, light pieces travelling farther. Sediment that arrives later buries the original layers and, in time, all the material is naturally cemented together or compressed into solid rock.

Banded ironstone
An ancient rock, it is made of layers of red chert and grey hematite.

Pisolitic ironstone

Flint spearheads
Spearheads were chipped carefully from flint to form a sharp edge and a tang to bind it to the spear.

Conglomerate
This coarse-grained rock is made of large rounded pebbles held together by finer material.

Chert
Chert is a tough, fine-grained rock made from material deposited on the ocean floor.

Breccia
This breccia consists of sharp rock pieces that erupted from a volcano and then cemented into rock.

LOOKING INSIDE

This sandstone has been sliced thinly and viewed through a polarising microscope to see its structure. It is composed of partly rounded quartz sand grains.

Shale
Sheets of shale sometimes have brown bands caused by rusty water seeping inward.

Banded jasper
This mineral is made from quartz and is a banded ironstone rock.

Breccia pebble
This rounded river pebble of breccia is perhaps on its way to becoming part of a conglomerate.

Paleolithic flint tools
Early humans used flint to make useful tools, including knives, spears and arrows.

Limestone
The calcium carbonate shells of tiny sea creatures are clearly seen in this piece.

Evaporite
When minerals like salt and gypsum crystallise as lakes and seas dry out, they are called evaporites.

Chert

Shale

Breccia
Sharp edges on these grains show they have not been carried far from their source.

Sandstone
This common rock is made of cemented sand grains, usually quartz.

FORMING A CANYON

Canyons, like the Grand Canyon cut by the Colorado River in the USA, are excellent places to see layers of sedimentary rock. Harder layers stand out clearly as steep cliffs while the softer layers erode to more gentle slopes.

Canyon forms Tectonic activity lifts the land surface above sea level, giving rivers plenty of energy to cut downward through the rocks.

Canyon deepens The river cuts down through the sedimentary layers to form a deep, narrow canyon with steep sides.

Canyon widens Softer layers of rock erode and are undercut, widening the canyon. This also causes the harder layers on top to collapse.

Metamorphic rock

Below the surface, rocks are continually changing from one kind to another in Earth's giant pressure cooker. They do not melt, but change slowly while staying solid. This is called metamorphism. Not much seems to happen at first, but then crystals in heated rocks join and grow larger. Metamorphic rocks like quartzite and marble are tougher and stronger than the rocks that formed them. Flat minerals such as mica regrow, turning their flat sides towards the pressure to form slate, phyllite and banded schists. At very high temperatures and pressures, new minerals such as garnet grow.

Quartzite
This rock is tougher than its sandstone parent because the quartz grains are joined together by heat.

Amphibolite
This consists of volcanic basalt with black amphibole minerals that have been heated and squeezed.

Blue marble
The blue-green colours in this marble come from serpentine that mixed with the limestone.

Banded gneiss
Easily recognised, this rock has thick, strongly folded bands of black mica and white feldspar.

Skarn
The raylike crystals in this skarn formed when sandy limestone was strongly heated.

Micaceous quartzite
When clay mixed in the original quartz sandstone, it caused mica to grow in this quartzite.

LOOKING INSIDE

Gneiss Under a microscope, this slice shows interlocking crystals of white, black and grey quartz, and brown mica.

Mylonite The banding in mylonite, caused by a sliding fault, is clearly seen in this magnified rock slice.

Anthracite coal
Anthracite is the highest-quality coal, and has been heated as well as squeezed.

▼ **Phyllite**
The original flat layers of shale rock were bent by pressure into tightly folded bands of phyllite.

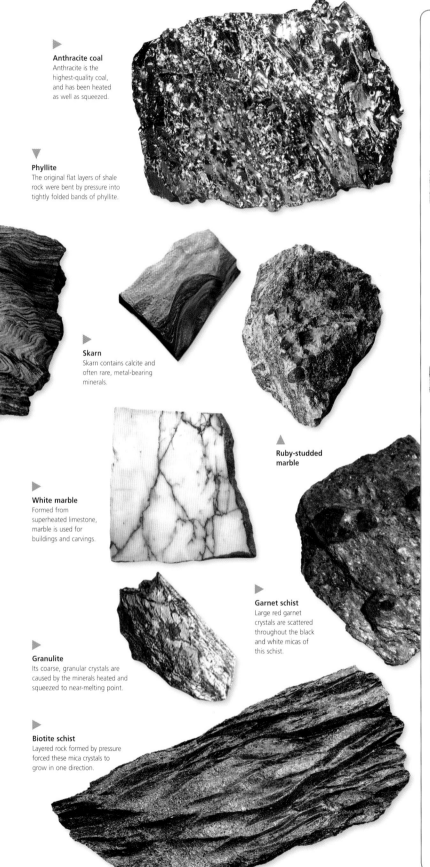

▶ **Skarn**
Skarn contains calcite and often rare, metal-bearing minerals.

▶ **White marble**
Formed from superheated limestone, marble is used for buildings and carvings.

▲ **Ruby-studded marble**

▶ **Garnet schist**
Large red garnet crystals are scattered throughout the black and white micas of this schist.

▶ **Granulite**
Its coarse, granular crystals are caused by the minerals heated and squeezed to near-melting point.

▶ **Biotite schist**
Layered rock formed by pressure forced these mica crystals to grow in one direction.

METAMORPHISM

There are two ways that rock can metamorphose, or change: by intense pressure, like being squeezed in a giant vice; or by intense heat, like being cooked by a blowtorch.

SQUEEZING
Sometimes rocks change when they are squeezed and pushed up into mountains by forces deep within Earth.

Shale
Sandstone
Limestone

Flat layers Sedimentary layers lie flat and straight as squeezing begins.

Schist
Marble
Gneiss

Folds Intense squeezing folds the layers tightly, like a rumpled carpet.

BAKING
Magma rises to the surface and cooks the surrounding rock. The rock is hardened and new minerals grow.

Shale
Sandstone
Limestone
Magma

Heating Hot magma begins to rise through the sedimentary rocks.

Hornfels
Quartzite
Marble
Magma

Baking Heat from the magma bakes the rocks and changes them.

Rocks in the landscape

The different kinds of rocks in the landscape are easy to recognise. Flat sedimentary rock layers in canyon cliffs look different from the pointed cones of volcanoes, or the folded metamorphic cliffs of a mountain range. Water, wind and ice change the landscape by eroding softer rocks away from harder ones. Granite is polished into smooth, rounded hills and mountains, while old basalt volcanic necks and lava flows form spectacular cliffs of straight, pipelike columns.

THE GRAND CANYON

Cut in the landscape by the Colorado River, the Grand Canyon, USA, is the largest desert canyon. The layered canyon walls are like the pages of a giant book that dates back more than 2 billion years. To follow the canyon's history, read the labels from the bottom of the illustration to the top.

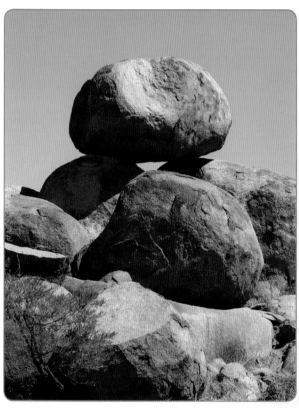

Granite can weather into smooth, rounded shapes that look like a stack of giant marbles.

Molten basalt from volcanoes cools and shrinks, forming beautiful six-sided columns.

Glaciers have carved steep cliffs out of solid granite mountains in Yosemite National Park, USA.

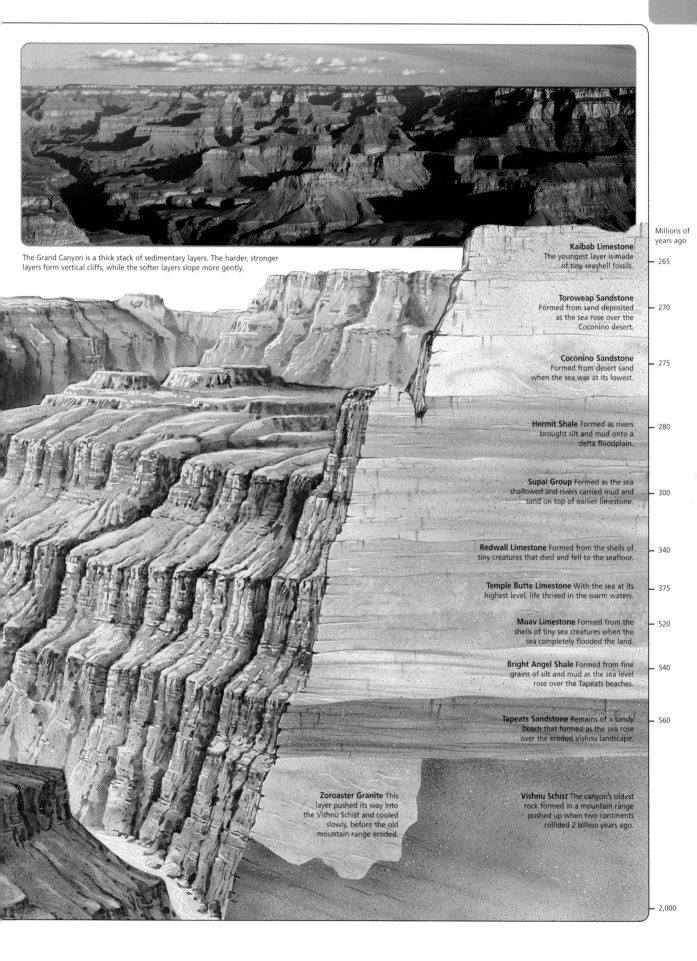

The Grand Canyon is a thick stack of sedimentary layers. The harder, stronger layers form vertical cliffs, while the softer layers slope more gently.

Millions of years ago

Kaibab Limestone The youngest layer is made of tiny seashell fossils. — 265

Toroweap Sandstone Formed from sand deposited as the sea rose over the Coconino desert. — 270

Coconino Sandstone Formed from desert sand when the sea was at its lowest. — 275

Hermit Shale Formed as rivers brought silt and mud onto a delta floodplain. — 280

Supai Group Formed as the sea shallowed and rivers carried mud and sand on top of earlier limestone. — 300

Redwall Limestone Formed from the shells of tiny creatures that died and fell to the seafloor. — 340

Temple Butte Limestone With the sea at its highest level, life thrived in the warm waters. — 375

Muav Limestone Formed from the shells of tiny sea creatures when the sea completely flooded the land. — 520

Bright Angel Shale Formed from fine grains of silt and mud as the sea level rose over the Tapeats beaches. — 540

Tapeats Sandstone Remains of a sandy beach that formed as the sea rose over the eroded Vishnu landscape. — 560

Zoroaster Granite This layer pushed its way into the Vishnu Schist and cooled slowly, before the old mountain range eroded.

Vishnu Schist The canyon's oldest rock formed in a mountain range pushed up when two continents collided 2 billion years ago.

— 2,000

Using rocks

Humans have long used rocks for tools and for building. Flint and volcanic rock are ideal for making tools because they break with sharp cutting edges. Great monuments, such as pyramids, palaces and temples, were built with granite, marble, slate, sandstone and limestone. Slate can be split into thin sheets and used for roofs or paving. Clay and shale are mined, shaped and fired in ovens to make bricks. Recently, other building materials have been developed, including glass and steel, to replace stone and brick in modern structures. However, polished slabs of granite and marble still decorate important buildings.

MAKING FLINT TOOLS

Early humans began making stone tools 2.5 million years ago to help them hunt animals for food. Their thumbs let them grip, hold and chip the rocks to make tools, such as knives, spear points and ax heads. About 50,000 years ago, humans learned to make better tools with fire.

The rocks are buried in sand and a fire is lit over the top.

Suitable rocks for tools are selected by smashing river pebbles.

Striking the rock with another breaks off thin, sharp flakes.

Slow heating and cooling make the stone easier to work.

Sharp edges are made when the stone is split in two.

Small pointed flakes are suitable for cutting and shaping.

Small pieces are sometimes wrapped to protect the fingers.

FAST FACT

Well-made knives and other tools were highly prized by early humans. The flaked edges of flint chips can be as sharp as steel. They are not as long lasting, however, because flint is brittle and the edges break.

BUILDING STONEHENGE

England's early inhabitants created the stone rings of Stonehenge about 5,000 years ago. The first pillars and lintels were cut from hard, local sandstone; later ones were made from dolerite brought from Wales.

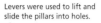

Levers were used to lift and slide the pillars into holes.

The pillars were pulled with ropes to stand perfectly straight.

Rock lintels, or cross-pieces, were raised on wooden platforms.

The lintel was shifted from the platform to the upright pillars.

PYRAMID OF THE MAGICIAN
The Maya started building the Pyramid of the Magician in Uxmal, Mexico, about 1,400 years ago. It was made of stone in five stages over 300 years – each time a new and bigger pyramid was built on top of the older one.

India's Taj Mahal, made of white marble and decorated with gems, was built in the mid-1600s by Emperor Shah Jahan as a monument to his wife.

The pyramid has an unusual oval shape, steep sides and two temples on the top.

Minerals

L ook closely at a rock and you may notice that is is made up of tiny pieces of one or more minerals. Minerals are the building blocks of rocks. They are solid chemical substances that occur naturally in Earth's crust. They are made up of chemicals called elements. A mineral that contains only one element is called a native element. There are thousands of different minerals, and they come in all colours, shapes and sizes. They include metals such as gold and silver, as well as valuable gemstones such as diamonds. Minerals may form regular, flat-sided shapes called crystals. Often, crystals of different minerals grow together, forming rocks. When minerals have plenty of space to grow, they form large, beautiful crystals.

COLOUR

Some minerals are always one unmistakable colour, while others, such as fluorite, may have many. Different elements or impurities in the mineral can cause colour variations.

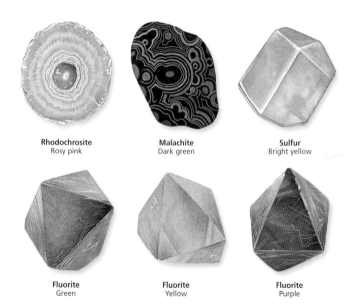

Rhodochrosite
Rosy pink

Malachite
Dark green

Sulfur
Bright yellow

Fluorite
Green

Fluorite
Yellow

Fluorite
Purple

HABIT

Habit is the shape formed by a mineral's crystals. Like a person, crystals can be short and fat, tall and thin, or somewhere in between.

LUSTRE

Lustre describes how the surface of a mineral looks. It may be shiny, glassy, waxy or just plain dull. The brightest lustre is that of a diamond.

Kaolinite
Dull

Asbestos
Silky

Galena
Metallic

Copper
Treelike

Labradorite
Rocklike

Garnet
Equal-sided

Calcite
Vitreous

Turquoise
Waxy

Amazonite
Vitreous

FLUORESCENT MINERALS

A few minerals, such as fluorite and opal, glow beautifully when an invisible ultraviolet light is shone on them.

EARTH'S CRUST
About 90 per cent of all the minerals found at Earth's surface are silicates – the building blocks of rocks.

Silicates 90%

Non-silicates 10%

CRYSTAL SYSTEMS
Minerals are grouped into six systems, based on the shape of their crystals. These systems determine the mineral's shape.

Vesuvianite
Tetragonal

Pyrite
Cubic

Amazonite
Triclinic

Selenite
Monoclinic

Beryl
Hexagonal

Barite
Orthorhombic

TRANSPARENCY
Transparency refers to how easy it is to see through a mineral. Many pure minerals are completely see-through. Opaque minerals cannot be seen through at all.

Quartz
Transparent

Moonstone
Semi-transparent

Chrysoprase
Translucent

Malachite
Opaque

MOHS SCALE OF HARDNESS

Mohs scale of hardness uses 10 minerals, from soft to hard, to help determine the hardness of other materials. If you scratch quartz against an unknown material and the quartz leaves a mark, then the mystery material is softer than quartz. You can also use the items on the right-hand side to test for hardness.

1 Talc

2 Gypsum

2.5 Fingernail

3 Calcite

3.5 Copper coin

4 Fluorite

5 Apatite

5.5 Glass

6 Orthoclase

6.5 Steel knife

7 Quartz

8 Topaz

8.5 Emery board

9 Corundum

10 Diamond

Ornamental minerals and crystals

Ornamental is the name given to attractive minerals and rocks that are not considered precious. These minerals, including agate, chalcedony hematite and lapis lazuli, are frequently used for carvings and jewellery. Minerals mined to extract metals are called ores and some, like the silvery cubes of galena (lead ore), can be very pretty. Ores are found in old mine dumps or collected with permission from working mines. Some collectors specialise in beautiful crystals, common minerals like quartz, or rare ones like rhodochrosite. Other collectors prefer miniature specimens, which are best seen with a microscope.

Kyanite
The gem mineral kyanite grows as long, light blue crystals in metamorphic rock.

Cinnabar
This mineral is a mercury ore and was used for red pigment called vermilion.

Desert roses
These flower-like crystal clusters of gypsum are often found in dry desert lakes.

Selenite gypsum
This soft mineral breaks along two cleavage planes.

Aragonite
Mollusk and coral shells are made from this mineral, which is a form of calcium carbonate.

Sulphur
This pretty mineral, too soft to be a gemstone, is used to make sulphuric acid.

Lapis lazuli
This is treasured for its rich blue colour.

Rhodochrosite
Crystals of this mineral are rare collectors items.

LAPIS LAZULI

Lapis lazuli was crushed to a fine powder and mixed with oil to make a highly prized blue pigment used in early paintings, jewellery and ornaments. Ancient Egyptians used the powder as eye shadow.

Rare and expensive lapis lazuli was used rarely in paintings, unless it was paid for by the wealthy. In this detail of *The Coronation of the Virgin*, painted in 1430, the robes of church officials contain the pigment.

Malachite
This delicately banded, deep-green ornamental mineral is an ore of copper.

SALT LAKES

The mineral we call 'salt' and use to flavour food is halite. Before refrigerators were invented, salt was used to preserve food and was as valuable as gold. Halite is deposited on the floor of lakes when the salt water evaporates.

This dry lake in Death Valley, California, USA, has a crust of evaporated salt. As the lake water dries up, salt is easily mined by just scraping it up.

Kaolinite
This clay mineral is used in ceramics and toothpaste.

Wulfenite
This ore forms heavy, yellow crystals.

Talc
One of the softest minerals, talc is crushed into fine flakes for talcum powder.

Cuprite
This attractive copper mineral is an important source of copper metal.

Wulfenite
Its crystals may also appear thin and table-like.

Galena
This heavy lead ore forms silvery blocks. The ancient Egyptians used it in their eye makeup.

Rock salt
This mineral grows in cubic crystals.

Amazonite

Pegmatite
This igneous rock, shown here with mica and fluorite, often has large gem crystals.

Precious and semiprecious minerals

In order to be called a precious gemstone, a mineral must satisfy three conditions: It must be beautiful, durable and rare. Diamond, ruby, sapphire and emerald are the four best known precious gemstones. Amethyst was once a gemstone and worn by royalty, but when large deposits were found in Brazil, it became too common. Sulphur is a striking yellow colour, but it would break if it were worn. Alexandrite is perhaps the rarest and most prized gemstone because of its strange ability to change colour from vivid green in the day to intense red at night. Semiprecious minerals, like tourmaline and quartz, are beautiful but quite common.

Azurite
This intense blue ore of copper is often polished for ornamental use.

Sapphires
Blue is the most common colour for sapphires, but orange and yellow stones are also found.

Diamond
This precious carbon mineral is the hardest of all gemstones.

Cat's-eye chrysoberyl
Fine needle-like fibres in this gem reflect a single bright line of light.

MAKING DIAMONDS

For carbon to form diamond crystals, it needs extremely high pressure. This is only found more than 150 km (90 miles) below Earth's surface.

RISING TO THE SURFACE
Kimberlite magma, formed in the mantle, moves up into the crust, bringing diamonds with it. It must travel quickly or else the diamonds will turn back to black carbon.

EXPLODING BUBBLES
Gas bubbles form as the magma nears the surface and begins to boil. Water in the surrounding rocks boils, too, causing an explosion like a shotgun blast.

FORMING DIAMONDS
Afterward, broken rock and magma harden in the volcano's funnel-shaped throat. Erosion carries some of the diamonds to nearby rivers.

Diamonds These come from explosive volcanoes that have burst through Earth's crust. Diamond locations are shown in purple.

Emeralds Emeralds are mined in several countries, but most come from Colombia in South America. Emerald locations are green.

Sapphires and rubies These heavy minerals are found in rivers near corundum-rich rocks. Ruby locations are red, sapphire blue.

Fosterite
A form of olivine, fosterite is the most abundant mineral in Earth's mantle.

Pyrite
This iron sulfide mineral, often called fool's gold, is made into beads and jewellery.

Amethyst
This is a violet or purple form of quartz.

Aquamarine
This delicate blue gemstone is related to emeralds.

Tourmaline
With a variable chemical makeup, tourmaline comes in many kinds and colours.

Imperial topaz
Deep orange crystals such as this are much harder to find than the pale blue variety.

Star ruby
Light shining off tiny needles in this ruby creates a floating starlike reflection.

Quartz
Perfectly formed crystals like this are prized by collectors.

Emerald
The most valuable emeralds have a rich green colour.

Quartz
This transparent gem also occurs in colours such as purple and yellow.

Galaxy opal
The colours in this huge opal, discovered in Australia in 1989, cover all the spectrum, from red to violet.

BIRTHSTONES

Birthstones go back to the time of Moses. He made a breastplate for his brother Aaron, a high priest, which was set with 12 coloured gemstones, representing the tribes of Israel. Gemstones later became associated with the months of the year, and the zodiac. Birthstones supposedly have magical power and bring the wearer good luck.

JANUARY
Garnet

FEBRUARY
Amethyst

MARCH
Aquamarine

APRIL
Diamond

MAY
Emerald

JUNE
Pearl

JULY
Ruby

AUGUST
Peridot

SEPTEMBER
Sapphire

OCTOBER
Opal

NOVEMBER
Topaz

DECEMBER
Turquoise

Metals

Native metals, such as gold, tin and copper, are found naturally in their pure form. The discovery that lumps of metal could be beaten or cast made it possible for people to create better tools and weapons. Gold was first worked about 8,000 years ago, but in its pure form it is too soft to be very useful. About 6,000 years ago, people in Mesopotamia discovered that when tin was added to molten copper, a stronger metal called bronze was formed. This metal mixture, or alloy, was durable and long-lasting. When people learned to extract iron from its rocky ore, it replaced bronze.

WORKING IN BRONZE

Over 3,000 years ago in China, people of the Shang Dynasty traded bronze objects. They used clay moulds to mass-produce ornately decorated vases and urns.

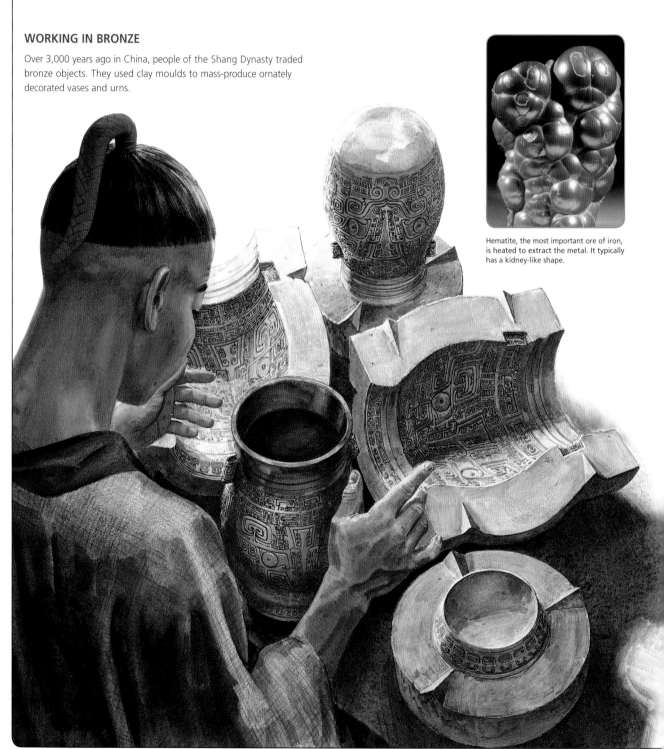

Hematite, the most important ore of iron, is heated to extract the metal. It typically has a kidney-like shape.

NATIVE METALS

NATIVE METALS

Gold, silver and copper are called native metals because they are found in their pure form. Other metals, such as aluminium or iron, have to be extracted from ores. Native metals do not break down or weather easily.

Iron, however, readily combines with oxygen – it rusts when exposed to air. Some metals, such as aluminium, need a lot of energy to extract them. As a result, they have only recently become useful to humans.

GOLD
Native gold is often found with quartz. It typically has treelike crystals and a bright metallic luster.

Gold has long been a precious metal. This death mask was made for Tutankhamen, an Egyptian king who began his reign in 1361 BC at age nine and died age eighteen. The mask is decorated with precious stones.

COPPER
Native copper is generally found in branching crystals. It is covered with a blue-green film where it has come in contact with the air.

The Hopewell culture of Ohio, USA, flourished from 300 BC to AD 500. Craftsmen used copper to make artifacts, such as this raven.

SILVER
Native silver forms long, thin crystal branches with a black tarnished skin.

Peru was once a rich source of silver. This pendant, engraved with a god wearing a feathered-ax headdress, is from the Chimu people. Their culture reached its peak in the 1400s.

Fossils

Most of what we know about life on Earth comes from the study of the fossilised remains of living things. Fossils are created over a long period of time. For a plant or animal to become a fossil, it must die in the right place, be covered by sediment and escape decay, scavenging animals, and erosion. The fossil record has many gaps. Organisms with hard body parts – such as shells, skeletons and teeth – are more readily fossilised than soft-bodied animals, and water dwellers are more readily fossilised than land dwellers. The fossil record makes exciting reading. As well as the stories of individual species, it charts the history of the whole living world, showing dead-end lines, periods of rapid growth and devastating mass extinctions.

CAUGHT IN SAP
These gnats were trapped about 40 million years ago by sticky tree sap that hardened to become amber. Many are missing legs and wings, which they lost as they struggled to free themselves.

Humans appear
NEOGENE

Bivalve mollusk

Tyrannosaurus rex

Archaeopteryx

Cycad leaves

Discosauriscus (amphibian)

PALEOGENE

23 mya

65.5 mya

CRETACEOUS

146 mya

JURASSIC

200 mya

TRIASSIC

251 mya

PERMIAN

FROM BONE TO STONE

All living things die, but few become fossils. Fossils form when the hard remains of living creatures are buried and protected beneath sediment. Soft-bodied creatures decompose too quickly to preserve well.

SAFE FROM SCAVENGERS
A dinosaur dies. Its body sinks to the bottom of a still lake. The soft parts decay, leaving the hard parts.

COVERED BY SAND
The dinosaur's hard parts are preserved, preventing them from decaying or washing away.

FOSSIL TIMELINE

In this spiralling timeline, each period after the long Precambrian era is highlighted by a fossil typical of that time. Fossils show us how life has changed over the ages, from simple cells to complex creatures like ourselves.

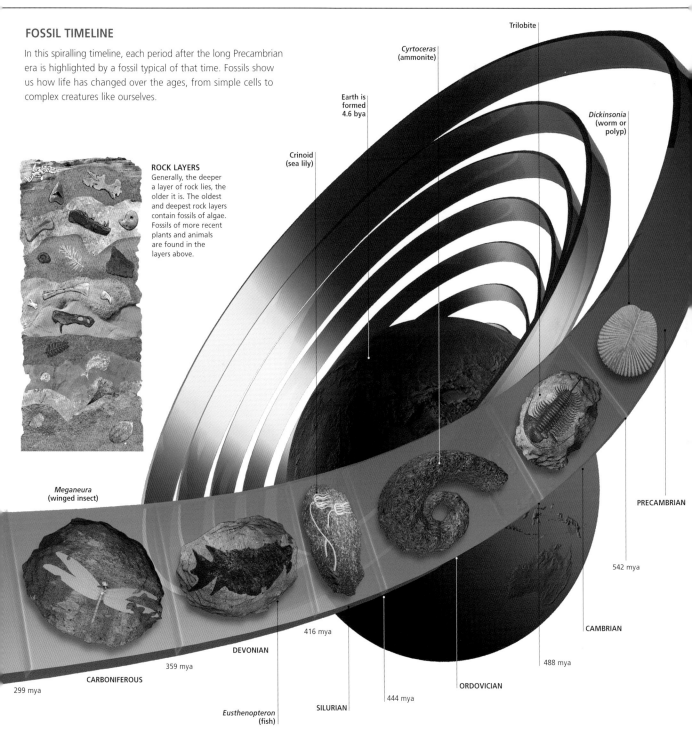

ROCK LAYERS
Generally, the deeper a layer of rock lies, the older it is. The oldest and deepest rock layers contain fossils of algae. Fossils of more recent plants and animals are found in the layers above.

Trilobite

Cyrtoceras
(ammonite)

Earth is formed 4.6 bya

Dickinsonia
(worm or polyp)

Crinoid
(sea lily)

PRECAMBRIAN

Meganeura
(winged insect)

542 mya

CAMBRIAN

488 mya

ORDOVICIAN

444 mya

416 mya

DEVONIAN

359 mya

Eusthenopteron
(fish)

SILURIAN

CARBONIFEROUS

299 mya

COMPRESSED LAYERS
Layers of sediment build up and flatten the skeleton; this slowly hardens into solid rock.

UPLIFT AND EROSION
After millions of years, the rock rises again to the surface and the bones are exposed.

Plants and invertebrates

When plants become fossils, they are petrified, or turned to stone. The fine details of delicate leaves can be preserved in mudstone. More durable plant parts, such as tree trunks and branches, can survive rough conditions. These are found in sandstone and volcanic ash. Invertebrates – animals without backbones – that have hard body parts like shells or spines are more commonly found as fossils than their soft-bodied relatives. Mollusks are one of the largest groups in the animal kingdom, and their fossils are common. These include clams and mussels, snails and ammonites. Coral fossils may be found in limestone.

Brachiopod
These two-shelled marine animals look like mollusks but are not closely related to them.

Tumulites

Pyritised ammonite
An ammonite shell has been completely replaced by beautiful, golden pyrite.

Nostoceras
As they grow, cephalopods like *Nostoceras* add chambers to their shell.

FROM TREES TO STONE

Sometimes whole forests can be petrified. This happens when water containing silica replaces the living tissue of the trees with minerals.

Bryozoan
These delicate fanlike creatures, dotted with tiny holes, are preserved in shale.

Hydnoceras **sponge**
While this is a soft sponge, it has a hard frame. This frame can be preserved as a fossil.

Fern leaf
A perfect impression of leaves and their veins is preserved between rock layers.

Gastropod
This spiralled snail, now fossilised in sandstone, once lived on the seafloor.

Hexactinellid sponge
This is a fragment of hard sponge skeleton.

Pieces of petrified wood from the Triassic are scattered over the ground at Petrified Forest National Park, Arizona, USA.

Trilobites
Trilobites lived in the oceans. They had well-defined body sections.

Burgess shale crinoid
This animal used tentacles to bring food towards its central mouth.

Coeloptychium **sponge**

Ammonite

Ginkgo wood
This section of fossilised wood from an ancient ginkgo tree shows its growth rings.

Spiny urchin
Sea urchin spines usually fall off before the shell is fossilised.

Amber
These gnats, now preserved in amber, flew in a coniferous forest 40 million years ago.

Mawsonites
Jellyfish are rarely found as fossils because their soft bodies decompose quickly.

Ammonite

Crinoids, or sea lilies, had spiny skin and were attached to the seafloor by a stem.

This fossilised maple leaf in stone shows a clear picture of its structure.

Fossilised stems and berries can reveal a lot about this basswood tree.

Growth chambers are clearly visible inside these ammonite shell fossils.

Vertebrates

Vertebrates are animals with an internal skeleton of hard bones. The oldest known specimens appeared about 500 million years ago. Vertebrate fossils include fish, amphibians, reptiles, dinosaurs, birds, mammals and humans. Vertebrates are not found as often as plant or invertebrate fossils, especially complete specimens. This is because their remains were usually eaten by scavengers soon after they died and the bones were scattered.

Archaeopteryx, a small feathered dinosaur, lived during the Jurassic. Like its modern descendants – birds – it had light, hollow bones for speed and agility.

This squirrel-like rodent, an early mammal, ate seeds and leaves like today's squirrels.

This frog lived 49 million years ago. The fossil was found in the Grube Messel quarry, Germany.

The fossil of this ancient python shows that it was very similar to modern pythons.

FOSSIL DETECTIVES

Parasaurolophus was a plant-eating dinosaur that lived in the late Cretaceous, between about 83 and 65 million years ago. It lived at a dangerous time when huge predators, such as *Tyrannosaurus*, were at large. It probably lived in herds for protection.

Scientists have studied the fossil to work out how *Parasaurolophus* used its unusual bony crest. They believe it was like a trumpet that warned others when predators were near.

The first fossil skeleton of *Parasaurolophus* was discovered in 1921 in Alberta, Canada. It is one of the most complete dinosaur fossils ever found and has been carefully preserved.

Missing bones are replaced with plaster.

THE FOSSIL SITE
The bones of *Baryonyx* were dug out of a clay pit in southern England. They were laid out in an outline of the animal so the missing pieces could be reconstructed.

Location of *Baryonyx* fossils

Original fossil remains

CHASMOSAURUS
This heavy, plant-eating dinosaur had horns and an armour-plated head for protection.

This heavy animal walked on four legs.

This three-toed animal ran on two legs.

ALLOSAURUS
It was a large, but agile, hunter with long, muscular legs for fast running.

Dynamic Earth

Volcanoes

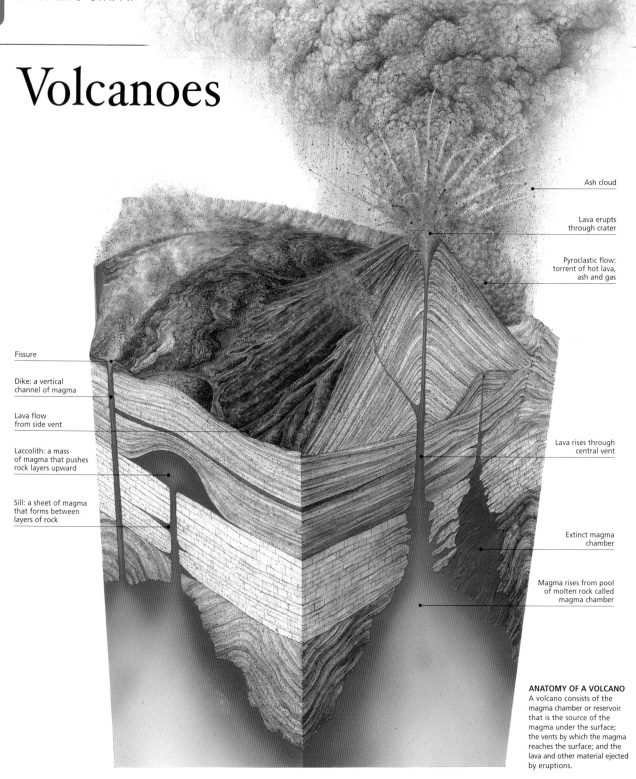

Ash cloud

Lava erupts through crater

Pyroclastic flow: torrent of hot lava, ash and gas

Fissure

Dike: a vertical channel of magma

Lava flow from side vent

Laccolith: a mass of magma that pushes rock layers upward

Sill: a sheet of magma that forms between layers of rock

Lava rises through central vent

Extinct magma chamber

Magma rises from pool of molten rock called magma chamber

ANATOMY OF A VOLCANO
A volcano consists of the magma chamber or reservoir that is the source of the magma under the surface; the vents by which the magma reaches the surface; and the lava and other material ejected by eruptions.

Volcanoes form where magma – incredibly hot, liquid rock – rises from Earth's upper mantle and collects in a chamber just below the crust. As more magma arrives, the pressure inside the chamber increases until the magma rises through fissures and overflows in an eruption. When it reaches the surface, magma becomes lava.

The type of eruption depends on the composition of the lava. If it is thick and contains large amounts of gas, the eruption releases cinders and clouds of ash in an explosion. If the lava is thin with little gas, it flows across the surface. If the magma comes into contact with water underground, the volcano explodes violently.

KINDS OF VOLCANOES

A fissure volcano forms where lava erupts along a fracture in Earth's surface. A shield volcano occurs when erupted material builds a low-angle hill. A cinder cone is made from cinders and ash erupted from a central vent. A composite volcano is made from layers of lava, ash and material eroded from the sides of the cone.

FISSURE VOLCANO
Fracture

Fissure

SHIELD VOLCANO
Magma chamber
Low-angle cone

CINDER CONE
Steep cone
Vent

COMPOSITE VOLCANO
Steep cone

HOW A LAVA TUBE FORMS
Lava hardens on exposure to air, but it continues to flow through tunnels beneath the surface. When lava stops flowing, the tunnels remain as hollow lava tubes up to 30 m (100 feet) wide and 15 m (50 feet) high.

1 Lava rivers These develop a hard skin soon after the lava starts flowing.

Cooling skin
Hot interior

2 Hard skin This becomes harder and forms a tube through which the lava keeps flowing.

Lava river
Hard tube
Lava tube

3 Hollow tube A hollow tube is left when the lava stops flowing.

Hollow lava tube

FLOWING LAVA

Magma is hot. When it reaches the surface, its temperature is usually about 1,200°C (2,200°F), which is why it glows red. Lava flowing down the sides of a volcano and across the nearby land is a mixture of molten rock and blocks of solid rock. Gases bubble out of cooling lava.

Pahoehoe
Lava that forms a smooth, flowing surface

A'a
Lava that hardens into lumps

Hot-spot volcanoes

Beneath Earth's crust, and far from the edges of tectonic plates, there are places where very hot material in the mantle rises all the way to the base of the crust. These are known as hot spots. The mantle rock is so hot it melts the solid rock and forms a magma chamber. Eventually, the magma erupts to the surface as a volcano. Tectonic plates move, but hot spots remain in the same place. When the plates move over a hot spot, a chain of volcanoes is created. An ocean hot spot can produce a line of volcanic islands. The volcanoes closest to the hot spot are active; those further away are extinct.

THE HOT-SPOT CYCLE

This diagram illustrates the birth, life and death of hot-spot volcanoes. At the front, active volcanoes are erupting above the hot spot. Behind lie older volcanoes that have been worn down by erosion. Those whose rims are fringed with coral are called atolls. Those that lie underwater are called seamounts.

Eroded, extinct volcano

Active shield volcano above hot spot

New volcano forming under the sea

Magma chamber

Feeder channel

Hot material in Earth's mantle

Coral atoll

Seamount

Continental plate

Oceanic plate
being pushed under
continental plate

Direction of
plate movement

Oceanic plate

LINKS IN THE CHAIN

As a tectonic plate passes over a
hot spot, a series of volcanoes forms.
Geologists can use these to trace the
movement of the plate.

Rising magma at a hot spot produces
a volcano on land or under the sea.

New volcanoes form as the plate moves
over the stationary hot spot; old ones die.

A chain of volcanoes or volcanic islands
marks the plate's passage over the hot spot.

HOT SPOTS OF THE WORLD
There are many hot spots. Prominent ones include those
at Yellowstone National Park and Hawaii, USA, Iceland,
the Galápagos Islands and the Azores.

NO RT H
AMERICA
PL AT E

EURASIAN PL   AT E

A FRICAN
PL AT E

INDIAN
PL AT E

PA CIFIC
PL AT E

PA CIFIC
PL AT E

SOMALI
PL AT E

SOUTH
AMERICAN
PL AT E

NAZCA
PL AT E

AUSTRALIAN PL   AT E

AN TA RCTIC PL   AT E

KEY
● Hot spot

An opening in the roof of a lava tube in Hawaii, USA, reveals
the furnace below. The islands are a chain of hot-spot volcanoes.

Iceland formed over a hot spot. Its landscape is littered with
bubbling mud pools, steaming craters and extinct volcanoes.

Kilauea

Kilauea, on the Big Island of Hawaii, is one of the world's most active volcanoes. It may have started erupting 600,000 years ago and has been erupting continuously since 1983. It can throw fountains of lava up to 600 m (2,000 feet) into the air. The volcano makes up more than 13 per cent of the area of the island, and its plumbing reaches 60 km (37 miles) deep into Earth. Because it is constantly erupting, Kilauea is still growing. But it is also falling apart as landslides carry huge amounts of debris away from the centre of the volcano towards the sea. According to Hawaiian legend, Kilauea is home to Pele, the volcano goddess.

HAWAII'S BIG ISLAND

Kilauea is located on Hawaii's Big Island. It is one of five volcanoes on the island. It is not the largest volcano – that honour goes to Mauna Loa – but it is the most active. Kilauea is also the most visited volcano on the planet.

Fountains of lava erupt from one of Kilauea's many craters and vents. Kilauea has been erupting constantly for more than 25 years.

Magma chamber
near Earth's surface

Site of current
eruption

Plants growing
on volcanic soil

Kilauea caldera

Earthquake

Earthquake

Oceanic crust

Magma-filled vent

Sea level

Earth's mantle

Earthquake

Earth's outer core

Earth's inner core

INSIDE KILAUEA

Kilauea is a Hawaiian-style, or shield
volcano. It shoots out almost continuous
eruptions of lava that can travel up to
10 km per hour (6 miles/h).

TYPES OF ERUPTIONS

There are five main kinds of volcanic eruptions.
Scientists name and describe them as follows.

Hawaiian Large amounts of runny lava erupt
and produce wide, low volcanoes.

Peléean Blocks of thick, sticky lava are
followed by a burning cloud of ash and gas.

Strombolian Small, sticky lava bombs and
blocks, ash, gas and glowing cinders erupt.

Vulcanian Violent explosions shoot out very
thick lava and large lava bombs.

Plinian Cinders, gas and ash are thrown great
distances high into the air.

Volcanoes around the world

Most volcanoes occur along the edges of tectonic plates. Where oceanic and continental plates collide, the denser oceanic plate is pushed under the lighter continental plate, a process known as 'subduction'. As well, new crust is continually formed by magma that rises to the surface and forces oceanic plates to separate. Both types of interaction between plates produce volcanoes and earthquakes. All the boundaries to the Pacific Plate are active, and form a nearly continuous line of oceanic volcanic mountains extending in a horseshoe shape for 40,000 km (25,000 miles). The volcanoes surrounding the ocean are often described as a 'Ring of Fire'. The ring includes many famous volcanoes – Fuji, Pinatubo, Tambora, Krakatau and Mount St Helens.

DANGER ZONES

Three-quarters of the world's active volcanoes, including some of the most violent, occur in the ring that surrounds the Pacific Ocean. The northward movement of the African Plate into the Eurasian Plate has created volcanoes in southern Europe, and in 1963 a volcano on the Mid-Atlantic Ridge produced the island of Surtsey, Iceland.

DUST AND ASH

Clouds of gas, dust and ash from extremely violent volcanic eruptions can sometimes rise above the troposphere and reach the stratosphere, where they can remain for months. They stop sunlight reaching Earth, and the world's climate becomes colder.

MOUNT PELEE, MARTINIQUE, 1902
An eruption on May 8, 1902, destroyed the town of Saint-Pierre and killed more than 26,000 people.

Novarupta, 1912

NORTH AMERICA

Mount St Helens, 1980

Mauna Loa, 1984

El Chickon, 1982

Mount Pelée, 1902

Santa Maria, 1902

PACIFIC OCEAN

SOUTH AMERICA

Mount Hudson, 1991

Wind direction

Volcanic dust and ash

Stratosphere

Troposphere

MAUNA LOA, HAWAII, USA, 1984
This is Earth's largest volcano and it has been active for thousands of years. Most recently, it erupted from March 24 to April 15 in 1984. No one lost their lives. Previous eruptions have destroyed villages.

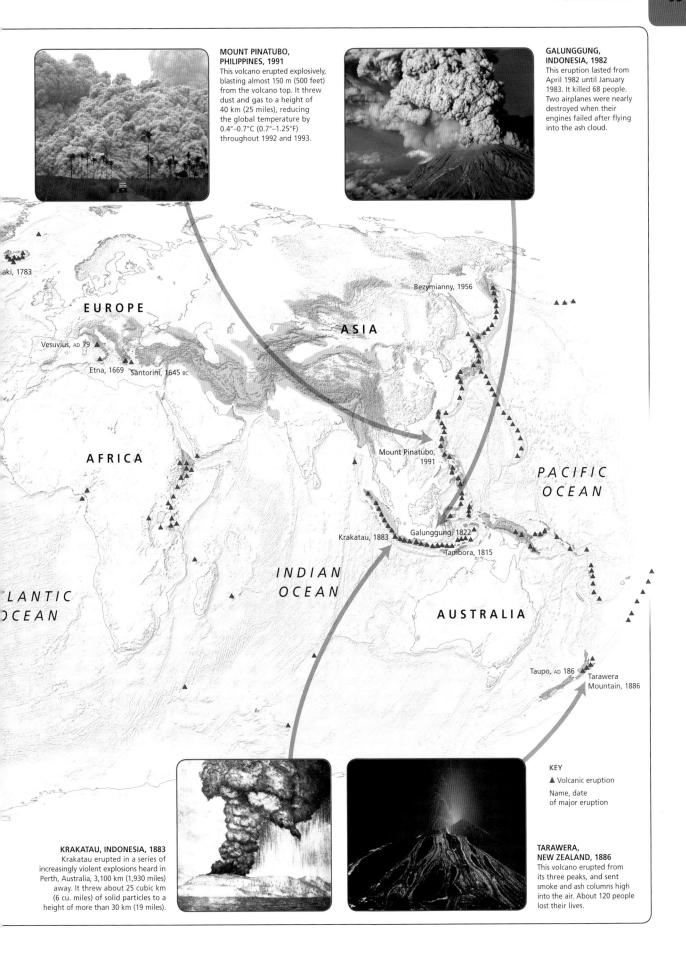

MOUNT PINATUBO, PHILIPPINES, 1991
This volcano erupted explosively, blasting almost 150 m (500 feet) from the volcano top. It threw dust and gas to a height of 40 km (25 miles), reducing the global temperature by 0.4°–0.7°C (0.7°–1.25°F) throughout 1992 and 1993.

GALUNGGUNG, INDONESIA, 1982
This eruption lasted from April 1982 until January 1983. It killed 68 people. Two airplanes were nearly destroyed when their engines failed after flying into the ash cloud.

aki, 1783

EUROPE

ASIA

Bezymianny, 1956

Vesuvius, AD 79

Etna, 1669
Santorini, 1645 BC

AFRICA

PACIFIC OCEAN

Mount Pinatubo, 1991

INDIAN OCEAN

Krakatau, 1883
Galunggung 1822
Tambora, 1815

ATLANTIC OCEAN

AUSTRALIA

Taupo, AD 186
Tarawera Mountain, 1886

KEY
▲ Volcanic eruption
Name, date of major eruption

KRAKATAU, INDONESIA, 1883
Krakatau erupted in a series of increasingly violent explosions heard in Perth, Australia, 3,100 km (1,930 miles) away. It threw about 25 cubic km (6 cu. miles) of solid particles to a height of more than 30 km (19 miles).

TARAWERA, NEW ZEALAND, 1886
This volcano erupted from its three peaks, and sent smoke and ash columns high into the air. About 120 people lost their lives.

Volcanic landscapes

When volcanoes spill molten rock across Earth's surface, they remake the surrounding landscape. The Deccan Plateau in India consists of a sheet of volcanic basalt that covers more than 500,000 square km (193,000 sq. miles) and is more than 1.6 km (1 mile) thick. The plateau was formed when, over a period of a million years, lava from a hot-spot volcano spread across a third of India. The lava hardened to form a thick layer of basalt. Eroded volcanoes are dramatic landscape features. Britain has no active volcanoes, but Arthur's Seat on the skyline of Edinburgh, Scotland, is an extinct volcano. Calderas, which are created when the top of a volcano collapses into its empty magma chamber, often fill with water and form distinctive lakes.

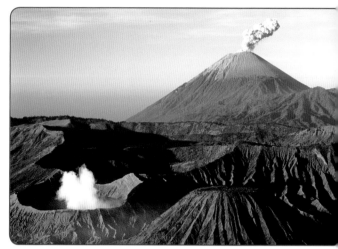

With the active volcano Gunung Semeru, the highest point on Java, Indonesia, in the distance and the smoking Gunung Bromo caldera in the foreground, this landscape is entirely volcanic.

READING THE CLUES

Landscapes contain evidence of past volcanic activity. The erosion of softer rocks exposes volcanic basalt, plugs of solidified lava and dikes of hardened magma. Sills are small lava sheets, usually up to about 30 m (100 feet) thick. Calderas may have small cinder cones, or craters, from later eruptions. When a caldera floods its cinder cone becomes an island.

Plug and dikes are formed by lava left in vents of a volcano.

Old lava flow

Caldera contains a small crater.

COLUMNS AND PLUGS

MAKING COLUMNS

Cooling lava
Lava cools from the surface downwards and shrinks as it hardens.

Vertical cracks
Cracks appear and grow towards each other and the hot centre.

Columns
These form when the cracks join up with each other.

The Giant's Causeway in Northern Ireland is an exposure of basalt columns.

MAKING PLUGS

Active volcano
Magma rises through a vent in the volcano.

Eruption ends
When the magma chamber is empty, any magma still in the vent solidifies.

Ship Rock

Plug forms
Erosion removes the outer layers of the volcano, and exposes the lava as a plug.

Ship Rock, New Mexico, USA, is a plug that formed inside a volcano.

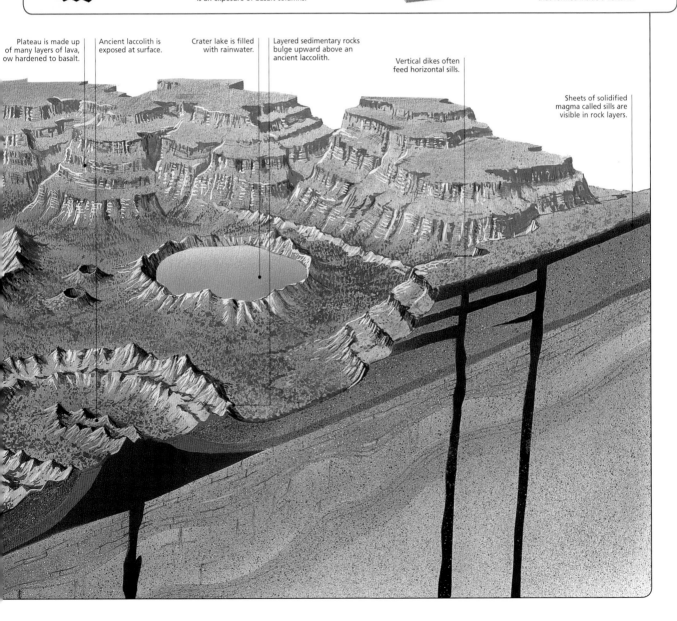

Plateau is made up of many layers of lava, ow hardened to basalt.

Ancient laccolith is exposed at surface.

Crater lake is filled with rainwater.

Layered sedimentary rocks bulge upward above an ancient laccolith.

Vertical dikes often feed horizontal sills.

Sheets of solidified magma called sills are visible in rock layers.

Craters and calderas

Craters are the funnel-shaped hollows or cavities that form at the openings, or vents, of volcanoes. The simplest craters occur on the top of volcanic vents and usually have a diameter of about 1 km (half a mile) or less. Sometimes, magma melts some of the rock around the mouth and carries it away, to create a crater at the side of the volcano. A caldera is formed when an eruption empties the magma chamber and its roof is not strong enough to support the weight of the volcano above. Later the volcano may become active again, erupting through the same vent to form a cinder cone inside the caldera.

1 BLOWING ITS TOP
A composite volcano grows above a magma chamber beneath the surface. Ash, gases and lava erupt through a central vent.

2 THE NEXT STAGE
The eruption becomes more violent, throwing ash and gas high into the air. The eruption reduces the amount of magma in the chamber.

HOW A CALDERA FORMS

Calderas are huge craters formed by a massive volcanic eruption. They are often more than 5 km (3 miles) in diameter. The world's largest, Mount Aso, Japan, is 27 km (17 miles) long and 16 km (10 miles) wide.

Mount Aso in Japan is the country's largest active volcano, standing 1,592 m (5,223 feet) above sea level. Its caldera measures 114 km (71 miles) if you walk around the rim.

A lake fills the caldera of Hare Shetan, Ethiopia. The aerial view reveals its circular shape and steep sides.

3 THE CLIMAX
The magma chamber is partly emptied. Magma sinks below the roof of the magma chamber, leaving an empty space.

4 THE COLLAPSE
The roof of the magma chamber can no longer support the weight of the volcano. It collapses downwards along faults around the central vent.

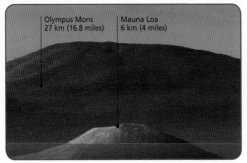

VOLCANOES ON OTHER PLANETS

Space probes have found nine volcanoes on Mars, five on Venus, four on Io, a moon of Jupiter, and many on Neptune's moon Triton. Not all of these resemble volcanoes on Earth. Some erupt sulphur, and volcanoes on Triton erupt liquid nitrogen or methane.

Olympus Mons
27 km (16.8 miles)

Mauna Loa
6 km (4 miles)

Olympus Mons on Mars is the Solar System's largest known volcano, and is more than four times higher than Mauna Loa, Hawaii.

From directly above, the extent of its lava flows can be seen. It is 500 km (310 miles) across, with a caldera 80 km (50 miles) wide.

Earthquakes

An earthquake is a violent release of energy in Earth's crust. When large rock masses move suddenly along faults below ground, the movement shakes the ground above. Earthquakes often happen because rocks are being pushed in two directions, usually because of the movement of tectonic plates. Volcanic activity can also cause earthquakes. The place in the crust where the break happens is called the hypocentre. The place on the surface immediately above the hypocentre is the epicentre. A shallow earthquake has a hypocentre less than 70 km (44 miles) below the surface; intermediate ones occur 70–300 km (44–186 miles) down; and deep earthquakes happen at depths greater than 300 km (186 miles).

5
6
7

People in Izmit, Turkey, search through the rubble for their possessions after the 1999 earthquake. This quake killed more than 17,000 people.

MEASURING EARTHQUAKES

The magnitude of an earthquake is usually measured by the Richter scale, based on the amount of energy released. The Mercalli scale is an alternative measure, devised in 1897 by Giuseppe Mercalli. It divides earthquakes into 12 categories, according to observations of the damage caused.

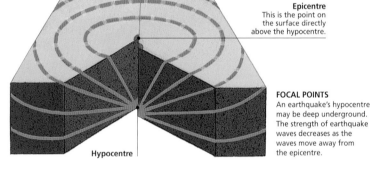

Epicentre
This is the point on the surface directly above the hypocentre.

FOCAL POINTS
An earthquake's hypocentre may be deep underground. The strength of earthquake waves decreases as the waves move away from the epicentre.

Hypocentre

I   People feel no movement beneath them.
II People on upper floors feel slight movement.
III Hanging objects swing, everyone feels the movement.
IV Windows and doors rattle, stationary cars rock.
V   Sleeping people wake, doors swing, dishes break.
VI Walking difficult, trees shake, slight structural damage.
VII Standing difficult, damage to poorly constructed buildings.
VIII Chimneys fall, tree branches break, furniture overturns.
IX   Structural damage to most buildings, ground cracks.
X   Large ground cracks, landslides, most buildings damaged.
XI Buildings collapse, underground pipes fracture.
XII Ground moves in waves, widespread devastation.

I   II   III   IV   V   VI   VII

THE RICHTER SCALE

Charles Richter developed this scale in 1935. Each step on the scale is a tenfold increase in earthquake power. That means that magnitude 7 is 10 times stronger than magnitude 6, and 100 times stronger than magnitude 5.

JAPANESE EARTHQUAKES

Under the islands of Japan, three tectonic plates jostle for position. To the southeast, the Philippine Plate slides beneath the Eurasian Plate. In the east, the Pacific Plate dives under the Eurasian Plate and the Philippine Plate as well. As a result, Japanese people experience regular earthquakes.

Traditional buildings called pagodas are designed to withstand earthquakes.

Traditionally, the Japanese blamed earthquakes on Namazu, a catfish. Usually the deity Kashima held Namazu down, but if he was distracted, Namazu thrashed about, shaking the ground.

A section of expressway was destroyed by a huge earthquake in Kobe in 1995.

SEISMIC WAVES

There are different kinds of earthquake waves. The most dangerous are surface waves.

P–waves
The first waves to arrive are called P-waves. They push and pull rocks in the ground.

S–waves
S-waves then move rocks up and down, and from side to side.

Surface waves
These make the surface move from side to side like a snake, or up and down like an ocean wave.

IX   X   XI   XII

Tsunamis

A tsunami – the name is Japanese for harbour wave – begins on the ocean floor with an earthquake or a large underwater landslide. The movement of the ocean floor sends shock waves through the water, like ripples on a pond, travelling at 645 km per hour (400 miles/h) or more, but only about 90 cm (3 feet) high. Sailors may not even notice these waves. When the waves enter shallow water, friction with the seabed slows them to about 50 km per hour (30 miles/h). The waves that continue to arrive push together, increasing the wave height. The wave trough may come ashore first, causing the sea to retreat, followed by a rapid rise of water sweeping inland. More waves follow. Sometimes a tsunami comes ashore as a vertical wall of water.

A TSUNAMI STRIKES

A tsunami has nothing to do with the tides, but it is more like a tidal movement than a breaker, hence its old name of 'tidal wave'. There are early warning systems to inform people of approaching tsunamis, but there are sometimes natural warning signs. Anyone seeing these signs should move to high ground immediately.

Incoming water advances farther up the shore than usual and remains still for several minutes.

The water retreats away from the coast much farther than normal. This is the first tsunami trough.

A white line on the horizon marks the tsunami wave crest, now approaching very fast.

A tsunami that hit Indonesia on December 26, 2004, killed more than 280,000 people. It was caused by a Richter magnitude 9.3 earthquake.

KILLER WAVE

A towering tsunami is a terrifying sight. As the wave reaches land, it collapses, smacking coastal buildings and hurling boats on land. Often, tsunamis are far more destructive than the earthquakes that caused them.

Earthquakes around the world

Earthquakes can happen almost anywhere. In most parts of the world they are rarely more than a tremor that rattles windows. But there are certain regions where earthquakes are much more violent. The shakiest parts of our planet lie on the boundaries of tectonic plates. The most active earthquake region is known as the 'Ring of Fire' around the Pacific Ocean. The northward advance of the Indian Plate into the Eurasian Plate generates another earthquake zone in central Asia, Malaysia and Indonesia. A third zone runs through Africa and into southern Europe, along the boundaries of four tectonic plates.

ALASKA, USA, 1964
At 9.2 magnitude this was the third-strongest earthquake ever recorded. It struck Prince William Sound and lasted about 4 minutes. Amazingly, only 131 people died.

Alaska, 1964, 9.2

NORTH AMERICA

San Francisco, 1989, 7.1

ATLANTIC OCEAN

Mexico City, 1985, 8.1

Guatemala City, 1976, 7.5

PACIFIC OCEAN

Nothern Peru, 1970, 7.8

SOUTH AMERICA

Valdivia, 1960, 9.5

MEXICO CITY, MEXICO, 1985
This magnitude 8.1 earthquake lasted 3–4 minutes and was followed by a magnitude 7.5 aftershock. It killed 9,000 people, injured 30,000 more and left 100,000 homeless.

RESCUE OPERATIONS

Nations respond to major earthquakes by sending emergency supplies and teams of doctors, fire fighters and specialist rescue workers. Some rescuers use dogs trained to find people trapped under rubble. Others use thermal imaging equipment. Heavy lifting gear moves pieces of buildings and rubble.

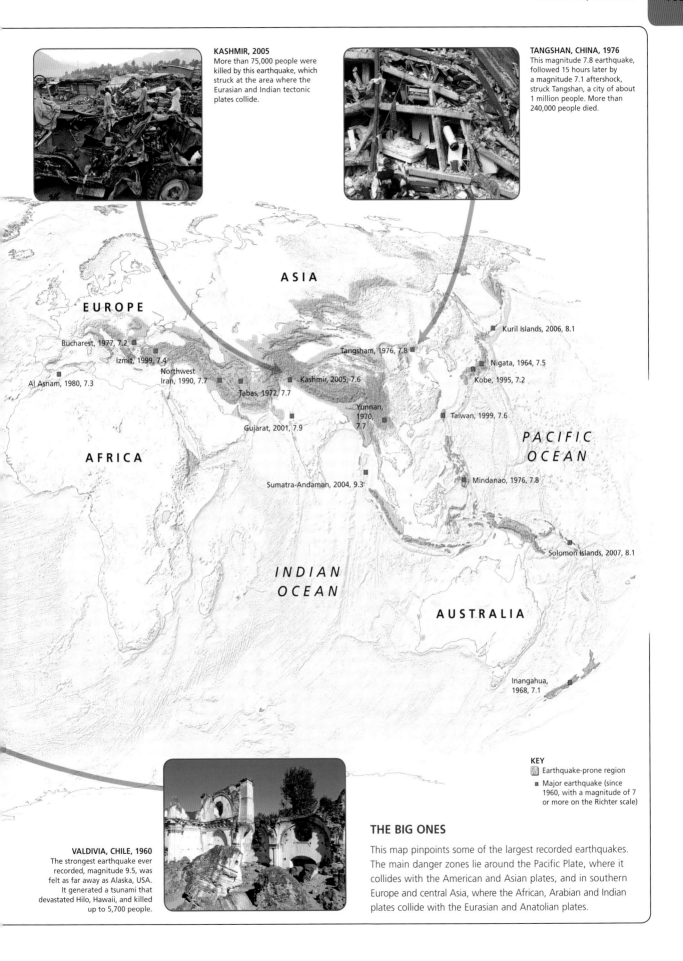

KASHMIR, 2005
More than 75,000 people were killed by this earthquake, which struck at the area where the Eurasian and Indian tectonic plates collide.

TANGSHAN, CHINA, 1976
This magnitude 7.8 earthquake, followed 15 hours later by a magnitude 7.1 aftershock, struck Tangshan, a city of about 1 million people. More than 240,000 people died.

ASIA

EUROPE

Bucharest, 1977, 7.2

Izmit, 1999, 7.4

Northwest Iran, 1990, 7.7

Al Asnam, 1980, 7.3

Tabas, 1972, 7.7

Kashmir, 2005, 7.6

Gujarat, 2001, 7.9

Tangsham, 1976, 7.8

Kuril Islands, 2006, 8.1

Nigata, 1964, 7.5

Kobe, 1995, 7.2

Yunnan, 1970, 7.7

Taiwan, 1999, 7.6

AFRICA

PACIFIC OCEAN

Sumatra-Andaman, 2004, 9.3

Mindanao, 1976, 7.8

INDIAN OCEAN

Solomon Islands, 2007, 8.1

AUSTRALIA

Inangahua, 1968, 7.1

KEY
- Earthquake-prone region
- Major earthquake (since 1960, with a magnitude of 7 or more on the Richter scale)

VALDIVIA, CHILE, 1960
The strongest earthquake ever recorded, magnitude 9.5, was felt as far away as Alaska, USA. It generated a tsunami that devastated Hilo, Hawaii, and killed up to 5,700 people.

THE BIG ONES

This map pinpoints some of the largest recorded earthquakes. The main danger zones lie around the Pacific Plate, where it collides with the American and Asian plates, and in southern Europe and central Asia, where the African, Arabian and Indian plates collide with the Eurasian and Anatolian plates.

Geysers and Hot Springs

The Grand Prismatic Spring in Yellowstone National Park is the largest hot spring in North America. Layers of bacteria create the bright colours around the edges of the hot pool.

Thousands of years after its last eruption, the area beneath a volcano may still be hot. In these areas, known as geothermal regions, heat rising from ancient magma chambers meets water trickling down through the ground. Water deep under the ground can be twice as hot as normal boiling water, but the pressure of the cooler water on top stops it from boiling. When water overflows at the surface, the pressure is released and the deeper, hotter water turns to steam and explodes upward. Depending on the pressure, the water and steam may expode as a giant fountain – a geyser – or bubble out gently as a hot spring.

When water at a hot spring mixes with soil and dissolved minerals, the result is a lake of boiling mud.

Japanese macaques relax in the warmth of a hot spring on the island of Honshu, Japan, escaping winter temperatures of below –15°C (5°F).

People bathe in Iceland's hot springs, even in winter, to soothe sore muscles and benefit from the water's minerals.

Draining
Cold water drains down and meets hot rock. Its temperature increases to above 100°C (212°F), but pressure prevents it from boiling.

Expanding
Hot water expands, rising through the fissures and pushing cold water upwards. This relieves the pressure on the superheated water.

Boiling over
Hot water boils with the pressure relieved, pushing cold water upwards. The water boils explosively, ejecting a column of water and steam.

Cold water

Magma chamber

Fissure

Heat

HOW GEYSERS ERUPT

Rainwater drains through rock fissures until contact with hot rock heats it to more than 100°C (212°F). Because of the weight of cold water above, high pressure prevents the water from boiling. The hot water expands, pushing cold water upwards through the fissures. This relieves the pressure and the hot water boils, violently expelling a column of water and steam.

Glaciers and Ice Sheets

Antarctica's ice sheet is the largest in the world. It holds approximately 70 per cent of the world's freshwater. If melted, it would raise the sea level by more than 55 m (180 feet).

A glacier is a huge amount of ice formed by the buildup of snow. When snow falls every year in a place where the temperature rarely or never rises above freezing, the snowflakes compress into ice. The pressure from newly fallen snow packs older snowflakes together and compresses them into solid ice. Each year's snowfall forms a band and scientists can tell the age of the ice by counting the bands. Because the ice is so heavy, a glacier flows downhill very slowly. If it is contained between the sides of a valley, it is a valley glacier. Ice sheets are dome-shaped glaciers that form when winter snowfall exceeds the amount that melts away in the warmer months.

Moraine

Head of glacier

Head of glacier

Head of glacier

Snout, or end, of glacier

U-shaped valley

Glacial lake

GLACIER ON THE MOVE

As a glacier moves slowly downhill, it carves out a wide U-shaped valley. It rips away loose rocks and pushes rock debris, called moraine, to its sides and in front of it.

SHAPING THE LAND

As they flow, glaciers scour away all the soil, then carve the underlying rocks into shapes an expert eye can recognise thousands of years later, long after the ice has disappeared. Glaciers cut U-shaped valleys, often with waterfalls entering high on their sides. They leave moraines and carry loose rocks long distances.

Between ice ages, the climate is warm and a range of mountains is covered by vegetation. Valleys are V-shaped, with steep sides, and the mountains are rugged.

During an ice age, the climate is too cold for plants and they disappear. Only the tops of the mountains are visible above the ice sheet. Ice flows through the valleys.

When the ice retreats, the valleys that remain are U-shaped. This is because they have been carved out by the slowly moving ice of glaciers.

Avalanches and Landslides

An avalanche tumbles down from Shispar Peak in the Huza region of Pakistan. The sides of the mountain are too steep for snow to form deep layers.

Mountain slopes and hillsides are not always stable. When rock, soil or mud start to move downhill, a landslide can occur. When snow slips from a slope or cliff, an avalanche occurs. The sliding material may move slowly or quickly. Gravity pulls it straight downwards, but part of the weight is directed downhill, along the edge of the slope. An avalanche or landslide occurs when the downhill force is greater than the strength of the material. A solid rock cliff face is perfectly stable, but material not firmly attached to it may move, especially if water makes the surface slippery. Landslides, rock falls, mudslides and avalanches can cause appalling damage. They can demolish buildings and bury entire villages.

MUDFLOWS

AFTER AN ERUPTION

In November 1985, the eruption of Nevado del Ruiz in Colombia melted ice and snow, which caused a devastating mudflow. Armero, 50 km (31 miles) away, was engulfed in a 40-m (131-foot) wall of mud and ash, which killed more than 23,000 people.

Nevado del Ruiz
This volcano is known by locals as the 'sleeping lion'.

Path of the mudflow
This streamed into the Lagunella River valley. It ended up spreading over 40 square km (16 sq. miles).

Town of Armero
Bodies were discovered here up to three weeks after the volcano erupted.

Weathering and Erosion

Wind has driven sand grains onto the solid rock of the Colorado Plateau, USA. This sandblasting has revealed the layers by eroding the softer rock faster than the hard rock.

When rock is exposed to the atmosphere, wind, rain and ice begin to wear it away. This is known as physical weathering. It grinds rocks into soil particles and grains of sand, and can reduce mountain ranges to level plains. Another type of physical weathering happens when extreme pressure and heat deep underground cause rocks to break apart.

Minerals in soil and bedrock can also be broken down when acidic rainwater soaks downwards. When a chemical reaction takes place, it is called chemical weathering. Rainwater reacts with granite, which consists mainly of feldspar, mica and quartz, to change the feldspar and mica to clay, but does not affect the quartz. Erosion is the removal of the products of weathering by wind or water.

Glaciers form from huge piles of snow. They gouge out wide, U-shaped valleys.

Rivers carve canyons and mesas, and wash away rocks and dirt.

Mesa

Canyon

Water can eat through some types of rock to form cave systems.

The ocean waves pound shorelines, cutting sea caves and columns called stacks.

In deserts, windblown sand wears away rock and forms shifting dunes.

WEAR AND TEAR

Weathering can change land in many ways. Glaciers grind out
valleys and transport rocks downhill. Rivers carve canyons and carry
away loose rocks and dirt. Acidic rainwater dissolves limestone to form
caves. Sand, the product of weathering, forms shifting dunes and is blown
against rock formations. Waves erode the coastal hills.

Eroded landscapes

Weathering and erosion reshape landscapes. At present, the world's fastest rate of erosion is found in the Himalaya. This mountain range, the highest in the world, is still rising as India pushes into Eurasia, but it is wearing away almost as fast. Over hundreds of millions of years, weathering and erosion will level these mountains until the region is a flat plain. Northern Canada, now a vast plain with a few low mountains, was once mountainous. Ocean waves are powerful agents of coastal erosion. Their action produces coastal cliffs, caves and stacks. In deserts, wind erosion creates strange landforms and salt weathering produces oddly shaped rocks.

PINNACLES

Rain seldom falls in the desert, but when it does it is often heavy and powerful. Erosion removes surface material, but in some places a covering of resistant rock shields the rock beneath, which is left as a column.

Thin cracks crisscrossing the rock are opened by falling water.

CANYONS

The force of water in rivers cuts canyons in the land, sometimes very quickly. The world's deepest canyon, Yarlung Zangbo Canyon in Tibet, cuts 5.3 km (3.3 miles) into the surface.

A river and its tributaries erode channels along the least resistant parts of sedimentary rock.

SEA STACKS

Where coastal cliffs are made from rocks with vertical joints or faults, waves can eat away at the cliffs, first creating then eroding a headland to make sea-level caves. This produces an arch in the rock, which can collapse and leave a stack.

Erosion creates a headland, which juts out into the ocean.

INSIDE A LIMESTONE CAVE

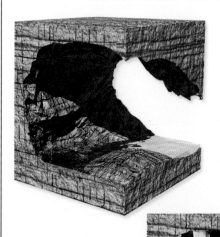

A CAVE FORMS
Acidic rainwater dissolves the calcium carbonate of limestone and carries it away, leaving behind a space that becomes a cave as the water erodes more and more material.

Stalactite

STALACTITES AND STALAGMITES
Water dripping from a cave roof contains dissolved calcium carbonate. As some of the water evaporates, it forms pointy stalactites hanging from the roof. As water drips down, calcium carbonate collects below and stalagmites grow upwards from the cave floor.

Stalagmite

Column

COLUMNS AND PILLARS
Stalactites and stalagmites grow an average 2.5 cm (1 inch) every 1,000 years. It is a very slow process, but eventually stalactites and stalagmites meet, forming pillars inside the cave. Over time, the pillars thicken and become columns.

KARST

Karst describes a hilly landscape, usually made of limestone, which has been eroded by acidic rainwater. Much of the surface rock has dissolved to form rugged, cone-shape peaks, and there are large underground caves, lakes and rivers.

Acidic rainwater dissolves surface limestone and carries it away.

cap rock breaks into sections
erosion widens the cracks.

Erosion removes the material between
the pinnacles and they become thinner.

Pinnacles in Monument Valley, USA, are made from layers of shale
and sandstone, and range in height from 120 to 300 m (400 to 1,000 feet).

he great force of fast-flowing
water deepens the channels
aster than it widens them.

Rocks fall from the nearly
vertical sides of the river valleys,
widening them into canyons.

The riverbed of the Rio Grande River in Texas, USA, is so deep it is almost
level with the land beyond the canyon.

Waves batter the headland, making
back-to-back caves either side.
These meet in an arch.

The arch collapses, leaving
a stack, separated from
the headland.

The Twelve Apostles are limestone stacks in Victoria, Australia. Several
have fallen and there are now only eight.

Erosion continues to sharpen karst
peaks, widen the channels into valleys,
and create a network of caves and
underground waterways.

The landscape of Guanxi, China, consists of steep-sided hills of karst.
The surface soil is thin and most water flows in underground rivers.

Oceans

World Oceans

Oceans and seas cover 71 per cent of Earth's surface. The average depth of the world's five oceans is approximately 3,730 m (12,240 feet), and combined they contain about 1,370 million cubic km (329 million cu. miles) of water. Continents extend for an average of 72 km (45 miles) beyond their coasts as gently sloping continental shelves beneath the water. At the edge of the continental shelves, the water is about 152 m (500 feet) deep. Beyond that the ocean floor slopes more steeply. The deepest point is at the bottom of the Mariana Trench, about 11 km (6.8 miles) below the surface of the Pacific Ocean.

WATER ON EARTH
Oceans hold 97.5 per cent of Earth's water. Of the remaining 2.5 per cent, 79 per cent is frozen in ice caps and glaciers, 20 per cent is below ground and only 1 per cent – 0.00025 per cent of all the water on Earth – exists as freshwater.

Oceans 97.5%   Freshwater 2.5%

Groundwater 20%

Ice caps and glaciers 79%

Accessible surface
freshwater 1%

Water in lakes 52%

Water vapour in
atmosphere 8%

Water in
soil 38%

Water in rivers 1%   Water in living
organisims 1%

SIZE OF THE OCEANS
The Pacific is by far the largest ocean. It makes up 46 per cent of the world's oceans. The Atlantic and Indian oceans are almost the same size, and the Southern and Arctic oceans are much smaller.

Pacific Ocean
155.6 million sq. km
(60.1 million sq. miles)
46%

Indian Ocean
68.6 million sq. km
(26.5 million sq. miles)
21%

Atlantic Ocean
76.8 million sq. km
(29.6 million sq. miles)
23%

Arctic Ocean
14.1 million sq. km
(5.5 million sq. miles)
4%

Southern Ocean
20.3 million sq. km
(7.9 million sq. miles)
6%

THE HEMISPHERES

Water is not distributed evenly on Earth because tectonic plate movements have carried the continents northwards into the Northern Hemisphere. More than two-thirds of Earth's land area is found here, while oceans cover nearly 80 per cent of the Southern Hemisphere. At present the Atlantic Ocean is growing wider and the Pacific Ocean is getting narrower.

NORTHERN HEMISPHERE

SOUTHERN HEMISPHERE

Pacific Ocean

The world's largest ocean extends from the Aleutian Islands in the north to the border of the Southern Ocean at 60°S latitude in the south. As well as having the largest area, covering about one-third of Earth's surface, the Pacific is the deepest ocean. It is also the coldest, with an average water temperature of 3.4°C (38.1°F) and the least saline, or salty. Its salt content averages 34.7 parts per thousand. Its vast area and depth mean the Pacific provides a wide variety of habitats for living organisms. Intense tectonic plate activity surrounding the Pacific has produced many volcanic islands.

NATURAL RESOURCES

The upwards flow of nutrient-rich water off the Peruvian coast sustains one of the world's largest fisheries. The North Pacific also supports important commercial fisheries for cod, sea bass, salmon and tuna. There are mineral, oil and gas reserves on continental shelves around the ocean.

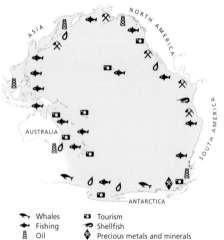

- 🐋 Whales
- 🐟 Fishing
- ⬛ Oil
- 💧 Gas
- ▣ Tourism
- 🦐 Shellfish
- ◆ Precious metals and minerals
- ⚒ Mining

Marine iguanas are sea-dwelling lizards that live only on the Galapagos Islands.

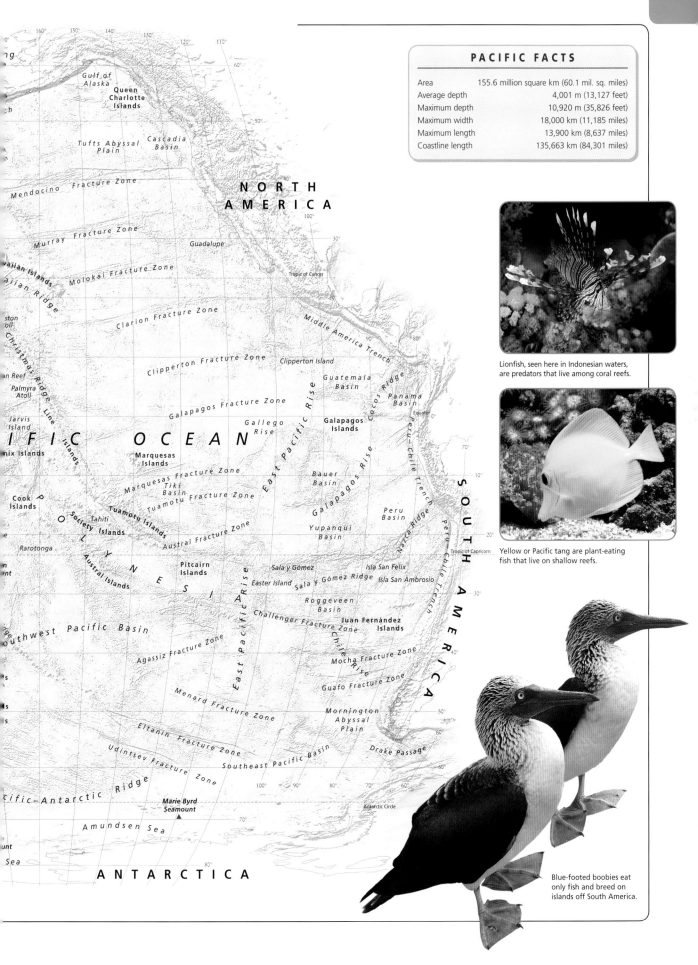

Gulf of Alaska

Queen Charlotte Islands

Tufts Abyssal Plain

Cascadia Basin

NORTH AMERICA

Mendocino Fracture Zone

Murray Fracture Zone

Guadalupe

Tropic of Cancer

Hawaiian Islands

Molokai Fracture Zone

Hawaiian Ridge

Clarion Fracture Zone

Christmas Ridge

Palmyra Atoll

Clipperton Fracture Zone

Clipperton Island

Line Islands

Jarvis Island

Galapagos Fracture Zone

Guatemala Basin

Cocos Ridge

Panama Basin

Phoenix Islands

PACIFIC OCEAN

Gallego Rise

Galapagos Islands

Equator

Marquesas Islands

East Pacific Rise

Galapagos Rise

Peru-Chile Trench

Bauer Basin

Cook Islands

Marquesas Fracture Zone

Tiki Basin

Tuamotu Fracture Zone

Peru Basin

POLYNESIA

Tahiti

Society Islands

Tuamotu Islands

Austral Fracture Zone

Yupanqui Basin

Nazca Ridge

Rarotonga

Austral Islands

Pitcairn Islands

East Pacific Rise

Sala y Gómez

Sala y Gómez Ridge

Isla San Felix

Tropic of Capricorn

Easter Island

Isla San Ambrosio

SOUTH AMERICA

Roggeveen Basin

Challenger Fracture Zone

Juan Fernández Islands

Southwest Pacific Basin

Agassiz Fracture Zone

Mocha Fracture Zone

Chile Rise

Menard Fracture Zone

Guafo Fracture Zone

Mornington Abyssal Plain

Eltanin Fracture Zone

Drake Passage

Udintsev Fracture Zone

Southeast Pacific Basin

Pacific-Antarctic Ridge

Marie Byrd Seamount

Antarctic Circle

Amundsen Sea

ANTARCTICA

Lionfish, seen here in Indonesian waters, are predators that live among coral reefs.

Yellow or Pacific tang are plant-eating fish that live on shallow reefs.

Blue-footed boobies eat only fish and breed on islands off South America.

Atlantic Ocean

The world's second-largest ocean, covering approximately one-fifth of Earth's surface, is the warmest, with an average water temperature of 3.7°C (38.7°F). It is also the saltiest; Atlantic Ocean water contains 34.9 parts per thousand of salt. Its deepest point is 8,605 m (28,233 feet) below the surface, at Milwaukee Deep in the Puerto Rico Trench. Along the ocean floor, from Iceland to about 58°S, a large underwater mountain range, called the Mid-Atlantic Ridge, divides the ocean into two sections, each consisting of several basins. The ocean is widening by about 2.5 cm (1 inch) a year as the seafloor spreads at the Mid-Atlantic Ridge.

NATURAL RESOURCES

The Atlantic has some of the world's richest shallow-water fisheries, although many have been over-exploited. There are oil and gas reserves off the African, Caribbean and Gulf of Mexico coasts and mineral reserves, including precious stones, off North and South America and Africa.

Fishing
Whales
Shellfish
Precious metals and minerals
Mining
Oil
Gas
Tourism

Atlantic walrus feed mainly on mollusks. They live in eastern Canada and the high Arctic.

Atlantic spotted dolphins inhabit tropical and subtropical Atlantic waters, and live in social groups called pods.

Hawksbill turtles inhabit tropical and subtropical oceans, including the western Atlantic and Caribbean.

ATLANTIC FACTS

Area	76.8 million square km (29.6 mil. sq. miles)
Average depth	3,605 m (11,828 feet)
Maximum depth	8,605 m (28,233 feet)
Maximum width	7,900 km (4,909 miles)
Maximum length	14,120 km (8,774 miles)
Coastline length	111,866 km (69,514 miles)

The Azores are a group of Portuguese islands in the North Atlantic.

Offshore oil rigs drill for oil found deep under the ocean bed. Workers can access the rig by ship or helicopter.

Sperm whales live in all the oceans. This pair, photographed near the Azores, is about to dive.

Indian Ocean

The Indian Ocean is the third-largest ocean and occupies 21 per cent of the total world ocean area. It is bounded by Africa to the west, the Arabian Sea and Bay of Bengal to the north, Indonesia and Australia to the east, and the Southern Ocean to the south. The Indian Ocean is divided from the Atlantic at 20°E, and it is separated from the Pacific at 147°E. North of the equator, the Indian Ocean climate is dominated by the monsoon winds. Tropical cyclones sometimes develop in the Bay of Bengal.

NATURAL RESOURCES

Warm waters restrict the growth of the marine algae on which fish feed. Fishing is therefore limited, aside from shrimp and tuna. There are large offshore oil and gas reserves. Beach sands contain minerals that several countries are exploiting.

Fishing
Shellfish
Whales
Oil
Gas
Mining
Precious metals and minerals
Tourism

Seychelles giant tortoises, once thought to be extinct, now survive only in captivity.

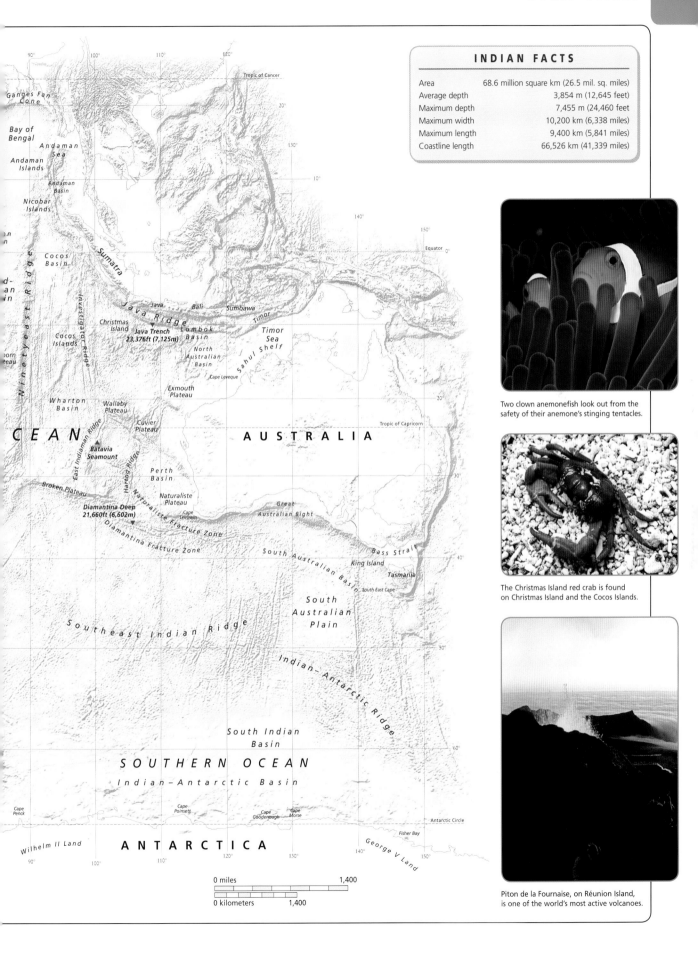

INDIAN FACTS

Area	68.6 million square km (26.5 mil. sq. miles)
Average depth	3,854 m (12,645 feet)
Maximum depth	7,455 m (24,460 feet)
Maximum width	10,200 km (6,338 miles)
Maximum length	9,400 km (5,841 miles)
Coastline length	66,526 km (41,339 miles)

Two clown anemonefish look out from the safety of their anemone's stinging tentacles.

The Christmas Island red crab is found on Christmas Island and the Cocos Islands.

Piton de la Fournaise, on Réunion Island, is one of the world's most active volcanoes.

Map labels: Ganges Fan Cone, Bay of Bengal, Andaman Sea, Andaman Islands, Andaman Basin, Nicobar Islands, Cocos Basin, Ninetyeast Ridge, Investigator Ridge, Sumatra, Java Ridge, Java, Bali, Sumbawa, Timor, Christmas Island, Java Trench 23,376ft (7,125m), Cocos Islands, Lombok Basin, North Australian Basin, Timor Sea, Sahul Shelf, Cape Leveque, Exmouth Plateau, Wharton Basin, Wallaby Plateau, Cuvier Plateau, OCEAN, AUSTRALIA, East Indiaman Ridge, Batavia Seamount, Hartog Ridge, Perth Basin, Broken Plateau, Naturaliste Plateau, Cape Leeuwin, Diamantina Deep 21,660ft (6,602m), Naturaliste Fracture Zone, Diamantina Fracture Zone, Great Australian Bight, South Australian Basin, Bass Strait, King Island, Tasmania, South East Cape, South Australian Plain, Southeast Indian Ridge, Indian–Antarctic Ridge, South Indian Basin, SOUTHERN OCEAN, Indian–Antarctic Basin, Cape Penck, Cape Poinsett, Cape Goodenough, Cape Morse, Antarctic Circle, Fisher Bay, Wilhelm II Land, ANTARCTICA, George V Land, Tropic of Cancer, Equator, Tropic of Capricorn

0 miles 1,400
0 kilometers 1,400

Arctic Ocean

The Arctic Ocean is the smallest and shallowest of the world's five oceans. It is almost completely landlocked by North America and Eurasia, and is connected to the Pacific through the Bering Strait and to the Atlantic through the Greenland and Labrador seas. The ocean is roughly circular and divided by a mid-ocean ridge into two basins, the Eurasian and North American. Most of the ocean is covered in ice during winter and some areas remain frozen in summer. In recent years the thickness and area of sea ice have been decreasing. The salt content of the Arctic Ocean varies seasonally as sea ice expands and retreats.

ARCTIC FACTS

Area	14.1 million square km (5.5 mil. sq. miles)
Average depth	1,430 m (4,690 feet)
Maximum depth	5,625 m (18,456 feet)
Maximum width	3,200 km (1,988 miles)
Maximum length	5,000 km (3,107 miles)
Coastline length	45,389 km (28,205 miles)

0 miles   1,000

0 kilometers   1,000

The polar bear, the largest of all bears, is superbly adapted to Arctic conditions.

A diver swims beneath the pack ice in the Canada Basin, off North America.

An Inuit man completes an igloo, which probably took two hours to build.

Brünnich's guillemots perch on a ledge in the Svalbard archipelago, Norway.

Colourful wooden houses are typical at Longyearbyen on Spitsbergen island.

Southern Ocean

The Southern Ocean did not officially exist until 2000, when the International Hydrographic Organisation formally defined its boundaries as the waters between latitude 60°S and the continent of Antarctica. Sometimes called the circumpolar sea or the Antarctic Ocean, it is the world's fourth-largest ocean. Surface sea temperatures range from about –2° to 10°C (28° to 50°F). With no continent to slow and deflect them, the winds in the Southern Ocean blow without interruption right around the world. The region is known for ferocious winds and high waves. Sea ice is widespread and the area and thickness of winter ice have increased in recent decades.

King penguins incubate their eggs on their feet under a warm fold of skin and waterproof feathers. Older chicks may try to snuggle back under.

SOUTHERN FACTS

Area	20.3 million square km (7.9 mil. sq. miles)
Average depth	4,500 m (14,450 feet)
Maximum depth	7,235 m (23,736 feet)
Maximum width	2,700 km (1,678 miles)
Maximum length	21,500 km (13,360 miles)
Coastline length	17,968 km (11,165 miles)

Maitri (India)
Novolazarevskaya (Russia)
Riiser-Larsen Peninsula
Antarctic Circle
Lützow-Holm Bay
Asuka (Japan)
Syowa (Japan)
Mizuho (Japan)
Molodezhnaya (Russia)
Thorshavnheiane
Maud Land
Enderby Land
Law Promontory
E a s t
Kemp Land
Mawson (Australia)
Mac Robertson Land
Prince Charles Mountains
Cape Darnley
Amery Ice Shelf
Mackenzie Bay
A n t
Zhongshan (China)
Davis (Australia)
Princess Elizabeth Land
C T I C A
Kaiser Wilhelm II Land
Davis Sea
a r c t
h Pole
dsen-Scott (USA)
Mirny (Russia)
Antarctic Circle
Queen Mary Land
i c
South Geomagnetic Pole
Vostok (Russia)
Shackleton Ice Shelf
arctic Mountains
Maud
♦ Kirkpatrick
55ft (4,528m)
Mill Island
Bowman Island
e Shelf
Vincennes Bay
Casey (Australia)
Cape Poinsett
Cape Waldron
Scott Base (NZ)
oss Island
McMurdo (USA)
Victoria Land
Wilkes Land
Sea
Terra Nova Bay (Italy)
Porpoise Bay
Adélie Land
Mt Minto
13,665ft (4,165m) ▲
George V Land
Dumont d'Urville (France)
Cape Keltie
Dumont d'Urville Sea
SOUTHERN OCEAN
Cape Adare
Leningradskaya (Russia)
Cape Cheetham
Mawson Peninsula
Cape Freshfield
Cape Gray
Balleny Islands
Antarctic Circle

This pair of wandering albatrosses perform a courtship 'dance'. They mate for life.

This seal stretches out to rest on the snow covering Brown Bluff, on the Antarctic Peninsula.

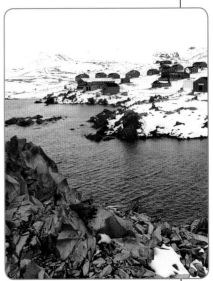

The Argentine research station and settlement Esperanza is home to about 50 people over winter.

The Spreading Seas

Ocean basins, or underwater depressions, cover about 65 per cent of Earth's surface. Layers of sediment cover the ocean floor, but beneath the sediment the oceanic crust is made from basaltic rocks. Continents contain rocks that are billions of years old, but no oceanic crust is more than 200 million years old. Mid-ocean ridges that run through all oceans mark the boundaries between tectonic plates that are moving apart. Oceans expand as magma pushes through the crust at these ridges. The oceanic crust does not remain intact because as some basins expand, others are shrinking to compensate. Dense oceanic crust is pulled beneath lighter continental crust where the two collide, and the oceanic crust sinks into Earth's mantle.

Direction of moving plate

Trench

Direction of moving plate

Mid-ocean ridge

Ocean basin

Continental crust

As the oceanic plates collide with the continents, they are forced downwards and form deep ocean trenches.

The seafloor is forced apart, slowly spreading on both sides of the mid-ocean ridge.

Magma seeps upwards through the ocean floor. Ridges form when it becomes solid.

CHANGING SHAPE

Oceans expand because two plates are moving apart along a mid-ocean ridge. Rising magma solidifies and forms new crust on the floor of the ocean basin. When sediment covers the floor and buries the mountains, an abyssal plain forms.

The abyssal plain is formed when sediment covers the ocean basin.

Direction of moving plate

Mid-Atlantic Ridge

South America

Africa

ON THE SEAFLOOR
The North American, Caribbean and South American tectonic plates are moving away from the Eurasian and African plates. This makes the Atlantic Ocean wider by about 2.5 cm (1 inch) each year. The plate boundary is along the Mid-Atlantic Ridge, where rising magma fills the gap.

PARTING THE LANDSCAPE

An ocean begins when plates move apart along a margin below a continent. This forms a rift valley that floods when the rifting crosses the coast, allowing seawater to enter.

Rift valley

Rifting This occurs when a section of crust falls between two sets of parallel faults, forming a rift valley.

Flooded rift valley

Flooding When the rift crosses the coast it floods. As plates continue to move apart, the rift widens. Rising magma hardens and forms the rift valley floor.

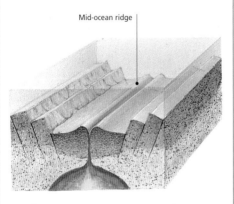

Mid-ocean ridge

Spreading As spreading continues, the flooded rift valley widens until it is a narrow sea, such as the Red Sea. Magma forms a central ridge in what will become an ocean.

Currents

This view from space shows Cape Hatteras in North Carolina, USA, looking south to where the Gulf Stream begins to swing eastward.

Warm air rises over the equator and falls in cooler regions to the north and south. This movement carries heat away from the equator and produces wind systems. Surface winds push seawater along and create ocean currents. These begin near the equator and flow from east to west in both hemispheres.

As they approach continents, currents turn away from the equator, then continue turning, forming circular patterns called gyres in the Atlantic, Pacific and Indian oceans. In the Arctic and Southern oceans, sea ice makes some water colder and saltier. This sinks below water that is less dense and flows away as a deepwater current.

SURFACE CURRENTS

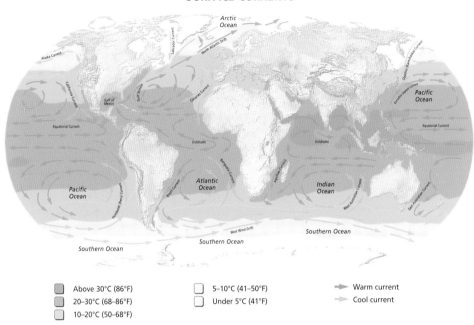

■ Above 30°C (86°F)	□ 5–10°C (41–50°F)
■ 20–30°C (68–86°F)	□ Under 5°C (41°F)
□ 10–20°C (50–68°F)	

➡ Warm current
➡ Cool current

DEEPWATER CURRENTS

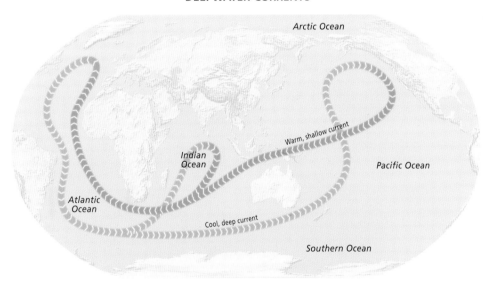

Seawater is densest when its temperature is just above freezing. When it freezes, salt is released from the ice, so water next to the ice is saltier, and therefore denser, than more distant water. The dense water sinks to form a deepwater current known as the Great Conveyor.

A current flowing south along Argentina's coast swirls into one heading north.

Clouds form over the Alaska Current, which brings warm water into contact with cold air.

The warm East Australian Current (pink) sweeps from the Coral Sea to the cool south.

THE GULF STREAM

The Gulf Stream is a warm ocean current that runs up the east coast of North America before it swings across the North Atlantic to Europe. It is like a river in the sea, 80–145 km (50–90 miles) wide. Also like a river, it forms curving meanders or circular eddies as it flows through the ocean.

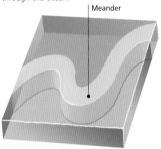

The Gulf Stream follows a curving path that eventually forms a meander.

The meander keeps curving until it almost surrounds a body of warm or cool water.

When the meander closes, its cuts off part of the current and forms an eddy.

Warm-water eddies spin clockwise and cool-water eddies spin anticlockwise.

Waves and Tides

Water at the top of a tall wave may travel faster than water at the bottom. The top then falls forwards and the wave curls as it breaks.

The gravity of the Moon works against Earth's gravity to produce two bulges – the tides – that move around Earth. The tides follow the orbit of the Moon, and raise and lower the surface of the ocean. One bulge is on the part of Earth facing the Moon and the other bulge is on the opposite side of Earth. The Moon takes 24 hours 50 minutes to complete one orbit, so high and low tides occur every 12 hours 25 minutes – exactly half of the Moon's orbit time. When tides pass around the coastline, their timing and magnitude – called the 'reach' – may change. While tides affect waves below the ocean, surface waves are caused by winds.

OCEAN TIDES

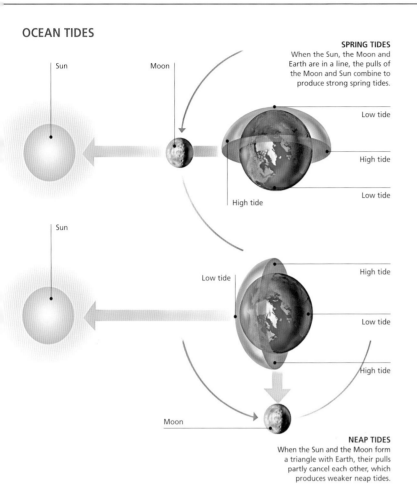

SPRING TIDES
When the Sun, the Moon and Earth are in a line, the pulls of the Moon and Sun combine to produce strong spring tides.

Sun

Moon

Low tide

High tide

Low tide

High tide

Sun

High tide

Low tide

Low tide

High tide

Moon

NEAP TIDES
When the Sun and the Moon form a triangle with Earth, their pulls partly cancel each other, which produces weaker neap tides.

The Bay of Fundy, Canada, has the world's largest tidal range. At low tide, rocks and ocean floor are visible and can be walked over.

At high tide, the ocean washes over the rocks and ocean floor.

FORMING A WAVE

Tides and movements along the thermocline produce waves below the surface, but surface waves are caused by winds that push the water forward. Their size depends on the strength of the wind and the distance over which it blows.

The thermocline is the ocean layer beneath the warm surface water and above the deep sea.

Tall, slow-moving waves occur within the thermocline.

Direction of wind

Surface waves are created by winds and storms.

Shoreline

Continental shelf

Surface waves are produced when particles of water move in circular patterns.

Ocean Zones and Habitats

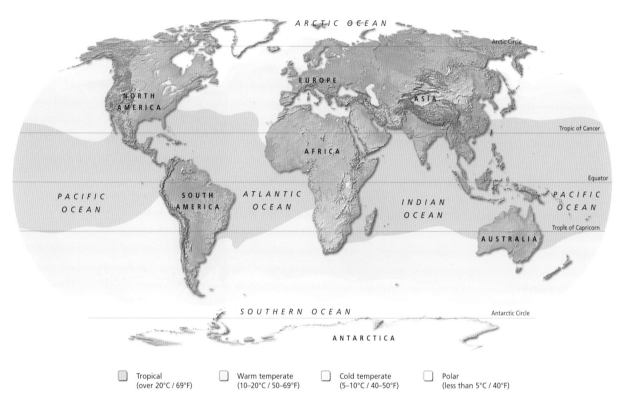

ARCTIC OCEAN

Arctic Circle

EUROPE

ASIA

NORTH
AMERICA

AFRICA

Tropic of Cancer

Equator

PACIFIC
OCEAN

SOUTH
AMERICA

ATLANTIC
OCEAN

INDIAN
OCEAN

PACIFIC
OCEAN

Tropic of Capricorn

AUSTRALIA

SOUTHERN OCEAN

Antarctic Circle

ANTARCTICA

☐ Tropical
(over 20°C / 69°F)

☐ Warm temperate
(10–20°C / 50–69°F)

☐ Cold temperate
(5–10°C / 40–50°F)

☐ Polar
(less than 5°C / 40°F)

Ocean zones can be arranged by water temperature. Warm and cool currents can affect the boundaries of the zones, but they generally follow degrees north and south of the equator.

A ll the oceans are connected, so there is a 'world ocean', and some of its inhabitants range widely through it. Most, however, stay within a particular part of the ocean. The oceans can be divided into geographical zones based on water temperature. A second set of zones is arranged by depth, based on the amount of light and nutrients. Each zone provides habitats for plants and animals. In some places on the ocean floor, hot water containing dissolved minerals spouts from the crust. Only very special life-forms can exist in these extreme habitats.

Tropical seas support coral reefs that are home to countless algae, fish and invertebrates.

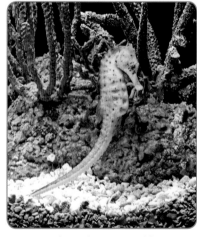

Temperate seas have underwater seaweed forests not far from shore, with many fish, including seahorses.

Polar seas teem with life, despite the cold. They support marine mammals, including whales. These are belugas, or white whales.

UNDER THE SEA

UNDERWATER LANDSCAPES

Beyond the shore, the seafloor slopes gently down the continental shelf until the water is about 150 m (500 feet) deep. The angle gets steeper on the continental slope. At the bottom lies the abyssal plain, a vast expanse of the ocean floor, more than 2,000 m (6,500 feet) below the surface. The ocean floor contains fracture zones, isolated hills called seamounts, mountains at the spreading ridges and deep trenches.

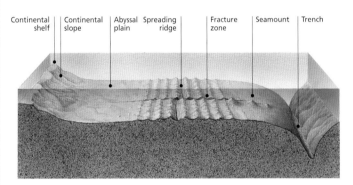

Continental shelf | Continental slope | Abyssal plain | Spreading ridge | Fracture zone | Seamount | Trench

THE DARK ZONE

Light is made up of the colours of the spectrum, each one with a different wavelength. Water absorbs red – the longest wavelength – quickly, followed by the other colours. Green and blue travel deepest, but eventually there is no light at all.

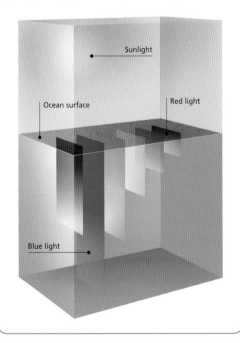

Sunlight

Ocean surface

Red light

Blue light

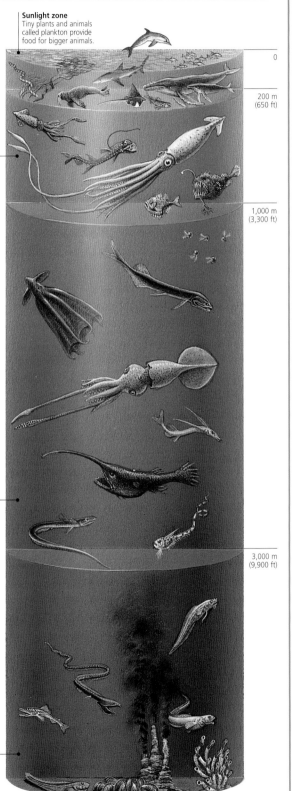

Sunlight zone
Tiny plants and animals called plankton provide food for bigger animals.

0

200 m
(650 ft)

Twilight zone
Many fish carry bacteria that produce light. This may be for camouflage or for identifying species.

1,000 m
(3,300 ft)

Midnight zone
Below 1,000 m (3,300 feet) is total darkness. The water is cold, still and sparsely populated. Many animals produce their own light.

3,000 m
(9,900 ft)

Abyssal zone
Covering 75 per cent of the ocean floor, this is a constant 4°C (39°F). Food particles rain down from above. Predators have lures and huge jaws for consuming prey larger than themselves.

Coral reefs

Coral reefs cover up to 600,000 square km (232,000 sq. miles) in tropical and subtropical seas. They grow best in brightly lit clear water at temperatures of 23–25°C (73–77°F). Coral polyps are small, soft-bodied animals that build an external skeleton called a corallite for protection. Reef-building polyps live side by side and their corallites fuse together into a corallum. As individual polyps die, others settle on top of the abandoned corallums. Little by little the structure grows into a coral reef. Algae grow on the outside of coral polyps. Together with waste products from the polyps, they form the basis of some of the world's richest ecosystems. Today, however, many coral reefs are fragile habitats.

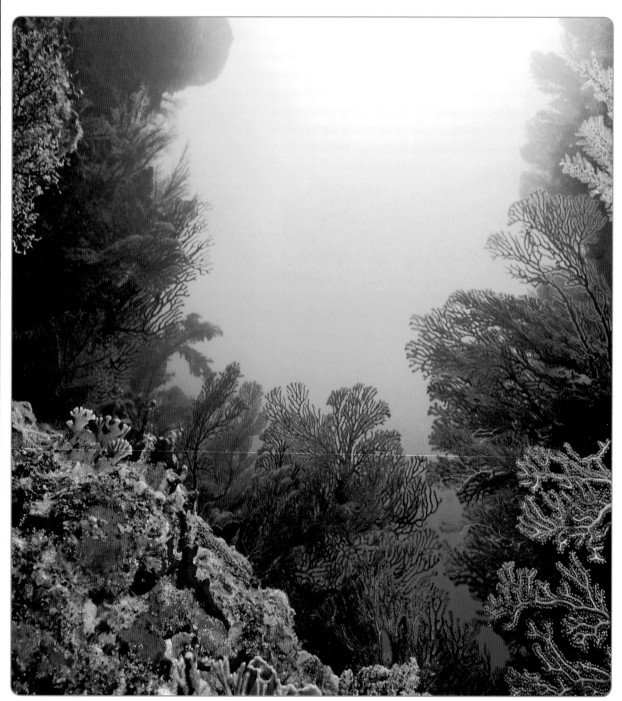

Almond Point Reef, found near Bequia on the St Vincent and Grenadine Islands in the Caribbean, is teeming with life. Sea fans fringe the sides and base of two coral outcrops.

CORAL REEFS OF THE WORLD

Coral reefs require clear water. Algae that live on the coral form a community that brings food to the polyps, and the algae need light to make their own food. Reefs rarely occur more than 60 m (200 feet) deep. Corals are sensitive to temperature, so they grow only in warm tropical and subtropical waters.

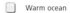 Warm ocean   Deep-water coral reefs   Warm-water coral reefs

KINDS OF CORAL

A colony of bubble corals looks like cream-coloured grapes. The 'bubbles' are filled with water.

Brain corals live in warm, shallow water. Their name refers to their appearance.

The tentacles of this soft coral look like the frilly petals of flowers, and the mouth looks like the stem.

Purple or Californian hydrocoral is a coastal species occasionally found in cold water.

HABITAT WATCH

Crown-of-thorns starfish, seen here feeding on coral polyps, attack reefs throughout the world. They have caused considerable damage to Australia's Great Barrier Reef. Reefs also suffer from bleaching, caused by the loss of their algae due to pollution.

INSIDE A CORAL POLYP

A polyp consists of a hollow digestive chamber attached to a disk at the base. The mouth is at the top, surrounded by tentacles used to capture food. Zooxanthellae are single-celled creatures that live and feed inside the chamber.

Zooxanthellae

Mouth

Tentacles

Sting cell

Thin layer of soft tissue

Digestive chamber

Limestone skeleton

Along the coast

The coast is where land and sea meet and interact. What happens depends on the energy of the waves and the resistance of the land. Sea storms hurl water against the shore with great force. Waves erode even the hardest rocks, cutting into hills to create sea cliffs. If the coast is sheltered by a headland or offshore sandbar, the waves exert less force, and plants and animals thrive in rock pools. Tides erode sandy beaches, but also build them elsewhere. Winds can drive dry sand inland to build coastal dunes.

HABITAT WATCH

Hong Kong is crowded, so the authorities are filling in the bay and building on top. The expansion already covers about 31 square km (12 sq. miles) and more is planned. Filling in the bay destroys the original underwater habitat.

A SANDY BEACH
A beach has distinct zones. The berm is a hill of sediment piled up by waves. Currents sometimes create a buildup of sand called a sandbar. Most sand grains are made from eroded quartz, but white sand consists of finely ground seashells.

Cliffs

Berm

Backshore

Foreshore

Offshore

Sandbar

LIVING ON THE EDGE

Seabirds roost and nest on cliff ledges close to the water that supplies their food. The tufted puffin nests in holes along northern North Pacific shores.

BETWEEN THE TIDES

IN A TIDAL ROCK POOL

Plants and animals living on the shore must cope with being dry and then exposed to salt water and rain. Rock pools in the zone between high and low tides are refreshed every time seawater flows in at high tide. Seaweeds grow in rock pools, and many animals live there permanently – among them sea anemones, hermit crabs, mussels and several kinds of fish.

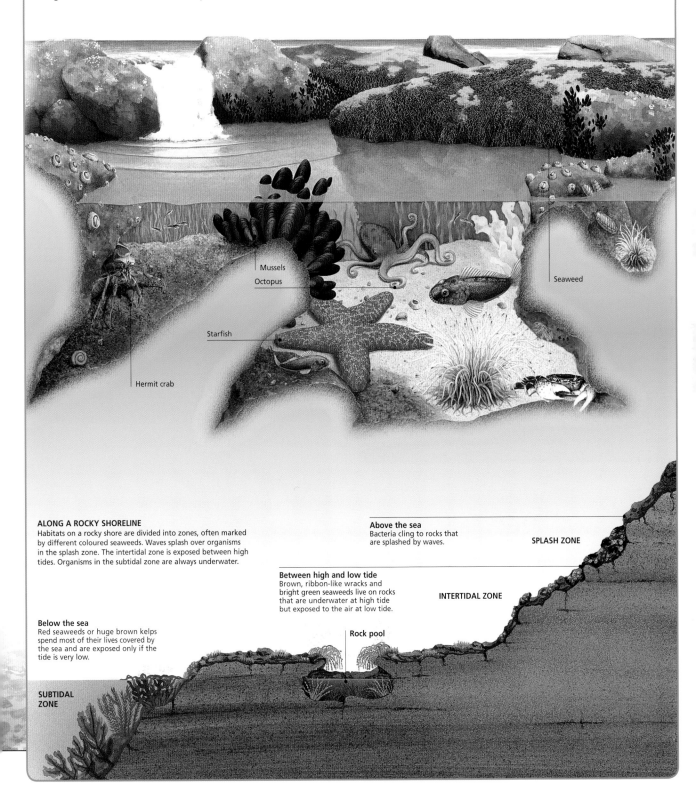

Mussels

Octopus

Seaweed

Starfish

Hermit crab

ALONG A ROCKY SHORELINE

Habitats on a rocky shore are divided into zones, often marked by different coloured seaweeds. Waves splash over organisms in the splash zone. The intertidal zone is exposed between high tides. Organisms in the subtidal zone are always underwater.

Above the sea
Bacteria cling to rocks that are splashed by waves.

SPLASH ZONE

Between high and low tide
Brown, ribbon-like wracks and bright green seaweeds live on rocks that are underwater at high tide but exposed to the air at low tide.

INTERTIDAL ZONE

Below the sea
Red seaweeds or huge brown kelps spend most of their lives covered by the sea and are exposed only if the tide is very low.

Rock pool

SUBTIDAL ZONE

Into the deep

With increasing depth the ocean becomes darker and colder, and the pressure becomes much greater. The ocean is divided into layers on the basis of these changes. Life is most abundant in the uppermost layer, where there is enough light for algae to make the sugars that provide their food. This is the sunlight zone above the continental shelves and extending to about 200 m (650 feet). Many of the fish living in darkness below the sunlight zone are marked with spots of light. They depend on food particles that sink from above and their bodies must withstand huge pressures. They cannot survive if they are brought to the surface.

STUDYING THE DEEP

Scientists use submersibles – specially designed submarines – to study the deep ocean and its inhabitants. These vessels have bright lights and mechanical 'arms' and 'hands' to collect samples. The American *Alvin* can reach nearly 4,575 m (15,000 feet) and the Russian *Mir* can reach 6,100 m (20,000 feet).

The Japanese submersible *Shinkai* can descend to 6,527 m (21,415 feet), the deepest of all.

HABITAT WATCH

Fishing fleets have caught such large numbers of fish in the sunlight and twilight zones of the oceans that stocks are seriously depleted. Southern bluefin tuna has been hunted to the point where it is in danger of becoming extinct.

Southern bluefin tuna

1 Seaweeds can grow only where there is light, so are rarely below 30 m (100 feet).

2 Butterflyfish feed on coral polyps in shallow waters.

3 Anchovies dwell in waters above 300 m (980 feet).

4 Bonito are fast-swimming fish above 200 m (660 feet).

5 Marlin are one of the fastest species of fish in the open ocean; they live down to 915 m (3,000 feet).

6 Jellyfish float in the surface layers, grazing on tiny plants and animals.

7 Requiem sharks prey on fish and turtles at depths up to 350 m (1,150 feet).

8 Dolphins hunt small fish, squid and crustaceans. They live above 180 m (590 feet).

9 Octopuses are stealth predators that live mostly in shallow coastal waters.

10 Sperm whales can dive to 3,000 m (9,850 feet) to catch large deep-sea squid.

11 Animals become fewer with increasing depth. The width of the cone shows the numbers at each level.

12 Lanternfish live 300–1,200 m (980–3,940 feet) during the

day, migrating upwards
at night to feed.

13 Squid are found from the surface
down to the depths.

14 Hatchetfish live down to a depth
of 1,525 m (5,000 feet). At night,
they feed on surface-living
zooplankton.

15 The mola mola has a distinctive
body shape and can be up to
3 m (10 feet) long.

16 Deep-sea rays feed on the bottom
of the sea, eating small mollusks,
worms and crustaceans.

17 Lanternfish have sensitive eyes
and lights on their undersides.
They live at 1,000 m (3,300 feet),
but swim upwards to feed.

18 Viperfish live above 4,400 m
(14,440 feet). They are ambush
predators of passing animals.

19 Anglerfish have a long, thin spine
with a bulb-shaped, glowing tip.

20 Ribbonfish reach up to 2.5 m (8
feet) long, feed on smaller fish
and squid, and live near
the ocean floor.

21 Filter-feeding sponges and soft
corals are found from the edge
of the sea down to 6,000 m
(19,680 feet).

22 Grenadiers feed on dead and
live material. They live between
200 and 2,000 m (660 and
6,600 feet).

23 Deep-sea eels are active predators
and scavengers that are found
down to 3,500 m (11,500 feet).

24 Giant squids are the largest
invertebrates in the world. They
can reach up to 20 m (66 feet)
in length.

25 Anglerfish dangle a lure at the
end of a long 'fishing rod'. Any
fish trying to bite the lure will be
trapped by the anglerfish's huge
mouth, filled with sharp teeth.

26 Mantas are related to sharks.
They grow to 7 m (23 feet) across
and are the largest species of ray
in the world.

27 Tripodfish live between 250 and
5,700 m (820 and 18,700 feet).

28 Deep-sea isopods are found at all
depths. Most species are found
in the deepest parts of the ocean
– between 1,000 and 5,000 m
(3,300 and 16,400 feet).

The ocean floor

Scientists once believed that the abyssal plain supported almost no life. That view changed with the discovery of hydrothermal vents and cold seeps. Hydrothermal vents are places at or near mid-ocean ridges where water heated by magma rises from the ocean floor. The water, usually heated to about 300°C (570°F), is rich in dissolved minerals, especially sulphides. Nearby, where the temperature is about 38°C (100°F), the minerals support a rich variety of organisms. Cold seeps are similar, but the water is cold and rich in dissolved methane or a mixture of hydrocarbons.

BLACK SMOKERS

Sulphur compounds rising from a hydrothermal vent darken the water, making a 'black smoker'. Minerals build a 'chimney' around a black smoker, up to 10 m (33 feet) high. The vent attracts animals, including beard worms, acorn worms, mussels, giant clams and crabs.

Smoking chimneys
Sulphur and other minerals deposited on the sides of the vents build natural chimneys.

INSIDE A BLACK SMOKER

Water heated by contact with magma and rich in sulphides rises from the ocean floor. The sulphides darken the rising water. Minerals form a chimney around the central vent.

Sulphide-rich plume of hot water

Main vent

Rock chimney

Side vent

Heated seawater

Hot rocks and magma

Circulation system
The arrows show how cold seawater seeps down through the ridge. Magma heats it to an amazing 300°C (570°F), then the water rises back up through the vent.

THE OCEAN FOOD WEB

A WEB OF SEA LIFE

Apart from the area around hydrothermal vents, all marine life, even in the deep ocean darkness, depends on photosynthesis, a process by which tiny plants – phytoplankton – turn the Sun's rays into food. Tiny animals – zooplankton – feed on phytoplankton, and larger animals feed on both types of plankton. The ocean food web shows that all marine organisms, as well as seabirds and mammals that spend time on land, are connected by the food they eat.

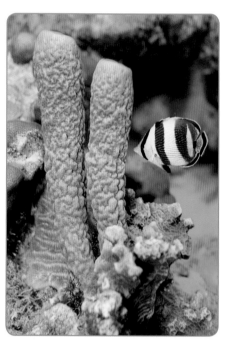

Sponges are clusters of specialised cells that feed on particles they filter from the water.

The Atlantic puffin has a beak with a sawlike edge that lets it carry several fish back to its young in the nest.

The Sun's energy drives the food web.

Seabirds feed on small fish.

Plants trap the energy of the Sun.

Phytoplankton trap the energy of the Sun.

Zooplankton graze on phytoplankton.

Small fish graze on zooplankton.

Killer whales feed on large fish and seals.

Large fish eat small fish.

Seals feed on large fish.

Land

Mapping Earth

EARTH FACTS

CIRCUMFERENCE OF EARTH AROUND THE EQUATOR
40 067 km (24,902 miles)

AREA OF SEA
362,033,000 square km (137,782,000 sq. miles)

AREA OF LAND ABOVE SEA LEVEL
148,021,000 square km (57,151,000 sq. miles)

OCEANS AND SEAS
Oceans and seas cover most of Earth's surface. Their average depth is about 3,730 m (12,240 feet). On the seafloor are mountains and valleys that dwarf anything on land.

CONTINENTS
There are seven major landmasses, or continents, on the planet. Europe and Asia are known as separate continents but they form a single landmass, called Eurasia.

NORTHERN HEMISPHERE

SOUTHERN HEMISPHERE

POLAR REGIONS
Earth's polar regions have extremely low temperatures. The frozen continent of Antarctica lies in the south and the ice-laden Arctic Ocean in the north.

HEMISPHERES
Hemisphere, meaning 'half ball', refers to the half of a planet's surface on either side of the equator. More than two-thirds of Earth's land area is found in the Northern Hemisphere.

Continents

Oceans and seas dominate the globe, covering 71 per cent of its surface. The land between these large bodies of water is traditionally divided into seven major landmasses or continents: Europe, Asia, North America, South America, Africa, Australia and Antarctica. Europe and Asia form a single landmass, known as Eurasia, but are conventionally identified as separate continents because of their distinct peoples and histories. Though technically a continent in itself, Australia is usually considered part of the large region of Oceania, which includes other islands of the southwestern Pacific.

North America

AREA: 22,078,049 SQUARE KM **(8,522,127** SQ. MILES)
POPULATION: 513,350,000

The continent of North America extends from just south of the North Pole to just north of the equator. It includes almost every kind of environment, from ice caps to forests, mountains, deserts and jungles. In the west, an almost unbroken chain of mountains stretches from Alaska to Costa Rica and includes the Rocky Mountains. The United States of America (the USA) and Canada are the largest of the continent's 23 countries.

```
0              1,000 miles

0     1,000 kilometres
```

WORLD RECORDS

WORLD'S LARGEST GORGE
Grand Canyon, USA, 446 km (277 miles) long, 16 km (10 miles) wide, 1.6 km (1 mile) deep

WORLD'S LARGEST FRESHWATER LAKE
Lake Superior, USA–Canada, 82,350 square km (31,800 sq. miles)

WORLD'S LONGEST CAVE SYSTEM
Mammoth Caves, USA, 565 km (351 miles)

WORLD'S LARGEST ACTIVE VOLCANO
Mauna Loa, Hawaii, USA, 4,170 m (13,680 feet) high, 120 km (75 miles) long, 50 km (31 miles) wide

WORLD'S LONGEST BORDER
US-Canadian border, 6,416 km (3,987 miles)

WORLD'S TALLEST ACTIVE GEYSER
Steamboat Geyser, Yellowstone National Park, USA, 115 m (380 feet)

NORTH AMERICAN MOUNTAINS AND RIVERS

Mount McKinley (Denali), USA 6,194 m (20,320 ft)

Mount Logan, Canada 5,951 m (19,524 ft)

Orizaba, Mexico 5,700 m (18,700 ft)

Mount St Elias, USA–Canada 5,489 m (18,008 ft)

Popocatépetl, Mexico 5,450 m (17,887 ft)

Mount Whitney, USA 4,418 m (14,495 ft)

Mississippi-Missouri 6,020 km (3,740 miles)
Mackenzie 4,240 km (2,630 miles)
Mississippi 3,780 km (2,350 miles)
Missouri 3,780 km (2,350 miles)
Yukon 3,185 km (1,980 miles)
Rio Grande 3,030 km (1,880 miles)

South America

AREA: 17,818,505 SQUARE KM **(6,877,943** SQ. MILES)
POPULATION: 375,441,000

From its tropical north, South America stretches 7,240 km (4,500 miles) to the chilly, storm-battered peninsula of Cape Horn, just 1,000 km (600 miles) from Antarctica. The Andes run the entire length of the continent's west coast. In the north, the Amazon (the world's second-longest river) snakes eastwards from the Andes to the Atlantic Ocean, through vast rain forests that once covered more than one-third of the continent.

Rain falls in the Atacama Desert just once or twice a century, and in some parts of the desert rain has never been recorded.

FAST FACT

Even though most South American countries have Spanish as their first language, more South Americans speak Portuguese. This is because Portuguese-speaking Brazil is the continent's largest country.

WORLD RECORDS

WORLD'S LONGEST MOUNTAIN CHAIN
Andes, western South America, 7600 km (4,700 miles)

WORLD'S DRIEST PLACE
Atacama Desert, Chile, average annual rainfall less than 1.3 mm (0.05 inch)

WORLD'S HIGHEST WATERFALL
Angels Falls, Venezuela, 985 m (3,230 feet)

WORLD'S HIGHEST CAPITAL CITY
La Paz, Bolivia, 3,631 m (11,913 feet)

WORLD'S HIGHEST NAVIGABLE LAKE
Lake Titicaca, Peru–Bolivia, 3,810 m (12,506 feet)

WORLD'S LARGEST RIVER BY VOLUME
Amazon, Peru–Brazil, discharges 200,000 cubic m per second (7,100,000 cu. feet/s) into Atlantic Ocean

WORLD'S LARGEST RIVER BASIN
Amazon Basin, nothern South America, 7,045,000 square km (2,720,000 sq. miles)

WORLD'S LARGEST LAGOON
Lagoa dos Patos, Brazil, 9,850 square km (3,803 sq. miles)

SOUTH AMERICAN MOUNTAINS AND RIVERS

Aconcagua, Argentina
6,960 m (22,834 ft)

Cerro Ojos del Salado, Argentina–Chile
6,908 m (22,664 ft)

Bonete, Argentina
6,872 m (22,546 ft)

Huascarán, Peru
6,768 m (22,205 ft)

Mount Illimani, Bolivia
6,462 m (21,201 ft)

Chimborazo, Ecuador
6,310 m (20,702 ft)

Amazon 6,450 km (4,010 miles)

Paraná-Río da la Pata 4,500 km (2,800 miles)

Purus 3,350 km (2,080 miles)

São Francisco 2,900 km (1,800 miles)

Paraná 2,800 km (1,740 miles)

Orinoco 2,500 km (1,550 miles)

Europe

AREA: 10,354,636 SQUARE KM **(3,997,929** SQ. MILES)
POPULATION: 689,546,932

Europe is not a self-contained continent, but the western part of Eurasia. Europe's boundaries are the Atlantic Ocean in the west, the Ural Mountains to the east, the Arctic Ocean in the north and the Mediterranean Sea to the south. Southern Europe has mild winters and warm, dry summers, while the northern climate is temperate with distinct seasons.

Swiss guards have protected Vatican City since the 15th century.

EUROPEAN MOUNTAINS AND RIVERS

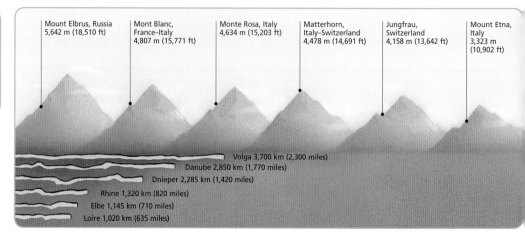

Mount Elbrus, Russia
5,642 m (18,510 ft)

Mont Blanc,
France–Italy
4,807 m (15,771 ft)

Monte Rosa, Italy
4,634 m (15,203 ft)

Matterhorn,
Italy–Switzerland
4,478 m (14,691 ft)

Jungfrau,
Switzerland
4,158 m (13,642 ft)

Mount Etna,
Italy
3,323 m
(10,902 ft)

Volga 3,700 km (2,300 miles)
Danube 2,850 km (1,770 miles)
Dnieper 2,285 km (1,420 miles)
Rhine 1,320 km (820 miles)
Elbe 1,145 km (710 miles)
Loire 1,020 km (635 miles)

Africa

AREA: 30,354,852 SQUARE KM (11,716,972 SQ. MILES)
POPULATION: 909,154,000

The world's second-largest continent extends from the southern shores of the Mediterranean Sea to Cape Agulhas. Africa consists of 53 independent sovereign countries. The largest is Sudan and the smallest mainland country is Gambia. The Seychelles, a group of islands off the east coast, is the smallest African country. Africa also contains the world's largest desert, the Sahara. Arab peoples form the majority of the population in the north. The south's mainly black population is made up of hundreds of native tribes.

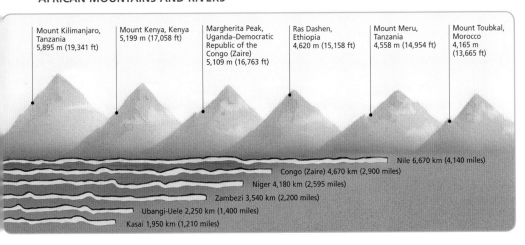

The Sahara, the world's largest desert, covers more than 9.2 million square km (3.5 million sq. miles). Vast seas of sand fill depressions in the landscape. Elsewhere, the surface is rock or gravel.

AFRICAN MOUNTAINS AND RIVERS

Mount Kilimanjaro, Tanzania
5,895 m (19,341 ft)

Mount Kenya, Kenya
5,199 m (17,058 ft)

Margherita Peak, Uganda–Democratic Republic of the Congo (Zaire)
5,109 m (16,763 ft)

Ras Dashen, Ethiopia
4,620 m (15,158 ft)

Mount Meru, Tanzania
4,558 m (14,954 ft)

Mount Toubkal, Morocco
4,165 m (13,665 ft)

Nile 6,670 km (4,140 miles)
Congo (Zaire) 4,670 km (2,900 miles)
Niger 4,180 km (2,595 miles)
Zambezi 3,540 km (2,200 miles)
Ubangi-Uele 2,250 km (1,400 miles)
Kasai 1,950 km (1,210 miles)

WORLD RECORDS

WORLD'S LARGEST DESERT
Sahara, northern Africa, 9,270,000 square km (3,579,000 sq. miles)

WORLD'S LONGEST RIVER
Nile, northern Africa, 6,670 km (4,140 miles)

WORLD'S LARGEST ARTIFICIAL LAKE
Lake Volta, Ghana, 8,482 square km (3,275 sq. miles)

WORLD'S HIGHEST TEMPERATURE
El-Azizia, Libya, shade temperature of 57.3°C (136°F) recorded on September 13, 1922

Asia

AREA: 44,391,162 SQUARE KM
(17,139,445 SQ. MILES)
POPULATION: 3,986,105,000

The world's largest continent covers 29.4 per cent of Earth's land surface and contains more than 60 per cent of the world's human population. It extends from the Ural Mountains and Suez Canal in the west to the Pacific Ocean in the east, where the narrow Bering Strait separates Siberia from Alaska, and from the Arctic Ocean to the Indian Ocean.

The Himalaya contain Mount Everest, the world's highest mountain. Climbers reached its summit in 1953.

WORLD RECORDS

WORLD'S HIGHEST MOUNTAIN
Mount Everest, China–Nepal, 8,850 m (29,035 feet)

WORLD'S LOWEST POINT ON LAND
Dead Sea, Israel–Jordan, 411 m (1,348 feet) below sea level

WORLD'S LARGEST LAKE BY AREA
Caspian Sea, western Asia, 371,800 sq. km (143,550 square miles)

WORLD'S OLDEST, DEEPEST, AND LARGEST (BY VOLUME) LAKE
Lake Baikal, Russia, 25 million years old; 1,637 m (5,371 feet) deep; 23,000 cubic km (5,500 cu. miles) of water

WORLD'S LARGEST COUNTRY BY AREA
Russia, 17,075,383 square km (6,592,812 sq. miles)

WORLD'S LARGEST COUNTRY BY POPULATION
China, population 1,313,974,000

WORLD'S LARGEST CITY BY POPULATION
Tokyo, Japan, population 35,197,000

WORLD'S LONGEST WALL
Great Wall of China, 3,460 km (2,150 miles)

WORLD'S LONGEST RAILWAY LINE
Trans-Siberian, Russia, 9,297 km (5,777 miles)

ASIAN MOUNTAINS AND RIVERS

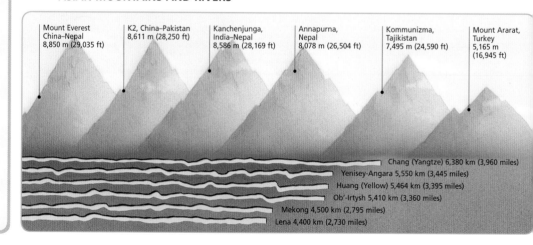

Mount Everest, China–Nepal, 8,850 m (29,035 ft)

K2, China–Pakistan, 8,611 m (28,250 ft)

Kanchenjunga, India–Nepal, 8,586 m (28,169 ft)

Annapurna, Nepal, 8,078 m (26,504 ft)

Kommunizma, Tajikistan, 7,495 m (24,590 ft)

Mount Ararat, Turkey, 5,165 m (16,945 ft)

Chang (Yangtze) 6,380 km (3,960 miles)
Yenisey-Angara 5,550 km (3,445 miles)
Huang (Yellow) 5,464 km (3,395 miles)
Ob'-Irtysh 5,410 km (3,360 miles)
Mekong 4,500 km (2,795 miles)
Lena 4,400 km (2,730 miles)

Oceania

AREA: 8,507,753 SQUARE KM **(3,283,993 SQ. MILES)**
POPULATION: 32,289,000

Oceania is a region in the South Pacific that consists of Australia, New Zealand, New Guinea, and the islands of Melanesia (including Fiji, Papua New Guinea, Vanuatu and Indonesia), Micronesia and Polynesia. Oceania has a land area of 8,507,753 square km (3,283,993 sq. miles). Australia, New Zealand, Christmas Island, Norfolk Island and the Cocos Islands make up a region called Australasia.

Uluru, the world's largest rock, is in Australia's Northern Territory. It is a sacred place for Australia's Aboriginal people.

OCEANIAN MOUNTAINS AND RIVERS

| Mount Wilhelm, Papua New Guinea 4,500 m (14,762 ft) | Mount Victoria, Papua New Guinea 4,073 m (13,363 ft) | Mount Cook, New Zealand 3,764 m (12,349 ft) | Mount Tasman, New Zealand 3,498 m (11,475 ft) | Mount Balbi, Papua New Guinea 2,743 m (8,999 ft) | Mount Kosciuszko, Australia 2,228 m (7,310 ft) |

Murray-Darling 3,750 km (2,330 miles)
Darling 3,070 km (1,905 miles)
Murray 2,575 km (1,600 miles)
Murrumbidgee 1,690 km (1,050 miles)
Lachlan 1,484 km (922 miles)
Sepik 965 km (600 miles)

WORLD RECORDS

WORLD'S LONGEST CORAL REEF
The Great Barrier Reef, Australia, 2,025 km (1,260 miles)

WORLD'S LARGEST ROCK
Uluru, Australia, 348 m (1,142 feet) high; 2.5 km (1.5 mile) long; 1.6 km (1 mile) wide

WORLD'S LARGEST SAND ISLAND
Fraser Island, Australia, 120 km (74 miles) long

Islands

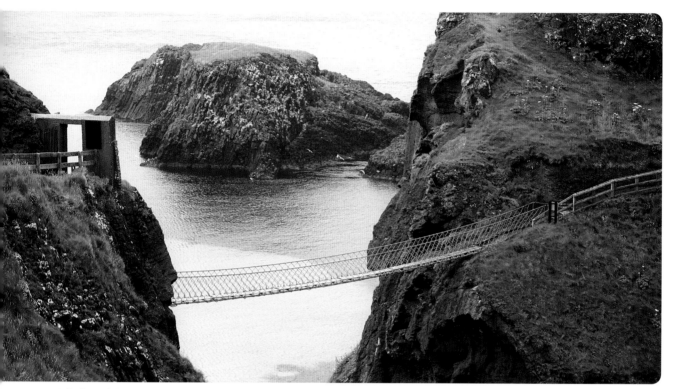

Ireland, part of the British Isles, is a continental island off the coast of Europe. Its lush green hills are the result of a mild climate and moist air coming in from the Atlantic Ocean.

An island is an area of land completely surrounded by water. They are found in every ocean and sea – from huge Greenland to tiny dots on the map. There are two kinds of islands: continental and oceanic. A continental island consists of high ground that rises above sea level from a continental shelf. Oceanic islands are not on continental shelves; they are active or extinct volcanoes that rise above sea level from the ocean floor. Because they are isolated from other landmasses, islands are 'laboratories of life' that are home to unique plants and animals.

HOW CONTINENTAL ISLANDS ARE FORMED

When the sea level rises, water flows across low-lying coastal plains. If there is high ground between the plains and the sea, some land may remain above water as an island on the continental shelf.

BEFORE THE ISLANDS ARE FORMED

Mountain

Sea level is low.

Mountain

Continental shelf

Coastal plain

AFTER THE ISLANDS ARE FORMED

Continental island

Reef

Sea level is high.

Continental island

Continental shelf

THE FIVE LARGEST ISLANDS

GREENLAND
Geographically, the world's largest island is part of North America, but historically it is linked to Scandinavia. It is a self-governing Danish territory.

2,175,600 sq. km
(840,004 sq. miles)

An iceberg forms a dramatic icy arch over water in the seas off Greenland's central ice sheet.

NEW GUINEA
This continental island separated from Australia when rising sea levels formed the Torres Strait about 5,000 years ago. Its wildlife is similar to Australia's.

808,510 sq. km
(312,167 sq. miles)

Buildings in New Guinea are made from local resources; palm trees are used for timber and roof thatch.

BORNEO
Borneo is part of Asia. It has about 15,000 species of flowering plants, 221 of mammals and 420 of birds, many found nowhere else.

745,561 sq. km
(287,863 sq. miles)

The high mountains and coral coasts of Borneo are home to more than 30 ethnic groups of people.

MADAGASCAR
There are highlands in the east, volcanic mountains in the north, plains in the west and a high, partly desert plateau in the southwest.

587,040 sq. km
(226,657 sq. miles)

Lemurs are found only in Madagascar. They are part of the island's unique wildlife.

BAFFIN ISLAND
An ice cap covers the centre of this Canadian Arctic island. Elsewhere the terrain is mountainous. The Norse called the island *Helluland*.

507,451 sq. km
(195,927 sq. miles)

The Arctic Circle crosses Baffin Island. Midsummer days are 24 hours long, but winters are dark.

HABITAT WATCH

Some island species may depend so completely on their environment they cannot tolerate disturbance. The dodo flourished on the African island of Mauritius until the island was discovered in 1507. It was flightless and easy to kill, and had been hunted to extinction by 1680.

Dodo

Mauritius is an oceanic island that was once an ancient hot-spot volcano. It lies in the Indian Ocean east of Madagascar.

Atolls

An atoll is a coral reef, usually circular, that projects above the surface of the sea and wholly or partly encloses an area of sea called a lagoon. There may be islands in the lagoon. Atolls begin to form when an underwater volcano rises above the surface. Corals build a fringing reef around the sides. When the rocks beneath the volcano cool and contract, the volcano sinks, but the corals continue to build upwards at the same rate. When most of the volcano has sunk below the surface, water fills the area enclosed by the reef to form the lagoon.

HABITAT WATCH

The coral atolls and islands of the Maldives, found in the Indian Ocean, make up the flattest country on Earth. The highest natural point is only 2.3 m (7½ feet) above sea level. This means that the Maldives are at great risk from even small rises in sea levels.

Ocean temperatures need to stay above 20°C (68°F) for coral to grow.

Barrier reef

The lagoon is too shallow for coral to grow there.

Beach of coral sand

To grow on an atoll, plants need shallow roots.

Limestone debris

Layers of basalt lava build up from volcanic eruptions.

Volcano's summit

Small patch reefs grow upwards and outwards from the shallow seafloor. They grow about 1 cm (½ inch) a year.

Bora Bora in Polynesia is a volcanic atoll surrounded by a lagoon and barrier reef.

The Cocos (Keeling) Islands consist of two main atolls and many smaller coral islets.

HOW ATOLLS FORM

An atoll is a coral reef that grows around the sides of an extinct volcano. As the volcano sinks, the coral grows and encloses a lagoon.

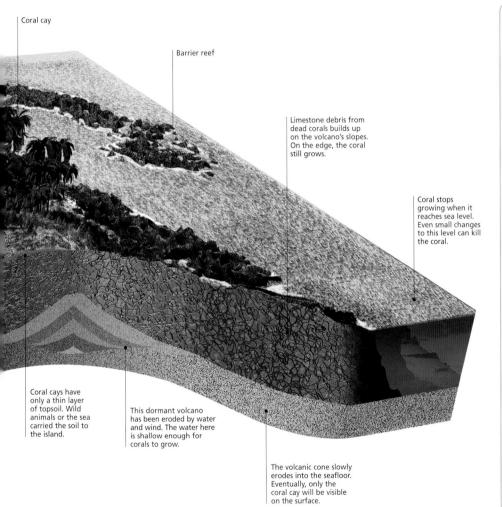

Coral cay

Barrier reef

Limestone debris from dead corals builds up on the volcano's slopes. On the edge, the coral still grows.

Coral stops growing when it reaches sea level. Even small changes to this level can kill the coral.

Coral cays have only a thin layer of topsoil. Wild animals or the sea carried the soil to the island.

This dormant volcano has been eroded by water and wind. The water here is shallow enough for corals to grow.

The volcanic cone slowly erodes into the seafloor. Eventually, only the coral cay will be visible on the surface.

CROSS SECTION OF AN ATOLL

Coral on the sides of an extinct volcano grows upwards as the volcano sinks. Birds drop seeds that germinate on the coral, which helps to form a shallow soil.

Active volcano This rises above the sea surface, fed by magma from beneath the ocean floor.

Fringing reef A reef forms as corals grow on the sides of the volcano just below sea level.

Lagoon The volcano sinks and erodes into the ocean floor, leaving the reef to enclose a lagoon.

Ecosystems

Almost every part of our planet is inhabited by an amazing variety of living things. There may be between 10 and 100 million kinds – or species – of plants and animals on Earth. All living things exist in the biosphere, which is made up of the land, oceans and atmosphere. Within the biosphere, there are many kinds of environments. Over millions of years, living things have gradually altered their bodies and behaviour to suit their environments. This process is called adaptation. Together, an environment and its inhabitants form an ecosystem. Members of an ecosystem depend on each other for food and resources.

THE LIVING WORLD

Each of Earth's environments has its own community of plants and animals. This illustration shows how ecosystems change between the tropical rain forests (far left) and the polar ice caps (far right).

OCEANS
Water covers almost 71 per cent of Earth's surface. Marine environments vary, depending on latitude and depth, and animals travel extensively.

TROPICAL FORESTS
Tropical forests require year-round warmth and abundant rain. Rain forests need rain all year. Seasonal forests are dry for part of the year.

SUBTROPICAL GRASSLANDS
Grasses tolerate a climate that is too dry for forests. Subtropical grasslands, called savannas, border tropical forests. They have both dry and rainy seasons.

DESERTS
A desert occurs where more water evaporates than falls as rain. Deserts occur in the subtropics, and on the west coast and interior of continents.

WORLD ECOSYSTEMS

MOUNTAINS
The higher the land, the fewer plants there are and the colder and windier it gets. Thick fur coats keep many mountain animals warm.

KEY
- Tropical forests
- Temperate and coniferous forests
- Grasslands
- Tundra
- Deserts
- Mountains
- Polar regions

TUNDRA AND POLAR REGIONS
No plants can survive on ice caps, where snow and ice persist throughout the year. Tundra vegetation occurs where the ground surface thaws in summer.

[TE]MPERATE GRASSLANDS
[T]emperate grasslands – prairie, [p]ampa, steppe and veld – occur [w]here winters are cool and rainfall [s]light. Scattered groups of shrubs [a]nd trees thrive.

TEMPERATE FORESTS
Trees grow well in wet temperate regions. In areas with cold winters, most of the trees are deciduous. Some animals migrate in winter.

CONIFEROUS FORESTS
Coniferous forests form a wide belt around the Northern Hemisphere where winters are long and the ground is frozen.

Tropical forests

Lowland regions near the equator that lie along river valleys and near coasts have a warm, wet climate. Rain falls fairly evenly through the year. This is the climate that supports tropical rain forest. In these steamy jungles, the air is always humid. Plant growth is dense, with tall trees covered in vines and smaller plants – epiphytes –growing on their trunks and branches. Tropical rain forests are home to more species than any other environment on Earth. Large areas of the tropics have distinct wet and dry seasons. There the forests are more open and a greater number of trees are deciduous.

Tropical forests

LIFE IN A BROMELIAD

The tank bromeliad grows on host trees high in the rain forest and produces food in its leaves. The leaves also collect water, which attracts many animals. They in turn deposit droppings, which provide nourishment for the bromeliad and help it to produce more food.

SHALLOW ROOTS

Some rain forest tree trunks have large finlike growths at the base called buttresses. They compensate for the shallow roots and can extend 10 m (30 feet) up the trunk to support the tree's weight.

Velvet worms have been discovered in bromeliads, far above their usual home on the forest floor.

A female poison-arrow frog deposits tadpoles into the water-filled bromeliad.

A mouse opossum eats a damsel fly larva from the bromeliad pool.

An alligator lizard drinks from the pool.

Beetle larvae prey on tadpoles.

A variety of land snails forage and hide between the leaves.

Predatory and scavenging ants patrol the area for anything they can find.

The roots of trees growing in poor soils remain near the soil surface, where they take the nutrients before they are lost at deeper levels.

Root tips attach themselves to fallen leaves.

Harpy eagle

Red howler monkeys

Linne's two-toed sloth

Geoffroy's spider monkey

Tree porcupine

Kinkajou

Silky (pygmy) anteater

Toco toucans

Emerald tree boa

Zebra butterfly

Tree frog

Anole lizard

SOUTH AMERICAN SCENE
This scene shows many typical rain forest features: tall trees with straight trunks and high crowns; buttress roots, vines and other creepers; bromeliads and other epiphytes; forest floor fungi; and a diverse range of creatures.

Brazilian tapir

Cock of the rock

Anaconda

Bushmaster snake

Capybara

Giant armadillo

Reticulated poison-arrow frog

Tropical forests

A tropical rain forest is thick with vegetation and teeming with animal life. The year-round warm, moist climate means there is no seasonal slowing of plant growth, and organic material lying on the ground decomposes rapidly. The tallest trees compete for sunlight – some are more than 30 m (100 feet) tall. Below them there are three layers of trees and shrubs that grow to different heights. Smaller plants – and many animals – flourish on the cool, damp and dark rain forest floor.

Bwindi Impenetrable Forest is an ancient rain forest in the East African country of Uganda. Half of the world's population of mountain gorillas live in its midst.

ON THE FOREST FLOOR

When a tree sheds a branch or falls to the ground, it starts to decompose. Fungi and beetles feed on the rotting wood, and bacteria feed on their waste. Mosses, ferns and small plants grow on the fallen branch or tree. Their roots obtain nutrients from pockets of soil trapped in hollows and crevices.

Birds find food among the leaf litter.

HABITAT WATCH

The Amazon basin holds the world's largest tropical rain forest, but about 23,310 square km (9,000 sq. miles) is cleared each year. Strenuous efforts are being made to reduce this.

Original rain forest

Current rain forest

USING THE FOREST

Tropical forests cover large areas of land that would support more people if it were converted to farmland. Many tropical trees yield valuable hardwood timber. Illegal logging opens up forest areas, providing many opportunities for exploitation.

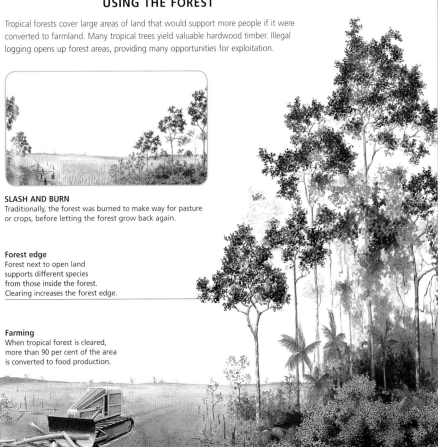

SLASH AND BURN
Traditionally, the forest was burned to make way for pasture or crops, before letting the forest grow back again.

Forest edge
Forest next to open land supports different species from those inside the forest. Clearing increases the forest edge.

Farming
When tropical forest is cleared, more than 90 per cent of the area is converted to food production.

Termites eat large amounts of plant litter, especially bark and wood.

Temperate and coniferous forests

Forests in Canada or Russia are different from the forests in France, India, Indonesia or Australia. Climate and soil influence the kind of trees that grow in a forest, and the trees determine what grows on the forest floor beneath them. In cold, northern latitudes, evergreen conifers grow in coniferous, or boreal forests (named after Boreas, the Greek god of the north wind), but few plants grow on these dark forest floors. In temperate regions of the world, spring flowers grow on the floor of deciduous forests, where the trees shed their leaves in winter. Mixed temperate forests of different kinds of conifers and flowering trees grow in some parts of the world.

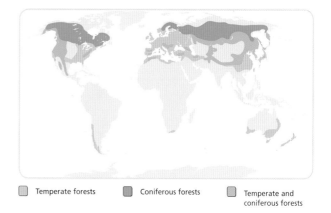

☐ Temperate forests   ☐ Coniferous forests   ☐ Temperate and coniferous forests

LIFE IN THE FOREST

The forest provides seeds, nuts, fruit and leaves for food, along with herbs and grasses in clearings, and holds nesting sites for many species. Plant eaters are prey for carnivores.

COLOUR BLAZE
A mixed forest in autumn is ablaze with the green leaves of evergreen trees and the brown, yellow, orange and red leaves of deciduous trees.

Burst of yellow dust
In spring, the male pine cone releases millions of pollen grains. A few days later, the male cone drops off the tree. Its job is finished.

Germination
If the seed finds a spot with enough warmth, moisture and light, it germinates and a new conifer grows.

THE CONIFER CYCLE
Conifers do not need water to reproduce. They rely on wind to carry pollen from the male cone to seeds in the female cone.

Sticky cone
The pollen lands on a sticky female cone. A pollen tube starts to grow and, up to a year later, the seeds are fertilised.

Swelling cone
The female cone grows to four times its size as the seeds grow inside. Two years later when the seeds are mature, the cone opens to release them.

Spreading seeds
Each seed has a wing and can take off in the wind. It also has food for germination inside a tough, outer casing.

HABITAT WATCH

About 8,000 years ago, forests covered about 70 per cent of Europe. Many were cleared to provide fuel, farmland and building materials.

Now they are being replanted by governments and private industry. The forested area of Europe is increasing by about 0.1 per cent a year.

Original forest cover

Current forest cover

Grasslands

Grasslands occur in areas that get more rain than deserts but not as much as forests. They have few trees and some have no trees at all. Grasses are hardier than trees and lose less water in dry winds than taller plants. Grasslands have different names in different parts of the world. The North American prairie once extended over much of the continent. When Spanish explorers first saw the South American pampa, they had to stand on the backs of their horses to see across the grass. Eurasia's grasslands, or steppe, extend from Hungary to China. Tropical grasslands, called savanna, grow on all continents, but are most famous in Africa. African savanna supports elephants, giraffes, zebras and lions.

☐ Grasslands

HABITAT WATCH

During the 19th and early 20th centuries, much of the North American prairie was plowed to grow cereal crops. Little of the original prairie survived, but some is now returning.

Original prairie cover

Current prairie cover

Bison, the native cattle of North America, were hunted almost to extinction. Now they are recovering. This herd is grazing on grassland in Grand Teton National Park, Wyoming.

GRASSLANDS AROUND THE WORLD

Grasses are the main plants in all grasslands, but the species are different on each continent, as are the other plants growing with them. They provide abundant food for herds of grazing mammals. Most temperate grasslands are used to raise livestock or grow crops. African savanna is unsuitable for farming.

A herd of antelope graze beneath a stormy sky on the African savanna.

Flowering plants beneath a clear blue sky bring colour to the Kazakhstan steppe.

Much of the pampa in Argentina is used to graze sheep and cattle.

Western gray kangaroos live in the western and southern grasslands of Australia.

AFRICAN SAVANNA

Open tropical grassland, with
scattered thorn trees, supports
herds of grazing mammals and
the predators that hunt them, as
well as birds and reptiles. Much
of the savanna is now protected
to conserve wildlife. However,
poaching remains a problem.

Tundra

Tundra exists beyond the limit of coniferous forest, where the climate is too cold and the gales too drying for forest trees to survive. A little way below the surface, a layer of soil remains permanently frozen – this is called permafrost. Tree roots cannot penetrate the rock-solid frozen soil, so the trees that do grow, such as birch and juniper, are only 90 cm (3 feet) tall. In summer, the surface thaws and sedges grow in pools and marshy areas. Lichens and mosses grow among the rocks. Grasses grow in the drier places and everywhere there are plants that flower and set seed before the ice returns.

☐ Tundra

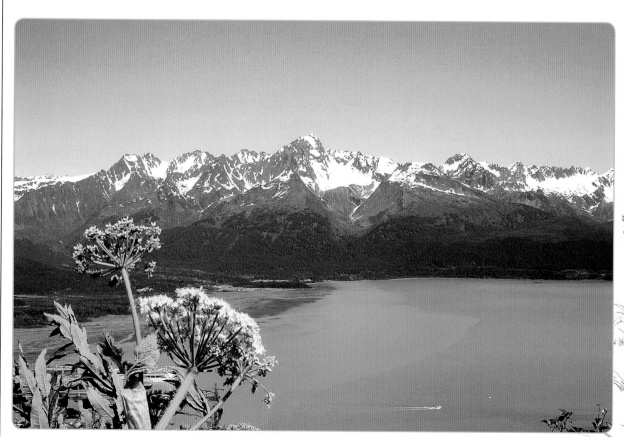

Flowering plants that emerged when the ice began to thaw on the slopes of Mount Marathon in Alaska, USA, are now setting seeds that will germinate next summer.

HABITAT WATCH

Polar bears live in the Arctic tundra and hunt seals on the pack ice offshore. As Arctic temperatures rise, coniferous forest expands northwards into the tundra, and the pack ice starts to melt. This reduces the polar bears' range.

Glacier ice recedes from the tundra on South Georgia Island, off the coast of Cape Horn.

ARCTIC TUNDRA

At the tree line, the trees are bare on the windblown side. Low-growing flowering plants, grasses, mosses and lichens survive better near ground level, where the temperature is warmer and the wind less chilling. In summer there is water and warmth for a short growing season.

COPING WITH THE COLD

The glacier buttercup has adapted to bitter cold and a short growing season.

White petals reflect sunlight to the centre of the flower.

Flowers move slowly around to trap sunlight throughout the day.

Dark flower centre absorbs heat to warm the flower.

Strong roots anchor the plant firmly in the soil.

Deserts

Deserts cover one-seventh of Earth's land surface. They are dry regions that on average receive less than 100 mm (4 inches) of rain per year. Because there are no clouds, the days are very hot. But when the Sun sets, the temperature drops quickly and the nights can be freezing cold. Only about a quarter of the world's deserts are made up of sand; most are rugged, rocky landscapes. The main subtropical deserts of the Northern Hemisphere are the Sahara, Arabian and Thar deserts, and the deserts of southwestern United States and Mexico. In the Southern Hemisphere, the major deserts are the Namib and Kalahari in Africa, the Atacama in South America and the deserts of central Australia.

☐ Deserts

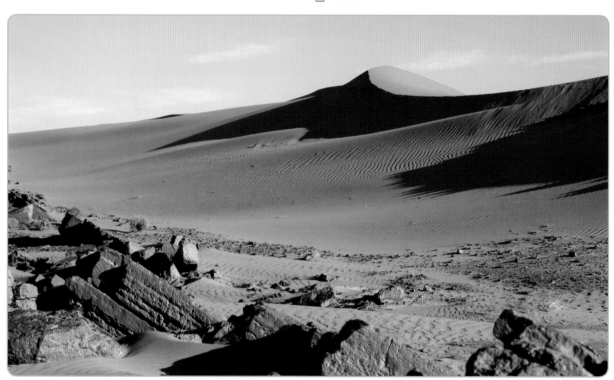

The sand dunes of the Sahara cover such a vast area they are called seas of sand. Like ocean waves, the dunes are constantly shifting.

HABITAT WATCH

From time to time, prolonged drought allows deserts to expand. When the rains return, plants appear and the land recovers. If livestock farmers are forced into smaller pastures, overgrazing may destroy the plant cover, making recovery difficult. This is called desertification. The map shows areas under threat in Africa.

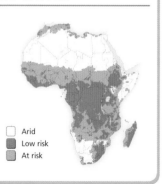

☐ Arid
☐ Low risk
☐ At risk

A poisonous gila monster suns itself beneath a prickly pear cactus in the Arizona Desert, USA.

ASIAN DESERT
The Thar Desert in northwestern India and Pakistan is covered by rolling sand dunes, with some rocky outcrops.

AUSTRALIAN DESERT
The Pinnacles Desert in Western Australia is covered in limestone formations, which are the eroded remains of ancient sea shells.

NORTH AMERICAN DESERT
Saguaro cactus grow in the Sonoran Desert, USA. This slow-growing plant stores food in its tall green stem.

HOT AND COLD

Rock and sand absorb heat quickly. During the day they can grow very hot. From late afternoon, as the Sun sinks lower in the sky, the desert surface loses heat by radiation faster than it absorbs it. Nights are cold.

By day the desert surface absorbs warmth rapidly and by noon it is very hot.

At night the surface loses the heat it absorbed by day and the temperature falls.

WHY DESERTS ARE DRY

Cool, moist air approaches a mountain range and drops over the mountains as rain. The air that reaches the other side is dry and sinks to the ground, where it heats up and becomes drier.

Hot, dry air rises from the desert.

Moisture falls as rain.

Dry air crosses the mountain.

Dry air sinks and becomes hotter.

Moist air approaches a mountain.

Windward side of mountain

Leeward side of mountain

FAST FACT
Antarctica is sometimes called the world's largest desert. Even though it contains 70 per cent of Earth's freshwater, this is trapped in huge ice sheets and rarely becomes liquid or evaporates into the air.

Deserts

In some deserts, rain may not fall for many years. Then, quite suddenly, a storm will break and there is a huge downpour that lasts just a few hours. The absence of moisture in the air means that clouds are rare and the skies are clear for most of the year. When the land is heated by the Sun, daytime temperatures can soar to 40°C (104°F). Plants and animals survive only if they adapt to the extreme heat and dryness, and make the most of the little rain that does fall. But, although they are dry and windy, not all deserts are hot. The cold winds that blow across the Gobi Desert of central Asia produce freezing conditions, but it is still considered a desert because it has very little rain.

GROWTH SPURTS
Saguaro cacti grow very slowly, with spurts during the summer rainy season. They flower and produce fruit after about 30 years and live 150 to 200 years.

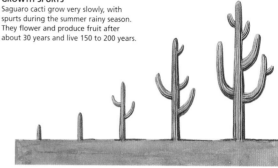

10 years 50 years 75 years 100 years 150–200 years

LIFE AMONG THE SPINIFEX

Spinifex is a kind of hummock grass, found in the desert areas of Australia. Each plant has a centre of dead, matted leaves, with green leaves covering the outside. Most are less than 90 cm (3 feet) tall, but they support many kinds of wildlife.

 The jewelled gecko feeds on termites that live in the spinifex.

 A legless lizard preys on smaller lizards and geckos.

 Small cockroaches find food and shelter in the spinifex.

The desert skink eats termites and other small creatures.

 The crimson chat visits spinifex to find insects such as cockroaches.

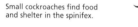 A tiny ninguai wriggles through spinifex to find insects.

WATER STORAGE
The succulent leaves and the soft fibre inside the trunk of the quiver tree store water. The white-powdered branches and pale trunk reflect the Sun's rays and stop the tree from overheating.

White-winged doves feed on the flowers and the moist, energy-rich ripening saguaro fruit.

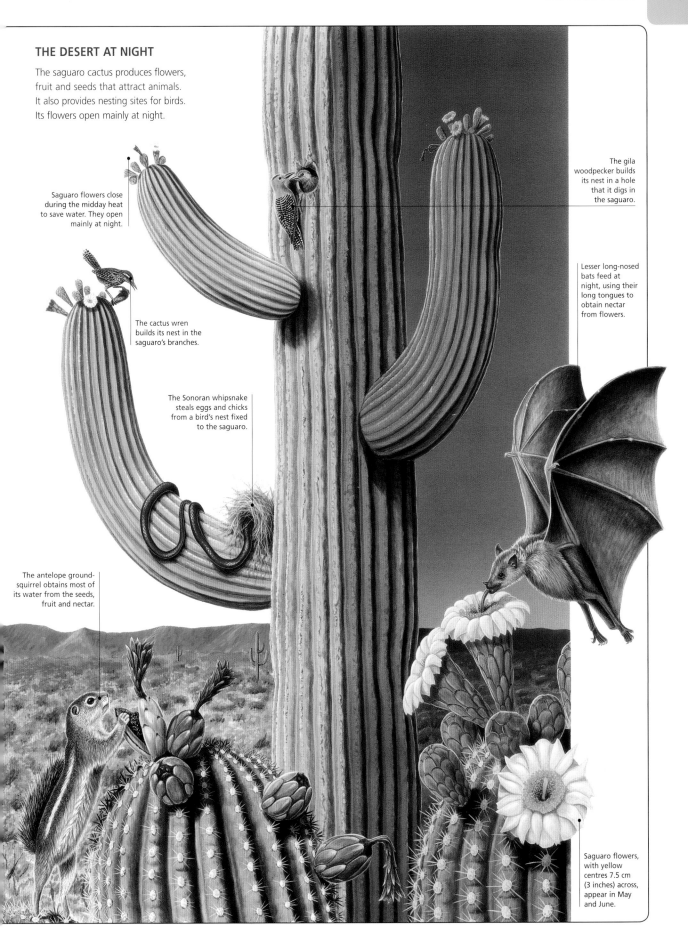

THE DESERT AT NIGHT

The saguaro cactus produces flowers,
fruit and seeds that attract animals.
It also provides nesting sites for birds.
Its flowers open mainly at night.

Saguaro flowers close
during the midday heat
to save water. They open
mainly at night.

The cactus wren
builds its nest in the
saguaro's branches.

The Sonoran whipsnake
steals eggs and chicks
from a bird's nest fixed
to the saguaro.

The antelope ground-
squirrel obtains most of
its water from the seeds,
fruit and nectar.

The gila
woodpecker builds
its nest in a hole
that it digs in
the saguaro.

Lesser long-nosed
bats feed at
night, using their
long tongues to
obtain nectar
from flowers.

Saguaro flowers,
with yellow
centres 7.5 cm
(3 inches) across,
appear in May
and June.

Mountains

Mountains make up about one-fifth of the land surface of Earth and are home to about a tenth of the human population. Most mountains form part of a chain or range. These may be linked to form a mountain belt, or cordillera (from the Spanish for 'little rope') and in turn may form part of a global mountain system. There are two main mountain systems. One circles the Pacific Ocean and includes the Andes of South America, the mountains of the American west, the icy mountains of Alaska and the mountains of Indonesia, Japan, New Guinea and New Zealand. The second includes the European Alps and the Himalaya Mountains in Asia.

 Mountains

The Matterhorn is one of Europe's highest mountains, with a distinctive, steep-sided shape. Its name comes from the German words *matt*, meaning valley, and *horn*, meaning peak.

HABITAT WATCH

Mount Everest attracts many climbers and some have discarded used packaging and equipment, rather than carry it, leaving large amounts of rubbish. Volunteers are clearing it and the Nepalese government now restricts access to the mountain.

The Himalaya Mountains are still rising, as the Indian tectonic plate moves northwards. They are the world's highest mountains, and are growing by about 0.5 cm (0.2 inch) a year.

THE HIMALAYA MOUNTAINS

About 71 million years ago, India broke away from the southern supercontinent of Gondwana and began moving northwards. The Indian Plate made contact with the Eurasian Plate about 30 million years ago and the mountains began to rise. The main episode of mountain building occurred 20 million years ago.

Eurasian Plate
Indian Plate today
10 mya
38 mya
Equator
55 mya
71 mya
Indian Ocean
Indian Plate
Sri Lanka

mya = million years ago

HOW THE HIMALAYA FORMED

India | Eurasia

Tethys Sea

1 INDIA STARTS ITS JOURNEY
Indian tectonic plate breaks away from Gondwana and moves northward towards Eurasia. The Tethys Sea begins to close.

Tethys Sea | India | Eurasia

Tethys seafloor is pushed under Eurasia.

2 ON THE MOVE
As the Indian continent moves, the Tethys seafloor is pushed beneath the Eurasian Plate, scraping off sedimentary rocks.

India

Seafloor sediments

3 COLLISION
The Tethys Sea finally disappears and the Indian and Eurasian plates collide, crumpling their rocks upwards.

Himalaya Mountains

Rocks compress and fold upwards.

4 FOLDING AND UPLIFT
As the Indian Plate pushes into the Eurasian Plate, the rocks compress. They fold and are pushed upwards.

Mountains

The rugged terrain, steep slopes and harsh climates of mountain regions make them hostile places to live permanently. There are vast areas that people rarely visit. Mountains are wild places, where only plants and animals that have adapted to the severe conditions can live and thrive. Above the tree line, the soil is thin and winds are strong, which restricts plant growth. This limits the food supply for animals. Wild sheep and llamas live in small flocks, but mountain pastures cannot support large groups of animals. Instead, small numbers of many species, all with different needs, share the resources.

North American Rockies These pikas live in the Rockies, part of a parallel chain of ranges that extend from New Mexico to British Columbia.

South American Andes The Andes run the length of South America. They are home to wild guinea pigs and these llamas, a kind of camel.

European Alps Occupying a large area in central Europe, the Alps are accessible to grazing animals such as the goatlike chamois.

African Atlas Mountains This forested and snow-capped range extends 2,400 km (1,500 miles) parallel to the Mediterranean coast.

Asian Tien Shan Mountains Between Russia and China, Asia's Tien Shan have snow-covered peaks rising to more than 6,100 m (20,000 feet).

ANIMALS OF THE MOUNTAINS

Many mountain animals are closely related to species found in the lowlands. Others, such as sure-footed mountain sheep, are found only among cliffs and narrow shelves where birds of prey and wild cats cannot reach them.

Transantarctic Mountains Extending 4,827 km (3,000 miles) across Antarctica, the mountains' bare rock peaks rise above the ice sheet.

New Zealand Southern Alps Rising more than 3,660 m (12,000 feet), this eroded range occupies the centre of New Zealand's South Island.

MOUNTAIN CREATURES

1 Rock hyrax
2 Golden eagle
3 Mountain goat
4 Puma
5 Poison-arrow frog
6 Grasshopper
7 White-tailed jackrabbit

Rivers

Rivers carry freshwater across the land and into the sea. Many begin their journey high in the mountains. They start as small streams that tumble over the rocks, growing larger as other streams join them. They can be quite large by the time they reach the lowlands. Other rivers start on lower ground, emerging as springs at places where groundwater rises to the surface. As rivers flow across plains and wide valleys, they slow down and widen, and often meander from side to side. Water draining into rivers from the surrounding land carries nutrients that allow aquatic plants to grow. These provide food for insects and fish, which in turn are hunted by larger fish and birds.

HABITAT WATCH

The sacred Bagmati River in Kathmandu, Nepal, is threatened by the city's human waste, garbage and sewage. Pollution by humans is the most serious problem facing all rivers. But rivers can be restored – the Thames in London, UK, has been cleaned up in recent years.

On level ground a river slows, widens and meanders. River meanders move slowly forwards as the river erodes one bank while depositing material on the other.

Angel Falls, Venezuela 985 m (3,230 feet)

Tugela Falls, South Africa 949 m (3,110 feet)

Yosemite, USA 436 m (1,430 feet)

Espelandsfoss, Norway 704 m (2,307 feet)

Empire State Building 443 m (1,454 feet)

WATERFALLS

A sharp, vertical drop in a river, usually produced by a fault in the underlying rocks, sends water tumbling down to the lower level and forms a waterfall. Angel Falls is the world's highest. Iguazú Falls, on the Brazil–Argentina border, is the widest at 2.7 km (1.7 miles).

Iguazú Falls contains 270 individual waterfalls that form a horseshoe around Devil's Throat (above).

DELTAS

FROM RIVER TO SEA

When large rivers cross a level plain before reaching the coast they lose speed. The slow-moving river divides to pass obstacles and deposits the silt it has carried from upstream, which forms new obstacles. Eventually, a complex, often fan-shaped, network of channels is formed. This is a delta.

HOW A DELTA GROWS
A river slows as it enters the sea. This causes it to drop its load of sediment. A major river will constantly deposit new sediment on top of earlier deposits, so its delta builds steadily outwards into the sea.

Delta system

Conglomerate

Sandstone

Siltstone

Shale

Area of illustration

The Nile is probably the best known delta. It begins near Cairo in Egypt. It is about 160 km (100 miles) long and 240 km (150 miles) wide at the coast.

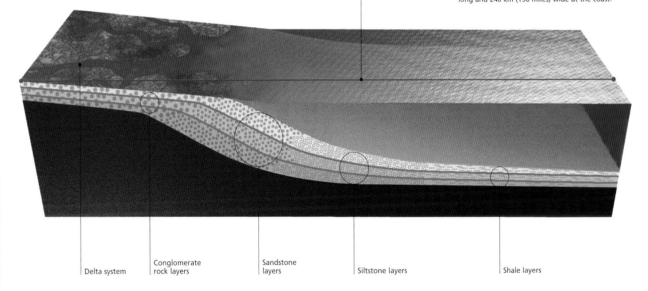

Delta system

Conglomerate rock layers

Sandstone layers

Siltstone layers

Shale layers

Braided delta Rivers that carry large pieces of sediment deposit them as they slow down, blocking their channels. The water flows around the obstacles, forming a braided pattern.

Meandering delta Rivers that carry fine sand and silt but few large pieces of sediment do not block their channels. They follow meandering paths that slowly change position.

Estuaries

An estuary occurs where the freshwater of a river meets the salt water of the sea. As the river enters the sea, it slows until it can no longer carry the material it has picked up along its journey. It deposits sand and coarser sediment, which form sandbars. Where fresh and salt water meet, reactions between them cause fine particles to clump together and settle, creating mud flats. Many estuaries are tidal. Where the tide is large, the fresh and salt water can form separate, parallel channels. Where the tide is small, the salt water may flow beneath the freshwater. The constantly changing conditions of an estuary attract many different kinds of life.

HABITAT WATCH

Large-scale shrimp farming is big business in Asia. Shrimp are grown in the mangrove swamps of Asia's estuaries, and most of these estuaries are now under threat. Malaysia alone lost 2,350 square km (910 sq. miles) of mangroves between 1980 and 1990 to shrimp farming and agriculture.

LIFE IN AN ESTUARY

Water birds, insects, worms, shellfish, crabs, fish and plants share the safe environment of an estuary, where there is always plenty of food.

A great white egret stalks the waters for fish.

A tributary of the river flows into the estuary.

Sea

The estuary is where river and sea meet.

Mangroves can grow in fresh or salt water.

River

VIEW FROM ABOVE

Freshwater from a river flows into a sheltered estuary, where it mixes with salt water from the sea. Mangroves grow on both sides of this estuary, with only a narrow channel between them.

Bluefish live in both fresh and salt water.

Blue crabs bury themselves into the mud over winter.

Avocets sweep their upturned beaks through the water for fish.

Buried ghost nippers nip attackers with their claws.

As the Maroochy River flows into the sea in Queensland, Australia, the shifting sandbars of the estuary are clearly seen.

KINDS OF ESTUARIES

Although a river empties into it, an estuary is really an inlet of the sea. There are four ways such an inlet can form.

Drowned river valley This forms where a rise in sea level has flooded an existing river valley.

Fjord This is a deep, steep-sided valley carved by a now-melted glacier, which carries a small river.

Bar-built estuary Sediment from a river creates a sandbar across its mouth with a lagoon behind.

Tectonic estuary This occurs where rock faults cause a section of coast to sink below sea level.

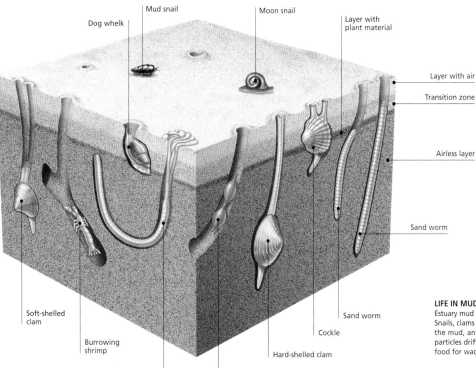

Mud snail
Dog whelk
Moon snail
Layer with plant material
Layer with air
Transition zone
Airless layer
Sand worm
Sand worm
Cockle
Hard-shelled clam
Soft-shelled clam
Burrowing shrimp
Lugworm
Peanut worm

LIFE IN MUD
Estuary mud is waterlogged and airless. Snails, clams and worms burrow into the mud, and feed at high tide on particles drifting past. They are then food for wading birds.

Wetlands

A wetland is any area of land that is wholly or partly covered by shallow water. The water can be fresh or salty. Swamps, marshes, bogs, lakes, rivers and estuaries are all wetlands. Wetlands offer many habitats for plants and animals that cannot survive in deep water or on dry land. They are a haven for birds, providing a wealth of fish, plants and insects for food, as well as reeds and rushes for nesting. As rivers continually deposit sediment and plants grow in the mud, wetlands are slowly changing all the time. Many wetlands are threatened, however, because they can be drained and used for farming, forestry or building. Others have been drained to control insect pests, such as mosquitoes.

HABITAT WATCH

The Pantanal in Brazil is the world's largest wetland. In summer, the rivers overflow their banks to form swamps and marshes that are home to thousands of plants and animals. However, 99 per cent of the Pantanal is privately owned by ranching cattle farmers, which threatens the delicate ecosystem.

The American alligator inhabits swamps, marshes, lakes and rivers across southeastern USA. There are about 1 million alligators in the Florida Everglades.

FROM LAKE TO SWAMP
When sediment builds up in a lake, the lake bed is raised and the water becomes shallower. Plants root in the mud and slowly creep out from the shore until the lake disappears.

Lake A lake is an inland body of water with plants growing in the shallow water around the edges.

Marsh As sediment builds up, plants advance farther into the lake. This makes a marsh around the edges.

Swamp The lake disappears. Plants cover almost the entire area, forming a marsh, or swamp if it is forested.

LIFE IN THE WETLANDS

Tall reeds and rushes growing close to a lake provide cover for nesting water birds and sheltered water where they can feed. Diving birds swim in the open water.

Sandpipers nest in wetlands and hunt for aquatic insects.

Reeds provide safe places for nesting and roosting.

Spoonbills, avocets and other birds gather food while wading in shallow water.

Curlew

Teals

Some birds, such as sandpipers, forage for food in the mud flats.

Grebes

Arctic regions

Around the shores of the Arctic Ocean, in the far north of North America and Europe, there is a short summer when the snow melts and herbs flower. This is the tundra. North of the tundra lies the permanent ice that extends from the coasts. It covers much of the ocean in summer and all of it in winter. This is the high Arctic, home to polar bears that feed mainly on seals they catch when they surface to breathe. The seals feed on fish, which prey on tiny animals called krill. North of the Arctic Circle, there is at least one night each year when the Sun does not set. This is called the 'midnight sun'. There is also one day in winter when it does not rise above the horizon.

Arctic regions

The snowcapped mountains and glaciers of Spitzbergen, in Norway's far north, are seen from the air. A Dutch explorer named the island Spitzbergen, which means 'jagged peaks'.

HABITAT WATCH

For people concerned about climate change, the Arctic is thought of as an early warning system. Rising ocean temperatures are already reducing pack ice in summer. This will affect the Inuit people of Greenland and Canada, who hunt on the ice. Their way of life may disappear.

Photographs taken at intervals through one summer night show that the 'midnight sun' travels around the horizon. It never sinks below it, but remains low in the sky.

INUIT HUNTER
The Inuit were once nomadic people who used dogsleds for transport. Today they are more likely to use snowmobiles and live in towns.

ARCTIC RESEARCH
Scientists travel to study the Arctic in icebreakers – special ships that are designed to travel through icy waters.

FIGHTING THE FREEZE

Arctic animals are well protected against the bitter cold. To prepare for winter, land mammals grow a thick layer of body fat to insulate them from the cold and give them energy. They have waterproof coats that trap a layer of warm air next to their skin and small ears to reduce heat loss.

CARIBOU
Caribou, or reindeer, have dense fur and a thick layer of body fat to keep them warm.

ARCTIC TERN
This migrating bird spends its summers in the Arctic and winters in the Antarctic.

POLAR BEAR CUBS
Cubs are born in the middle of winter, but are nursed by their mother in a snow den until spring.

WALRUS
It uses its two long tusks to anchor itself to the ice, or keep fishing holes open.

HARP SEAL
Like all seals, it has a thick insulating layer of blubber for warmth in winter.

Antarctic regions

Isolated from all other continents by the vast and stormy Southern Ocean, Antarctica is the coldest place on Earth. It has dry valleys where lichens and mosses survive, with a few species of insects and mites. The continent provides no food for larger animals. Birds visit and penguins breed on the ice, but they feed at sea, where life is abundant. Algae growing on the underside of the floating ice shelves provide food for shrimplike krill. Fish, seals and whales feed on the krill; penguins feed on fish; and fast, fearsome leopard seals hunt penguins and smaller seals. The land is permanently covered with ice and snow, which melt in summer only in a narrow coastal area. The ocean freezes each winter.

 Antarctic regions

Emperor penguins, the continent's most famous inhabitants, are clumsy until they dive into the sea. Then they maneuver effortlessly through the water.

UNDER THE SURFACE

Ice floats because frozen water is less dense than liquid water. When most icebergs float, about 85 per cent of their volume is below the water's surface.

The part of the iceberg above the water is made up of compressed snow.

The cold core of ice has a constant temperature of about −15° to −20°C (5° to −4°F).

TRAVELLING TO THE ANTARCTIC

Antarctica has become a tourist destination. Visitors land on the Antarctic Peninsula, so they can say they have set foot on the continent. They cannot travel overland. Their numbers are controlled to protect the environment.

More than 15,000 tourists visit Antarctica each year, for its scenery and wildlife.

HABITAT WATCH

1985   1990   2000   2006

Earth's ozone layer absorbs UV rays in sunlight. Over Antarctica the ozone thins naturally each spring, but in 1985 scientists observed a much larger loss, nicknamed the 'ozone hole'. This was caused by gases used in aerosol cans, called CFCs. The largest hole ever was recorded in 2006.

KINDS OF ICEBERGS

Tabular Broken-off pieces of ice shelves are wide, flat-topped and white or blue in colour.

Dry dock An iceberg this shape is called a dry dock. The centre lies below the waterline.

Pinnacle A pinnacle iceberg has sharp spires that project high above the water's surface.

Agricultural areas

Rye was first cultivated in southwest Asia about 13,000 years ago. This was the beginning of one of the most important changes in human history: from finding food by hunting animals and gathering plants to producing it by tending livestock and growing plants. Farmers cleared away the existing plants, plowed the land to destroy weeds and sowed seeds of crop plants. This was the most radical change to the natural environment humans have ever made. European farmers replaced their forests with crop fields and pasture. In North America, farmers cleared the prairie grasses for cereal crops. Because cereals are also grasses, this change to the environment was less extreme. Today, when tropical forests are cleared it is almost always to provide land for farming.

HABITAT WATCH

Most farmers use fertilisers to supply nutrients to their crops. This increases the farmer's yield, but when water carrying fertiliser drains into a river or the sea, it can kill the aquatic plants. When the plants die, there is less oxygen in the water, killing fish.

Although the first farms were usually small, modern farms in some countries can be huge and mechanised. Farmers use tractors to haul heavy machinery for harvesting grain.

TERRACED HILLS

Farmers in Asia learned long ago that the best way to cultivate a hillside is to plow around the slope (not up and down) and to build level terraces for their crops. Unfortunately, clearing plants from hillsides can speed up soil erosion.

American prairie farms are vast and need irrigation. Here, water is supplied in a circular pattern from automatic sprinklers. The fields are also sown in circles.

European farms, like this one in England, often contain many small fields enclosed by hedges. This region was once forested.

Urban areas

When people began to farm the land, they also began to settle in one place. They built villages that grew into towns and cities. In cities, not everyone was needed to produce food, so other activities could flourish. Cities produced craft workers of all kinds, as well as teachers, priests, artists, musicians, inventors and scholars. More and more people moved to the cities in search of work and access to services such as health and education. Today, more than half of the entire human population are city dwellers. In many developing countries, cities are growing too quickly for there to be enough basic services, such as clean drinking water and electricity. As a result, millions of people live in extreme poverty and unhealthy conditions.

HABITAT WATCH

City dwellers burn fuel and generate a lot of waste. Both cause pollution unless they are managed. Air pollution from traffic fumes is a health hazard in many cities. Separating trash from recycling can ease the waste disposal problem.

MODERN CITIES

The skyscrapers of New York, USA, let more than 8 million people live in a small area.

Kolkata, India, has 4.6 million inhabitants, but one-third live in slums, mostly in poverty.

ÇATALHÜYÜK

Around 6000 BC, several thousand people lived in Çatalhüyük, one of the first villages, in what is now Turkey. Their houses were so tightly packed that people entered through doors in the roof.

A CROWDED WORLD

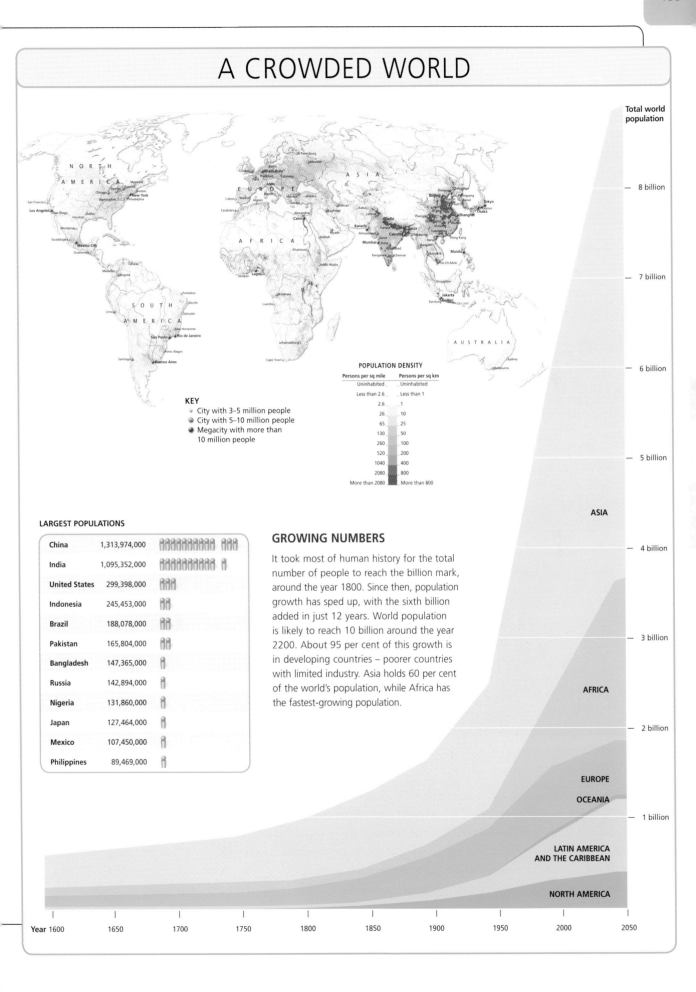

KEY
- City with 3–5 million people
- City with 5–10 million people
- Megacity with more than 10 million people

POPULATION DENSITY

Persons per sq mile	Persons per sq km
Uninhabited	Uninhabited
Less than 2.6	Less than 1
2.6	1
26	10
65	25
130	50
260	100
520	200
1040	400
2080	800
More than 2080	More than 800

LARGEST POPULATIONS

Country	Population	
China	1,313,974,000	
India	1,095,352,000	
United States	299,398,000	
Indonesia	245,453,000	
Brazil	188,078,000	
Pakistan	165,804,000	
Bangladesh	147,365,000	
Russia	142,894,000	
Nigeria	131,860,000	
Japan	127,464,000	
Mexico	107,450,000	
Philippines	89,469,000	

GROWING NUMBERS

It took most of human history for the total number of people to reach the billion mark, around the year 1800. Since then, population growth has sped up, with the sixth billion added in just 12 years. World population is likely to reach 10 billion around the year 2200. About 95 per cent of this growth is in developing countries – poorer countries with limited industry. Asia holds 60 per cent of the world's population, while Africa has the fastest-growing population.

Total world population

— 8 billion
— 7 billion
— 6 billion
— 5 billion

ASIA

— 4 billion
— 3 billion

AFRICA

— 2 billion

EUROPE
OCEANIA

— 1 billion

LATIN AMERICA
AND THE CARIBBEAN

NORTH AMERICA

Year 1600 | 1650 | 1700 | 1750 | 1800 | 1850 | 1900 | 1950 | 2000 | 2050

Biodiversity

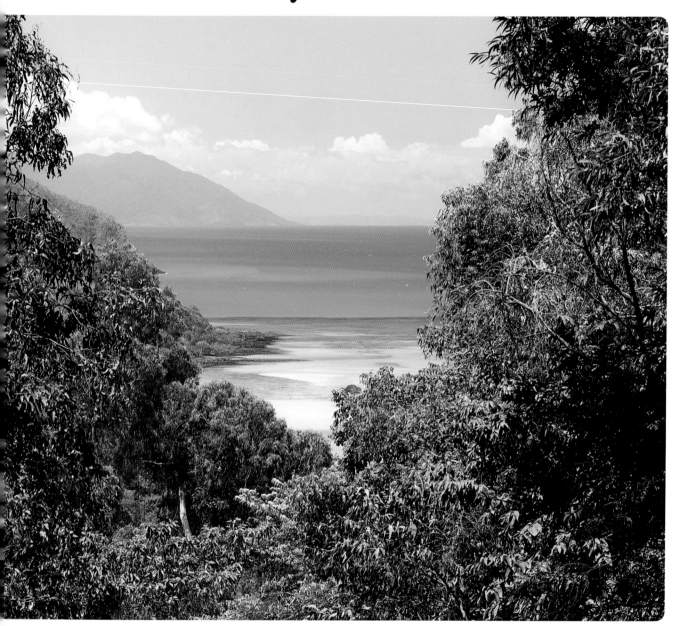

The Daintree, in Australia's northeast, is one of the oldest rain forests on Earth. Offshore lies the Great Barrier Reef, the largest structure made by living organisms.

Biodiversity is short for 'biological diversity'. It refers to the incredible variety of living things that exist on Earth, where they live, and how they interact. It is not just how many species live in one area, but how varied a particular species is, or how complex an ecosystem, or community, is. Rain forests are the most diverse ecosystems in the world. Pollution makes life difficult for some animals and plants, which reduces their biodiversity in the affected area. Changing the use of land, by clearing forests for farmland, for example, may reduce or increase biodiversity depending on the circumstances. Scientists agree that we should preserve as much biodiversity as possible.

WORLD VIEW

This map shows the biodiversity of different countries, as researched by their governments. Biodiversity is greater in countries with warm climates than countries with cold ones. It is lowest in extreme habitats, such as deserts and polar regions.

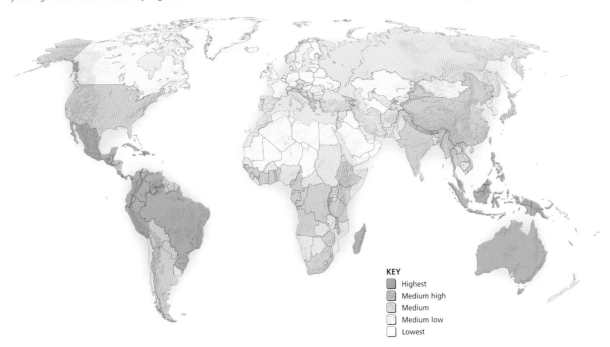

KEY
- ■ Highest
- ■ Medium high
- ■ Medium
- □ Medium low
- □ Lowest

LIFE IN DANGER

The World Conservation Union publishes a Red List of endangered animals and plants. It currently lists more than 16,000 species at risk.

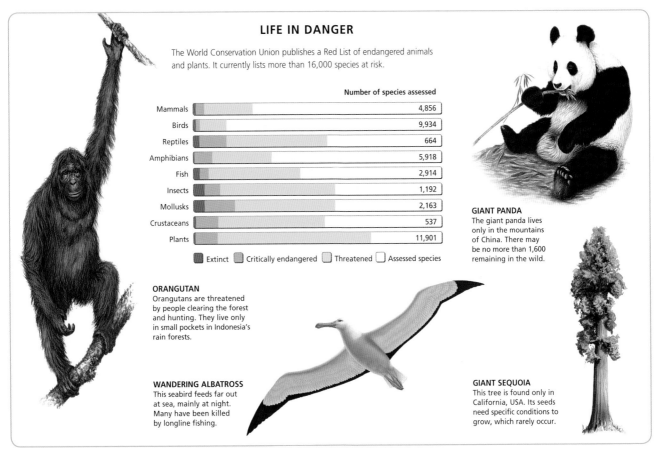

Number of species assessed

Mammals	4,856
Birds	9,934
Reptiles	664
Amphibians	5,918
Fish	2,914
Insects	1,192
Mollusks	2,163
Crustaceans	537
Plants	11,901

■ Extinct ■ Critically endangered □ Threatened □ Assessed species

ORANGUTAN
Orangutans are threatened by people clearing the forest and hunting. They live only in small pockets in Indonesia's rain forests.

WANDERING ALBATROSS
This seabird feeds far out at sea, mainly at night. Many have been killed by longline fishing.

GIANT PANDA
The giant panda lives only in the mountains of China. There may be no more than 1,600 remaining in the wild.

GIANT SEQUOIA
This tree is found only in California, USA. Its seeds need specific conditions to grow, which rarely occur.

Global Environment

There are now so many people in the world – and the industries supplying our needs are so large – that we are having a significant effect on the natural environment. Many scientists believe we are altering the global climate, although others disagree. Traffic fumes reduce air quality in many cities. In some places, factories pollute both air and water. Gases emitted by many factories and power stations make rain more acid, which damages lakes and rivers. Poor land management erodes the soil and can allow nearby deserts to expand. None of these problems is irreversible, but to solve them all we need to improve the way look after our planet.

Only 26 per cent of forests in Tasmania, Australia, remain after years of logging.

PLANET IN PERIL

Industry and development can cause serious environmental damage, such as pollution of the air, land and sea. The problems of industrialised countries are now reappearing in developing regions.

HOLDING BACK THE DESERT
Deserts expand and contract naturally. Careful livestock and crop management along the edge can provide permanent plant cover that gradually forces the desert to retreat.

SAVING THE FORESTS
Temperate forests are expanding, but tropical forests are disappearing. This can sometimes be reduced if local people are allowed to profit from the standing forest.

REDUCING AIR POLLUTION
Older industrialised countries now set strict limits to factory and vehicle emissions. The limits are becoming tighter and are being introduced worldwide.

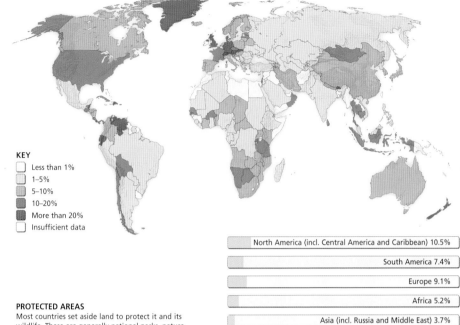

KEY
- Less than 1%
- 1–5%
- 5–10%
- 10–20%
- More than 20%
- Insufficient data

Overgrazing destroys plant life. In regions such as Rajasthan, India, it can allow land to become desert.

PROTECTED AREAS
Most countries set aside land to protect it and its wildlife. These are generally national parks, nature reserves and other protected areas. The amount of protected land in a region varies greatly. The need for land to be protected also differs; it is greater in more densely populated areas, such as cities.

North America (incl. Central America and Caribbean) 10.5%

South America 7.4%

Europe 9.1%

Africa 5.2%

Asia (incl. Russia and Middle East) 3.7%

Oceania 7.1%

WORLD 6.4%

☐ Area protected   ☐ Total area

When forests are cleared from hillsides, the soil erodes. It washes downhill into rivers, killing fish.

ELIMINATING ACID RAIN
Acid rain, caused by factories, power stations and vehicles, has been brought under control in many countries, although its effects are slow to disappear.

SAVING THE OZONE LAYER
Scientists discovered that gases, called CFCs, used in aerosol cans created a hole in the ozone layer. CFCs are now banned and the ozone layer will recover.

KEEPING OUR WATER CLEAN
Governments no longer allow waste to be dumped in rivers or the sea. International agreements aim to reduce and prevent water pollution.

Weather

World Weather

It is likely, wherever you live, that one of the first things you do each day is check the weather. Weather affects our lives in many ways, from what we wear and how we feel to what we grow in our gardens. But what makes weather? Weather is, simply, air that moves over Earth's surface. Images from satellites in space show how air swirls over landmasses, bringing wind and cloud, rain and snow, storms and hurricanes. Generally, people in a particular region experience similar weather from year to year. This regular pattern of weather over an extended period of time is called a region's climate.

Hurricanes are huge storms. This picture clearly shows Hurricane Fran's counterclockwise spiral wind pattern as it approached the Florida coast in 1996.

Winds do not blow over obstacles but try to find ways around them. This creates a complex pattern of swirling eddies, which can be seen from above in a cloudy sky.

Cold air moving across Antarctica and the Southern Ocean causes large areas of ice and snow to form over parts of the Weddell Sea to the northwest of the continent.

Climate Zones

Different regions of the world have different climate patterns, and smaller areas within those regions also have their own kinds of climate. We call these regions and areas climate zones. Near the equator are tropical zones; they have hot and wet climates. At the other extreme are the north and south poles, which are extremely cold and dry. In between are warm subtropical zones; dry desert, or arid, zones, where days are hot and nights cold; high mountain zones, with cold, snowy winters; and temperate zones, where conditions are generally moderate year-round.

Most snow in one year
1,224 inches (31,102 mm)
on Mt Rainier, Washington,
USA, 1971–72

Greatest temperature change in a day
100°F (56°C), from 44°F (6.7°C)
to –56°F (–49°C),
at Browning, Montana,
USA, 1916

Strongest measured wind gust
231 mph (372 km/h)
on Mt Washington,
New Hampshire, USA, 1934

NORTH AMERICA

SOUTH AMERICA

Driest place
0.02 inch (0.5 mm) per year
in Quillagua, Atacama Desert,
Chile, 1964–2001

HOT AND COLD, WET AND DRY

This map shows the world's eight main climate zones. Even within the same region, there can be more than one kind of climate.

ADAPTING TO CLIMATE

Plants and animals are found in most places on Earth, even in locations where weather patterns are extreme. Over time, living things have developed ways of dealing with, or adapting to, the climate in which they live.

PLANTS
Cactus plants grow in some arid desert regions. They have few or no leaves, an extensive root system and store the little water they get in fleshy green stems.

Fleshy green stem

Extensive, shallow root system

ANIMALS
The snowshoe hare's short ears help it retain heat in snowy environments. Long ears allow the desert-dwelling antelope jackrabbit to lose excess heat in hot weather.

Snowshoe hare

Antelope jackrabbit

Mountain zones may be cold, wet and windy.

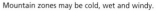

Polar zones are very cold all year round.

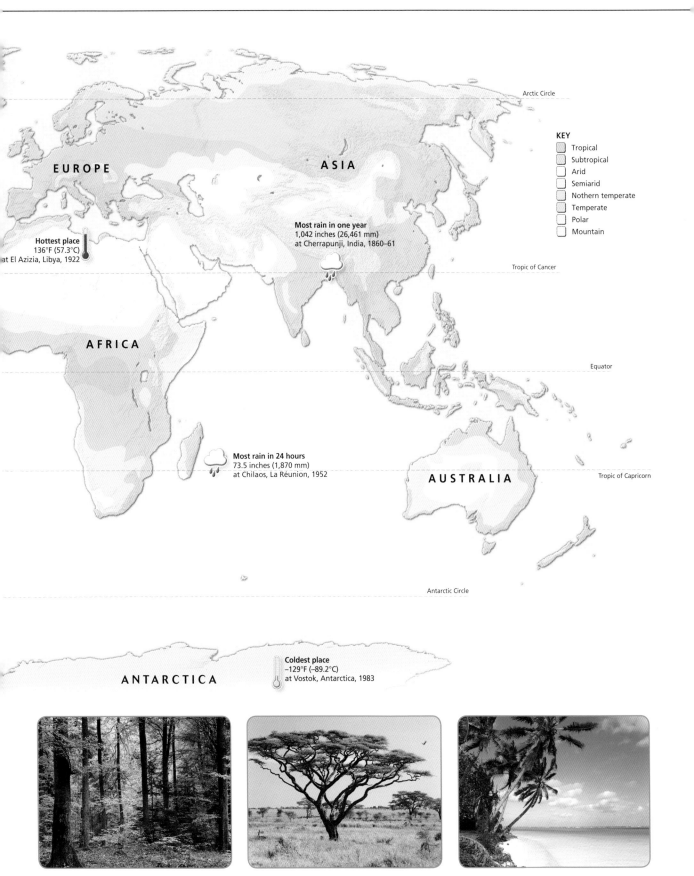

KEY
- Tropical
- Subtropical
- Arid
- Semiarid
- Nothern temperate
- Temperate
- Polar
- Mountain

Arctic Circle

EUROPE

ASIA

Most rain in one year
1,042 inches (26,461 mm)
at Cherrapunji, India, 1860–61

Hottest place
136°F (57.3°C)
at El Azizia, Libya, 1922

Tropic of Cancer

AFRICA

Equator

Most rain in 24 hours
73.5 inches (1,870 mm)
at Chilaos, La Réunion, 1952

AUSTRALIA

Tropic of Capricorn

Antarctic Circle

ANTARCTICA

Coldest place
−129°F (−89.2°C)
at Vostok, Antarctica, 1983

Temperate zones have cold winters and cool summers.

Semiarid zones usually have grasslands with few trees.

Tropical zones are warm and wet all through the year.

Weather Engine

The Sun fuels our weather. Earth's surface is warmed by sunlight. The tropics on either side of the equator receive the most intense heat, while the poles receive the least. Earth's surface absorbs half the available energy from the Sun; the atmosphere absorbs the rest or reflects it back into space. Bright white snow, which reflects most of the Sun's energy, retains very little heat. Dark green tropical rain forests absorb much more. Temperatures on land vary more than those in the oceans. These differences generate winds. Winds set in motion the vast circulation of the atmosphere, which produces the world's weather.

THE LAYERS OF THE ATMOSPHERE

Thermosphere
Above 80 km (50 miles)
This is the atmosphere's outer layer. Gases here are very thin.

Mesosphere
50–80 km (30–50 miles)
The mesosphere is much colder than the stratosphere.

Stratosphere
15–50 km (9–30 miles)
The stratosphere has dry, warm air.

Troposphere
0–15 km (0–9 miles)
The air here contains lots of water vapour and dust. Most of the world's weather occurs here.

THE SUN AND THE SEASONS

Because Earth's axis is tilted at an angle of 23.5 degrees, the amount of solar energy that reaches different parts of the globe varies as the planet orbits the Sun. These variations create our seasons, which are opposite in the Northern and Southern hemispheres.

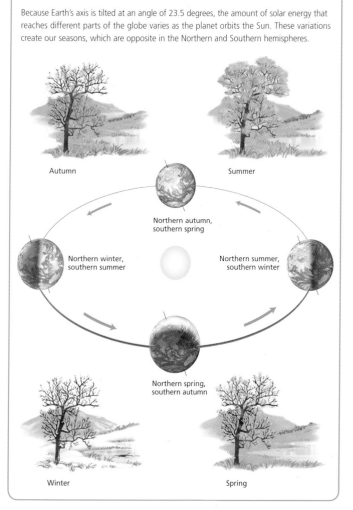

Autumn

Summer

Northern autumn, southern spring

Northern winter, southern summer

Northern summer, southern winter

Northern spring, southern autumn

Winter

Spring

HEAT FROM THE SUN

Air is warmed more at the equator than at the poles. Depending on the season, rays of sunlight fall on small circular areas near the equator. At the poles, however, the rays hit Earth at an angle and are spread over a wider area, which weakens them.

- ▢ Light travelling to equator
- ▢ Light travelling to poles

EARTH'S CLIMATE

At the equator, the Sun's rays hit Earth almost directly all year long. This is the hottest zone on Earth. Farther away from the equator, the rays hit at more of an angle and the climate is cooler.

This diagram shows how the Sun's rays hit Earth during the northern winter (southern summer).

This diagram shows how the Sun's rays hit Earth during the northern summer (southern winter).

SEASONAL CHANGES

The Sun's path creates the seasons, which change the appearance of the land, from the new growth of spring to the bare trees of winter.

Spring

Summer

Autumn

Winter

World winds

The Sun heats the tropics year-round, which causes the air at the equator to rise. It then spreads out, cools and sinks to the surface around 30° north and south of the equator. From there, some air flows back towards the equator at ground level. This completes a circular pattern of airflow, called a cell. Similar cells exist between 30° and 60° and between 60° and the poles. The movement of air at ground level within these cells creates Earth's major wind patterns. As the winds move north and south, they are deflected by the planet's rotation: to the right in the Northern Hemisphere, to the left in the Southern Hemisphere. This is known as the Coriolis effect.

WIND CELLS

Wind cells nearest the equator are called Hadley cells, after the English scientist George Hadley, who described them in 1753. Ferrel cells are named after American scientist William Ferrel, who first noted them in 1856.

WIND PATTERNS

Because hot air rises and cold air sinks, the Sun's uneven heating of Earth's surface causes air to circulate as shown in the diagram below. Winds are important influences on climate.

Polar cell
Cold air at the poles sinks and travels towards the equator before rising upon meeting the Ferrel cell.

Jet stream
Strong, high-altitude, westerly winds

Hadley cell
Warm air rises from the equator and spreads towards the poles, before sinking at around 30° north and south.

Ferrel cell
Some of the air from the Hadley cells continues towards the poles, before rising at about 60° north and south.

Warm and cold air meet, creating a belt of stormy, wet weather.

Cold easterly winds blow from the poles.

Upper air cools and sinks, creating dry conditions.

Warm, moist air rises at the equator, clouds form and rain falls.

Air flows poleward from the southwest.

Air flows towards the equator from the northeast.

60°N

30°N

Equator

Polar easterlies
Cold easterly winds blow from the poles to 60° north and south.

CORIOLIS EFFECT
In the Northern Hemisphere, the Coriolis effect causes air to move clockwise and down around high pressure, and counterclockwise and up around low pressure. It is the opposite in the Southern Hemisphere.

THE MONSOON

Patterns of global air flow influence local winds such as the monsoon. This seasonal wind brings heavy rain to many subtropical parts of the world, especially India and Bangladesh.

People who live in India and Bangladesh have to cope with heavy monsoon rain.

Dry season In winter, high pressure creates winds that push moist air away from India and Bangladesh.

Doldrums
The windless area at the equator

Trade winds
Easterly winds blow towards the equator.

Westerlies
Warm, moist winds blow from the west.

Wet season In summer, inland low pressure draws moist air in from the ocean, bringing torrential rain.

The water cycle

The way water moves between the atmosphere, land and sea creates a cycle of moisture that shapes our weather and provides us with a continuous supply of freshwater. When the Sun heats the oceans, lakes and rivers, some of that water turns into water vapour, which is released into the atmosphere. Water contained in plants is also released as part of photosynthesis. The release of water from all these sources is known as evaporation. This water vapour forms clouds, which in turn produce rain. Some rain is absorbed by soil and plants, while the rest flows back to the sea in rivers and underground channels.

Heavy clouds bring rain and mist to rain forests in Colombia, South America.

FROM THE SEA AND BACK AGAIN

Water that evaporates from oceans and other sources condenses as clouds. Winds carry the clouds inland, rain then falls on the land, and the water makes its way back to the sea. This completes the cycle.

Clouds build
up over land.

Water evaporates
and forms clouds.

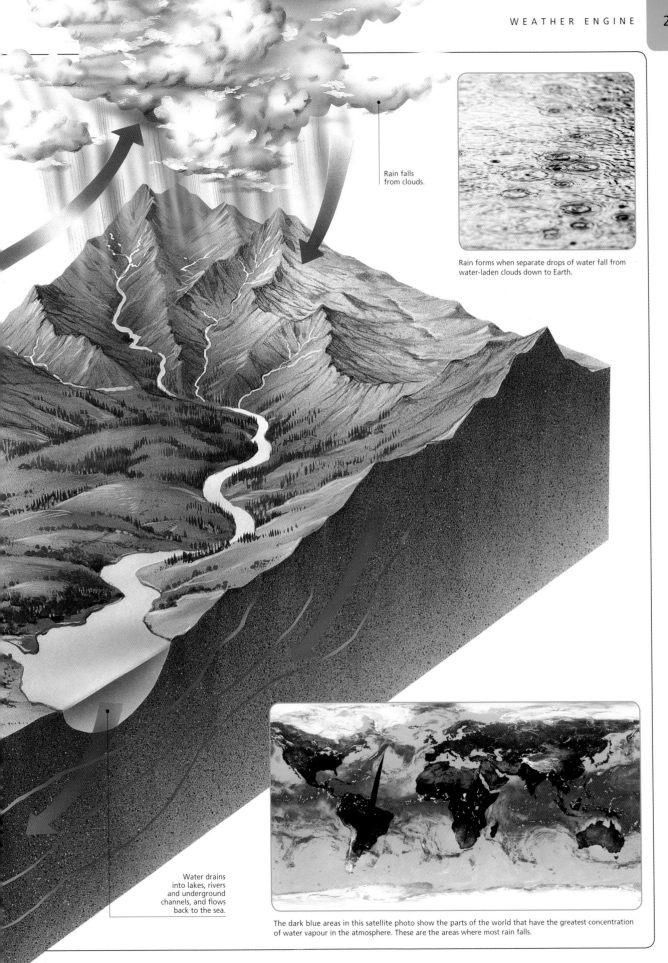

Rain falls
from clouds.

Rain forms when separate drops of water fall from
water-laden clouds down to Earth.

Water drains
into lakes, rivers
and underground
channels, and flows
back to the sea.

The dark blue areas in this satellite photo show the parts of the world that have the greatest concentration
of water vapour in the atmosphere. These are the areas where most rain falls.

Clouds

Clouds are masses of water droplets and ice crystals that float in the sky. They are formed by a process that begins when warm, moist air rises. As the warm air cools, it is unable to hold water vapour. Some of the water vapour condenses around dust particles and forms minute water droplets. These tiny drops make up clouds. The sky can be covered with a blanket of cloud that is formed when a mass of warm air rises above cooler air and causes the water vapour to condense. Clouds also form when warm air is forced to rise over mountains, or when warm air blows over a colder surface such as cool water. On hot days, storm clouds appear when warm, moist air rises and then cools rapidly.

THE COLOURS OF CLOUDS

Water droplets in clouds scatter all the colours in white sunlight equally, so clouds appear white, except when they are in shadow or blocking out the light.

Water droplets in cloud

Colours that make up white sunlight

Thick cumulonimbus clouds will soon bring a storm with heavy rain over Lake Poopo in Bolivia.

HOW CLOUDS FORM

Clouds usually form as a result of warm air that rises from the ground. When the warm air meets colder air higher in the atmosphere, the water vapour in the rising air condenses to form clouds. This happens in three main ways: by convection currents, over mountains and through frontal activity.

Condensation level

Convection Heating of the ground warms air near the surface, causing an air mass to rise.

Condensation level

Over mountains If air meets a mountain range it is forced upwards, and clouds form over the mountaintops.

Condensation level

Frontal activity When two air masses meet, the warmer air rises and forms clouds.

Cirrocumulus

Cumulonimbus

A SKY OF CLOUDS

Clouds are named according to their height and shape, by combining the prefixes *alto* and *cirro* with the Latin names *stratus* (flat), *cirrus* (wispy) and *cumulus* (puffy). Rain-bearing clouds are called *nimbus*, and depending on shape are known as *nimbostratus* or *cumulonimbus*.

16,500 feet (5,000 m)

Altostratus

Altocumulus

6,500 feet (2,000 m)

Cumulus

Stratocumulus

Stratus

Sea level

Kinds of clouds

No two clouds are exactly the same. They are usually grouped according to how high they are above the ground. Although they vary in shape and size, they can be divided broadly into two kinds: heaped, fluffy clouds and layered clouds. Heaped clouds are formed when pockets of warm air drift upwards, while layered clouds are created by moist air moving horizontally between cooler layers. It is important to identify kinds of clouds because they give us information about the weather. White, puffy cumulus clouds are associated with warm sunny days. Cirrus clouds may be followed by lower altostratus clouds and low stratus rain clouds, which cover the entire sky in a solid grey sheet.

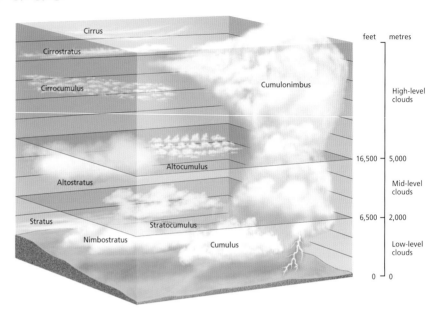

Cirrus
Cirrostratus
Cirrocumulus
Cumulonimbus
Altocumulus
Altostratus
Stratus
Stratocumulus
Nimbostratus
Cumulus

feet   metres

High-level clouds

16,500 — 5,000

Mid-level clouds

6,500 — 2,000

Low-level clouds

0 — 0

HIGH CLOUDS

CIRRUS
Streaky cirrus clouds, blown by strong winds, can signal an approaching storm.

SUPERB CIRRUS
Large cirrus clouds form when upper-level winds are weak and the clouds are not dispersed.

CIRROCUMULUS
Cirrocumulus clouds consist of ice crystals and the clouds have a cellular appearance.

MIDDLE CLOUDS

ALTOCUMULUS
Altocumulus clouds form when there is a lot of moisture, but only light winds are blowing.

ALTOSTRATUS
Near the polar regions, thick layers of cloud can cover the sky and bring snow.

LOW CLOUDS

STRATOCUMULUS
In subtropical coastal places, sheets of stratocumulus move inland from the moist oceans.

STRATUS
This mountain slope is covered with a thick layer of stratus cloud as cold air moves across the region.

SHALLOW CUMULUS
Flat-topped shallow cumulus clouds like these are a common sight on a fine day.

Winds

Air begins to move when the Sun heats the land and warms the atmosphere. Molecules in the air move faster when they are heated and the air starts to expand. Like a huge, invisible bubble, warm air rises through the surrounding cooler air. At the same time, cooler, heavier air is drawn in to replace the rising air. This circulation of air is called convection. Wind speed depends on air pressure. Wind blows from areas of high pressure to areas of low pressure. Meteorologists use the Beaufort scale to measure the force of wind, ranging from 0 (calm) to 12 (strong winds associated with hurricanes).

Jet streams are fast-moving ribbons of air blowing at high level. This photograph from space shows a jet stream above Egypt.

THE BEAUFORT SCALE

FORCE	SPEED (PER HOUR) KM	MILES	DESCRIPTION	EFFECT
0	1	1	Calm	Smoke moves straight up
1	5	3	Light air	Smoke slightly bent
2	11	7	Light breeze	Leaves rustle
3	18	11	Gentle breeze	Leaves move
4	30	19	Moderate breeze	Small branches move
5	39	24	Fresh breeze	Small trees sway
6	50	31	Strong breeze	Large branches move
7	61	38	Moderate gale	Whole trees sway
8	74	46	Fresh gale	Twigs break off
9	87	54	Strong gale	Roofs damaged
10	102	63	Gale	Trees uprooted
11	117	73	Storm	Widespread damage
12	120+	74+	Hurricane	Widespread destruction

Going down
Air sinks over cool areas, such as the sea.

From the sea
Wind blows from the sea as cool air flows towards the city to replace the rising warm air.

LAND AND SEA BREEZES
Coastal winds blow in from the sea during the afternoon. These create cooling sea breezes, which are strongest in the late afternoon. At night, the winds blow in the opposite direction, from the land and out to sea.

AFTERNOON
Thin clouds offshore

Warm air over land

Cool air over sea

Strong sea breeze

NIGHT
Clouds

Air over land cools quickly.

Air over sea cools slowly.

Weak land breeze

DAY BREEZES

On warm, sunny days, sea breezes blow on the coast. These onshore breezes are caused by differences in temperature between the hot land and the cooler water.

On the move
Warm air spreads out at high altitudes.

MOUNTAIN WINDS

Cool winds enter mountain valleys both during the day and at night, but in different ways. In the daytime, the wind descends into the centre of the mountain valley. At night, it flows down the sides of the mountains.

When the Sun heats the mountain slopes, warm air rises. The air then cools and falls into the valley to replace the rising air.

At night, warm mountain air loses its heat and flows down the mountain slopes into the valley to create a cool wind.

Moving up
The air over the land, particulary city areas, warms during the day. This warm air rises into the atmosphere.

Rain, hail and snow

Water or ice that falls from clouds is called precipitation. It may
be in the form of rain, drizzle, sleet, snow or hail. The conditions
within a cloud, and the temperature outside it, control the kind of
precipitation that falls. Water droplets in a cloud can turn into ice
if the cloud is at a height that is called the freezing level. This can
be as low as 300 m (1,000 feet) or as high as 5,000 m (16,500 feet)
above the ground. Snow falls from very cold, low clouds when the
air temperature is around freezing; this allows the ice crystals to
reach the ground without melting.

SNOWFLAKES
Snowflakes are loose clusters
of ice crystals. They are usually
six-sided (hexagonal), but their
exact shape depends on the
temperature of the air.

RAIN
Rain forms when water
droplets collect around
ice crystals until they are
heavy enough to fall.

HAIL
As strong air currents circulate
and cause layers of ice to build
up around small ice crystals, they
become larger and form hail.

SNOW
Snow forms in low-level
clouds, where ice crystals
do not melt before they
hit the ground.

Upper layer In very cold
temperatures, clouds are
spread out and are formed
mainly of ice crystals.

Middle layer Strong air
currents carry ice crystals
and water droplets high
into the atmosphere.

Lower layer This layer is
close to freezing. Water
vapour from the ground
condenses to form a cloud.

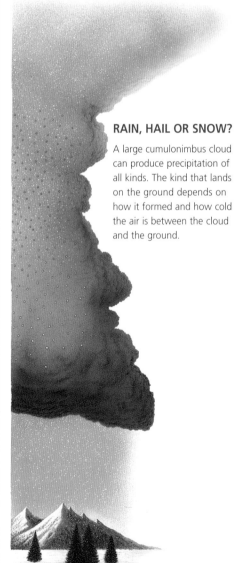

RAIN, HAIL OR SNOW?

A large cumulonimbus cloud
can produce precipitation of
all kinds. The kind that lands
on the ground depends on
how it formed and how cold
the air is between the cloud
and the ground.

FLOODS

CAUSE AND EFFECT

Rivers can flood when so much rain falls over a prolonged period that they overflow their banks. A severe flood occurred in October 2000, when torrential rain caused huge streams of water to engulf houses in northeastern Italy. Roadways turned into fast-flowing rivers. Dams designed to trap floodwaters collapsed as water levels reached their highest point in more than 30 years.

PREVENTING FLOODS

For thousands of years, humans have tried to reduce the risks of flooding by building structures to block and channel rising waters and the flow of rivers and oceans.

Levees Banks of earth built up beside rivers are called levees. Erosion, earthquakes or high rainfall can cause levees to fail.

Tidal barriers These are large walls, or barriers, built in low-lying areas, to control tidal flooding and block large waves.

Dams Concrete walls built to block rivers are called dams. They are strong to hold back the water that builds up behind them.

YANGTZE IN FLOOD

This satellite photo shows the pinkish ribbons of China's Yangtze River before a flood surged down it in August 2002.

In this photo, taken after the 2002 flood, the extent to which the flood waters spread across the land can be clearly seen.

Storms

Storms are created when warm, rising air currents and water vapour combine with colder air at middle and upper levels of the atmosphere. As rising, moist air cools, the water vapour turns into cloud. This cloud will continue to grow into a cumulonimbus, or thundercloud, if strong, warm updrafts meet cold air at middle and upper levels. The cold air in the upper part of the thundercloud starts to sink, creating downwards air currents called downdrafts. The combination of updrafts and downdrafts causes water droplets and ice crystals to grow and form rain and hail. It also creates the electrical charges that cause lightning.

Warm front   Cold front   ● City / town

CHANGING WEATHER

This diagram shows a low-pressure system over northern Europe. Its precise location is shown in the map above right. The cold front is creating stormy conditions over western Europe. Farther east, a warm front is bringing light rain to much of Poland. As the fronts move eastward, they can either strengthen or weaken.

Behind the cold front, the air clears and the temperature falls.

Warm air rises rapidly along the cold front, forming thunderstorms.

Warm air rises gradually along the warm front, producing widespread cloud.

Lille

Bonn

Prague

THE STORM CYCLE

There are usually three main stages in the progress of a thunderstorm. They involve the formation of cumulus clouds and then the opposing updrafts and downdrafts of air currents. The entire cycle may last for only about 15 minutes or it could last for several hours.

Building up Rising air currents cause water vapour to condense and form cumulus clouds.

Updraft

Downdraft

Anvil

At its peak The cumulonimbus cloud forms an anvil, or flat top. Air begins to sink, creating downdrafts.

On the wane Downdrafts outnumber updrafts. The storm's supply of warm, rising air is finally cut off.

Spreading cloud produces light rain and snow over Poland.

The leading edge of the warm front creates a band of high cloud.

Prevailing winds push the system towards Belarus and the Ukraine.

Kraków

Kiev

Tornadoes

A tornado – also called a twister or a whirlwind – is one of the most powerful forces on Earth. Hot and humid conditions are ideal for a tornado, which starts with an enormous thundercloud. From its dense, black base, a spinning, funnel-like form snakes down to the ground. When it touches, it gathers up a huge, billowing cloud of dust and debris. This can measure up to 1.6 km (1 mile) across, move at up to 105 km per hour (65 miles/h) and generate winds of up to 480 km per hour (300 miles/h). It can be powerful enough to flatten buildings and lift cars, trees and people high into the air.

WHERE AND WHEN
This United States map shows where and when tornadoes are likely. It indicates the number of tornadoes per year that normally occur in different areas.

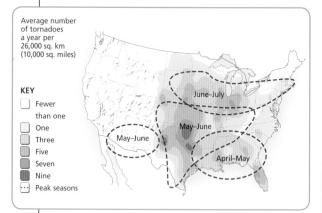

Average number
of tornadoes
a year per
26,000 sq. km
(10,000 sq. miles)

KEY
- ☐ Fewer than one
- ☐ One
- ☐ Three
- ☐ Five
- ☐ Seven
- ☐ Nine
- ⌐⌐⌐ Peak seasons

June–July
May–June
May–June
April–May

FORMATION OF A TORNADO

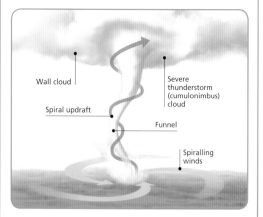

Wall cloud
Spiral updraft
Severe thunderstorm (cumulonimbus) cloud
Funnel
Spiralling winds

Tornadoes typically look like an elephant's trunk, or funnel, hanging from the base of a storm cloud. Very low air pressure inside this funnel causes moisture in the atmosphere to condense, making it visible. The bulge at the base of the thunderstorm is known as the wall cloud. Severe weather conditions may produce a line of storms that result in a series of tornadoes.

As this tornado sweeps through Pampa in Texas, USA, debris is thrown in all directions, extending well outside the funnel. The color of a tornado's funnel depends on the dust and debris it gathers up.

Hurricanes

A hurricane is a huge, spinning storm system that begins as a cluster of thunderstorms over the tropics. If the cluster drifts beyond 5° north or south of the equator, it starts rotating. The farther away from the equator it moves, the hurricane spins faster and becomes more powerful. Hurricanes can measure up to 800 km (500 miles) across and can produce torrential rain, winds up to 300 km/h (190 miles per hour) and an enormous high tide called a storm surge. The calmest place in a hurricane is its centre, or eye, which is free of cloud and strong winds.

Hurricane Katrina hit the USA's south coast in 2005. As it passed low-lying New Orleans, the city's protective levees broke, flooding most of the city for several weeks.

INSIDE A HURRICANE

Hurricanes start life as small thunderstorms over warm water.

Eye of the storm

As the hurricane rotates, it continues to draw in moist air from the ocean, gaining energy all the time.

Warm water heats the air and creates a rising current of moist air.

Cool air is pulled in to replace the rising current.

Huge banks of cumulonimbus clouds build up.

HURRICANE LIFE CYCLE

Day 1
A storm cluster forms.

Day 2
The storm begins to spin.

Day 3
A spiral shape develops.

Day 6
The eye of the storm emerges.

Day 12
The storm begins to fade.

WILD WINDS
Strong winds are a feature of all hurricanes. A hurricane can last for weeks and cover thousands of miles.

Lightning

Lightning is probably the most dramatic feature of a thunderstorm. We still do not know exactly what causes lightning, but we do know that it involves an increase of positive and negative electrical charges inside a thundercloud. It is likely that the updrafts in a storm carry positive charges to the top of the cloud, and downdrafts pull negative charges to the bottom. These opposite charges are attracted to each other. The attraction grows stronger until, eventually, the electricity leaps, or discharges, from one area to the other. We see this as a lightning bolt.

CLOUD-TO-CLOUD LIGHTNING

Most lightning occurs within clouds. Often, the positive charge in one cloud is attracted to the negative charge in another. Lightning leaps between them. Lightning can also occur in the same cloud.

Positive charge in upper cloud

Negative charge at base of cloud

CLOUD-TO-AIR LIGHTNING

Negative charge in atmosphere

Positive charge in cloud

A positive charge that builds up at the top of the cloud is close to a negative charge in the atmosphere next to the cloud. Lightning eventually jumps between them.

Most lightning bolts discharge about 100 million volts of electricity. A strike in a city, such as this one in Istanbul, Turkey, can cause sudden power surges that may disrupt power supplies.

CLOUD-TO-GROUND LIGHTNING

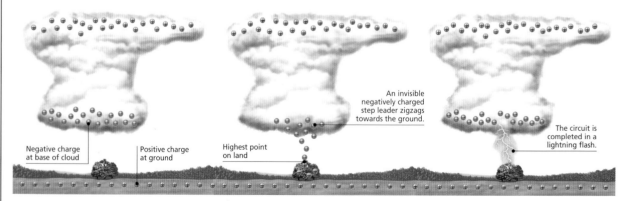

Negative charge at base of cloud

Positive charge at ground

Highest point on land

An invisible negatively charged step leader zigzags towards the ground.

The circuit is completed in a lightning flash.

Sometimes the strong negative charges along the bottom of cumulonimbus clouds can cause equally strong positive charges on the ground below. The two charges eventually meet in the form of lightning. This may strike open ground or tall objects such as trees.

COLOURS IN THE SKY

HOW RAINBOWS FORM
When sunlight passes through glass or water, it bends slightly, or refracts, and breaks up into the separate colours that make up white. A rainbow forms when sunlight is refracted as it enters raindrops, is reflected from the rear of the drop and is refracted a second time as it leaves.

WHY THE SKY IS BLUE

Sunlight is a mixture of all the colours of the spectrum: red, orange, yellow, green, blue, indigo and violet. Particles in the atmosphere scatter these colours one by one, beginning with violet. When the Sun is high in the sky, only violet, indigo, blue and a little green are scattered – so the sky looks blue.

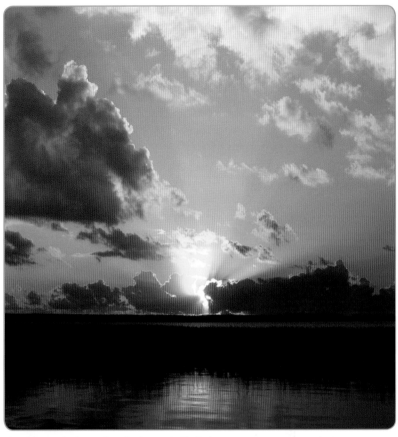

Blues, yellows and reds are reflected in the water in this glowing sunset scene.

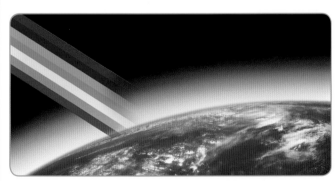

At about noon, the Sun is high in the sky and only bluish colours in the spectrum are scattered.

Towards sunset, sunlight travels farther through the atmosphere. Red and yellow are scattered.

Sunrise can produce reddish skies near the horizon and blue skies higher up.

Global Freezing

Earth's climate has changed many times in the last few million years. During periods of severe cold, known as ice ages or glacials, ice crept across the land. It gouged out hollows as it pushed soil and rocks ahead of it. Sea levels dropped greatly as much of the water froze. During the warmer periods between the ice ages – called interglacials – the ice melted and the huge hollows filled with water to become lakes. Evidence about past climates comes largely from animal and plant fossils, found in sediments from ocean beds.

THE LITTLE ICE AGE

Between 1430 and 1850 northern Europe experienced a 'Little Ice Age'. The River Thames in London, England, froze over in winter. From 1607 to 1814, people held events called frost fairs on the ice, with food stalls, games and dancing.

ICE AGE ANIMALS
One ice age, called the Würm Ice Age, lasted from 120,000 to 20,000 BC. During this time, huge elephant-like mammoths lived on the cold plains of what is now Siberia.

A CLIMATE TIMELINE
This timeline shows the major climate changes that have occurred during Earth's 4.6-billion-year history. The wavy line on the chart indicates the temperature relative to today's average, which is marked by the straight horizontal line.

3.7 bya Climate 10°C (18°F) warmer than today

330 mya Start of long ice age

2.7–1.8 bya
Ice sheets widespread

450 mya
Brief ice age

245 mya
Climate warms;
dinosaurs appear.

Present average temperature   bya = billion years ago   mya = million years ago   ya = years ago

Stalls and booths were set up.
People sold food, drink and
even souvenirs of the ice fair.

Depending on the severity
of the frost, the ice could
be up to 6 m (18 feet) thick.

0 mya

65 mya Gradual
cooling begins;
dinosaurs vanish.

1.6 mya Cooling continues; ice ages
occur roughly every 100,000 years.

Brief, warm interglacial periods
occur between ice ages.

AD 900–1100
Brief warm period

18,000 ya
Peak of last ice age;
mammoths disappear.

6,000 ya
Warm climate encourages
development of farming.

1450–1850
Little Ice Age

Global Warming

arth's climate may be changing as a result of human activity. Earth has steadily been getting warmer since the end of the 'Little Ice Age' in the 1800s. Last century, global temperatures rose by 0.6°C (1°F). This increase is called global warming, and it may be caused by greenhouse gases. Greenhouse gases – such as water vapour and carbon dioxide – occur naturally in the atmosphere and keep our planet warm by trapping heat from the Sun. However, when fuels such as coal and oil are burned to create electricity and power cars, extra carbon dioxide forms. More carbon dioxide means more heat is trapped in the atmosphere and Earth heats up.

INSIDE A GREENHOUSE
Greenhouses are made of glass and have slanted roofs to allow the maximum amount of sunlight to enter. The Sun's heat is trapped inside, which raises the temperature inside the greenhouse and helps the plants to grow.

THE GREENHOUSE EFFECT

Greenhouse gases absorb heat from the Sun and warm the planet. However, some greenhouse gases, such as carbon dioxide and methane, have built up in the atmosphere. As a result, the natural 'greenhouse' has become warmer.

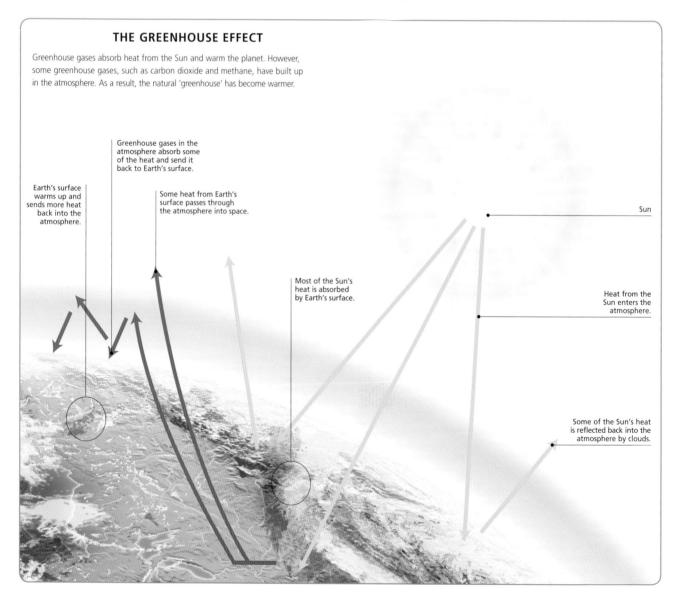

Greenhouse gases in the atmosphere absorb some of the heat and send it back to Earth's surface.

Earth's surface warms up and sends more heat back into the atmosphere.

Some heat from Earth's surface passes through the atmosphere into space.

Most of the Sun's heat is absorbed by Earth's surface.

Sun

Heat from the Sun enters the atmosphere.

Some of the Sun's heat is reflected back into the atmosphere by clouds.

CARBON DIOXIDE EMISSIONS

The United States, with less than five per cent of the world's population, is responsible for more than a quarter of human greenhouse gas emissions. This graph shows the total carbon dioxide gas emissions divided by the population of a number of countries. Each American emits more than 20 t (22 tons) each year. Australians are the next worst offenders.

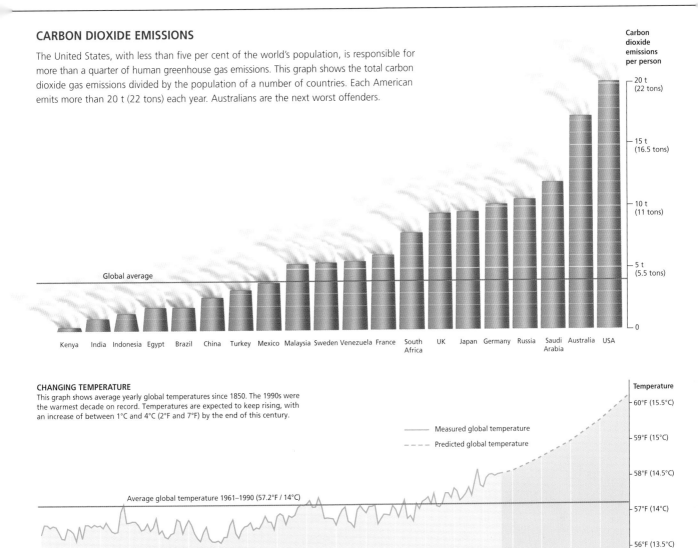

Carbon dioxide emissions per person

- 20 t (22 tons)
- 15 t (16.5 tons)
- 10 t (11 tons)
- 5 t (5.5 tons)
- 0

Global average

Kenya · India · Indonesia · Egypt · Brazil · China · Turkey · Mexico · Malaysia · Sweden · Venezuela · France · South Africa · UK · Japan · Germany · Russia · Saudi Arabia · Australia · USA

CHANGING TEMPERATURE

This graph shows average yearly global temperatures since 1850. The 1990s were the warmest decade on record. Temperatures are expected to keep rising, with an increase of between 1°C and 4°C (2°F and 7°F) by the end of this century.

Temperature

—— Measured global temperature
- - - Predicted global temperature

Average global temperature 1961–1990 (57.2°F / 14°C)

- 60°F (15.5°C)
- 59°F (15°C)
- 58°F (14.5°C)
- 57°F (14°C)
- 56°F (13.5°C)
- 55°F (13°C)

Year 1860 1870 1880 1890 1900 1910 1920 1930 1940 1950 1960 1970 1980 1990 2000 2010 2020 2030 2040 2050

Cars and trucks are big contributors to greenhouse gas emissions. Heavy traffic is common in industrialised countries, and more people are buying vehicles in the developing world.

Coal-fired power stations, such as this one in the UK, are one of the biggest emitters of carbon dioxide and other polluting chemicals into the atmosphere.

Effects of global warming

Earth has heated and cooled naturally in cycles for millions of years. What is different about the heating cycle we are currently experiencing is that many experts now agree that humans are the cause. Most societies in the world are dependent on burning coal for electricity. The increased amounts of greenhouse gases that result are causing the atmosphere to overheat. If this trend continues, the effects could be devastating. As ice sheets and glaciers melt, sea levels will rise and flood islands and coastal regions. Rainfall patterns may change, causing drought in Africa and India. To slow down this climate change, most industrialised countries signed the Kyoto Protocol in 1997 and agreed to reduce greenhouse gas emissions.

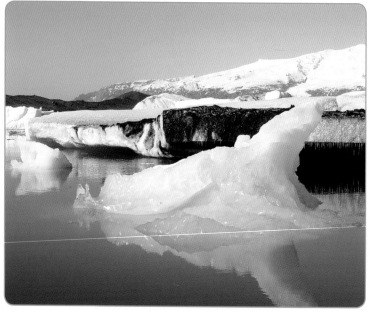

Jökulsárlón is the largest glacial lake in Iceland. It appeared in 1934, and has steadily increased in size as more of the glaciers that feed it melt.

HOT SPOTS OF GLOBAL WARMING
Scientists have noted many changes in Earth's climate. These include changes in Arctic temperatures and ice, patterns of floods and droughts, the saltiness of the oceans, wind patterns and extreme weather such as heat waves, wildfires and hurricanes.

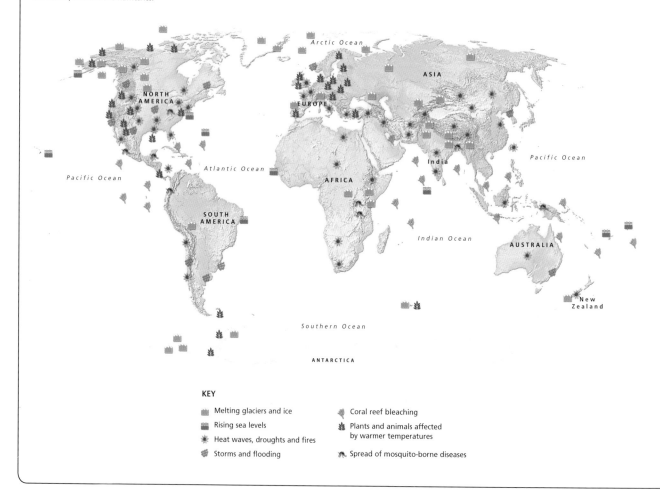

KEY

- Melting glaciers and ice
- Rising sea levels
- Heat waves, droughts and fires
- Storms and flooding
- Coral reef bleaching
- Plants and animals affected by warmer temperatures
- Spread of mosquito-borne diseases

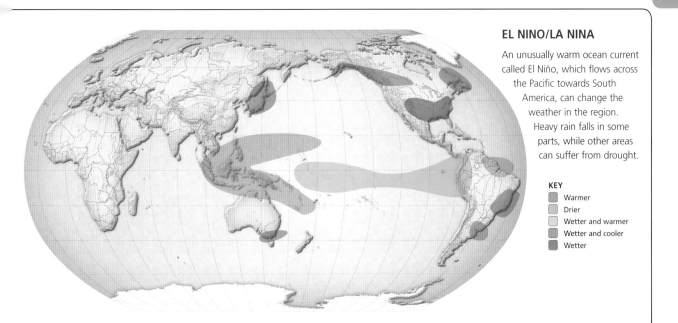

EL NINO/LA NINA

An unusually warm ocean current called El Niño, which flows across the Pacific towards South America, can change the weather in the region. Heavy rain falls in some parts, while other areas can suffer from drought.

KEY
- Warmer
- Drier
- Wetter and warmer
- Wetter and cooler
- Wetter

This fishing boat was once moored by the shores of the Aral Sea in Kazakhstan. Now it lies miles from the shrinking sea.

The Arctic ice caps have been getting smaller, because more ice is melting than is being replaced by snowfalls.

Changing rainfall patterns may cause droughts in some regions. These parched conditions increase the risk of wildfires.

RETREATING GLACIERS

Glaciers supply essential water to people in areas such as central Asia, Peru and Nepal. If the glaciers melt and disappear, people in these regions will face serious water shortages.

1917 The peak of Mount Kilimanjaro in Tanzania was covered by glaciers.

2007 More than 80 per cent of Mount Kilimanjaro's glaciers have melted away.

Scientists predict that the mountain's glaciers will disappear completely by the middle of this century.

Earth's Riches

Earth provides us with the resources we need to live. If we manage them carefully, some of these resources – water, plants and animals – will never run out. These are renewable resources. Others, such as fossil fuels (coal, oil and gas), minerals and precious stones, are not renewable. Fossil fuels supply most of the energy we need to light and heat our homes and to fuel our cars. These fuels are 'fossil' because they are the remains of animals and plants buried deep underground. Because some resources may run out soon, scientists are trying to find new ways to supply the energy we need.

SUPPLY AND DEMAND
The three fossil fuels – coal, oil and gas – are by far the most important sources of energy. The United States uses about a quarter of all the world's energy.

SOURCES OF ENERGY

Oil 33%
Coal 24.5%
Gas 22%
Nuclear 7%
Hydro 2%
Firewood 11%
Other 0.5%

USERS OF ENERGY

USA 24.5%
China 9%
Russia 7%
Japan 5.5%
Germany 4%
Rest of world 50%

WHERE TO FIND RESOURCES

As supplies of coal, oil and gas decline, other energy sources, such as wind and solar power, become more important.

Oil and gas
Found together in rock layers in Earth's crust, oil and gas are extracted by drilling from land and sea.

Coal
Coal, the most plentiful fossil fuel, can be collected by digging at the surface or by mining deep underground.

Nuclear power
Certain elements, such as uranium, emit high-energy particles that are converted into electricity at nuclear power plants.

Geothermal power
In some regions, groundwater is heated by hot, volcanic rock to create steam that is used to generate power.

KEY

▓ Forest and woodland
░ Arable land
▒ Grazing
□ Marginal or nonproductive
⛏ Oil field
◕ Coal field
◊ Natural gas field
⚛ Nuclear energy
≈ Hydroelectric energy
◉ Geothermal energy
✳ Wind energy
☽ Tidal energy
☀ Solar energy
◆ Precious metals and minerals
⊗ Metallic minerals
⊠ Non-metallic minerals

EARTH'S RESOURCES

For thousands of years, people have used the resources that Earth provides. Recently, humans have used more of these resources and at a much faster rate.

Hydroelectric power
Hydroelectric power is created when water passes through electricity-generating turbines at the bottom of a dam.

Wind power
Wind turbines convert the power of the wind into electricity. The wind turns the turbine blades, which drive electrical generators.

Solar power
Clusters of mirror-like solar panels reflect the Sun's rays onto a solar furnace, where the intense heat is converted into electricity.

Sea power
Water passing through narrow tunnels in a tidal barrage, which is like a dam, drive huge turbines that produce power.

Oil and gas

The most sought-after resources are oil and natural gas. New fields are being searched for and found all the time. Countries that have large reserves of oil and gas under their land or in nearby seas sell to countries that need these resources. This trade affects the economy of the whole world. Modern industries, and the growing number of people on Earth, use an ever-increasing amount of oil and gas. However, as it takes millions of years for oil and gas to develop, there are only limited amounts remaining. When they are all used up, we will have to find other sources of energy, such as solar energy or the power of moving wind and water.

This huge machine, called a pump jack or nodding donkey, lifts oil through a bore hole from deep underground reserves in in Alberta, Canada.

LIMITED SUPPLY

The graph below shows the number of years that known supplies of fossil fuels are expected to last, if they continue to be used at the present rate.

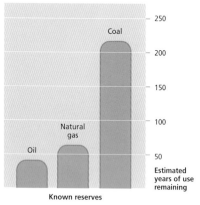

Known reserves

Coal
Natural gas
Oil

- 250
- 200
- 150
- 100
- 50

Estimated years of use remaining

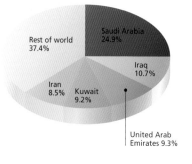

Revolving crane

Flare

ON AN OIL RIG

An oil platform is like a huge steel and concrete hotel in the middle of the ocean. Several hundred workers can live there for weeks at a time. Most platforms stay in position for about 25 years.

Well heads
These transport oil and gas to the platform.

Processing equipment

FOSSIL FUEL RESERVES

The whole world relies on fossil fuels, but only a few countries produce and supply them. Most of the world's oil and gas comes from Middle Eastern countries.

NATURAL GAS RESERVES

Russia 30.7%
Iran 14.8%
Qatar 9.3%
Rest of world 37.3%
United Arab Emirates 3.9%
Saudi Arabia 4.0%

OIL RESERVES

Saudi Arabia 24.9%
Iraq 10.7%
Kuwait 9.2%
Iran 8.5%
Rest of world 37.4%
United Arab Emirates 9.3%

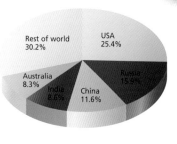

COAL RESERVES

USA 25.4%
Russia 15.9%
China 11.6%
India 8.6%
Australia 8.3%
Rest of world 30.2%

HOW OIL AND GAS ARE FORMED

Oil and gas form when the decayed remains of tiny sea creatures are crushed beneath layers of rock. The process takes millions of years.

Mud and silt cover dead sea creatures and turn into rock.

As layers pile up, the sea creatures slowly turn into oil and gas.

Oil and gas rise towards the surface until they are blocked by layers of rock.

They pool under the rock with the gas on top of the oil.

Derrick
This carries the crown block and supports the weight of the drill string.

Crown block

Helicopter
People and supplies are taken to and from the oil rig by helicopter.

Cabins

Drill pipes

Lifeboat

Satellite dishes

Helicopter pad

Coal

Coal is one of the most widely used fuels. It is burned for heat and energy. Coal consists of the remains of ancient swamp plants. As the plants decay in mud, they turn into a moist, spongy substance called peat. Sometimes, sedimentary rock forms on top of the peat and compresses it. The crushed peat then turns into a dark brown rock called lignite, or brown coal. As more layers of rock press down on it, lignite becomes bituminous coal. Under extreme pressure, bituminous coal changes into anthracite – a hard, shiny, black coal. The more coal is compressed, the harder it becomes and the more energy it releases when burned.

Upcast shaft and fan

Coal is taken to the surface in a large metal container called a skip.

The broken coal falls onto a conveyor belt that takes it to the upcast shaft.

A machine called a cutting head tears into the coal with its sharp-toothed wheel.

While most coal is mined deep underground, some is mined near the surface. Mines like this one in Germany are called open-pit mines.

HOW COAL IS FORMED

Over thousands of years, buried plant material can become compressed and lose most of its water, oxygen and other gases. During compression its carbon content gradually increases and it turns into coal.

Peat

Lignite, or brown coal

Bituminous, or black coal

Anthracite

Decayed plants become peat. This material consists mainly of moisture and gases.

Layers of sedimentary rock compress the peat, turning it into lignite, or brown coal.

Increased pressure turns lignite into bituminous, or black, coal.

Anthracite, the highest quality coal, is the most compressed, and contains little water or gas.

Coal is loaded onto rail cars for transportation.

Miners take the downcast shaft to reach the coal face. Fans supply them with air.

The miners dig tunnels through the rock. They use metal pillars to support the roof.

The miners descend to the coal face in a metal elevator known as a cage.

MINING COAL

Today, machines do most of the digging involved in mining coal. The method shown here, known as continuous mining, is used in most coal mines.

MAKING STEEL

Steel is a mixture of iron and carbon, which combine when heated with coal. We use it to make many objects, tools and utensils, cars and trains.

THE RAW INGREDIENTS

To make steel, iron must be removed from iron ore.

Coke – a type of heated coal – heats iron ore to extract molten iron.

Limestone removes impurities from the molten iron.

THE PRODUCTION PROCESS

Coke and iron ore are heated together in a large furnace. When the molten iron sinks to the bottom, limestone is added.

In another furnace, oxygen is blasted into the iron to reduce the amount of carbon and turn it into steel.

The molten steel is tipped into a continuous casting system. Steel is shaped into long sections by being squeezed between rollers.

THE END RESULT

Flexible wire is an important steel product.

Sheets of steel are used for many products.

Steel girders provide support in large buildings.

Many types of pipes are made of steel.

Solar and wind energy

The Sun is a powerful source of energy. It could, in fact, supply the whole world's energy needs – Earth receives 20,000 times as much energy from the Sun as we currently use. Energy from the Sun –called solar energy – can be harnessed in many ways. Satellites in space have large panels covered with solar cells that turn sunlight into electrical power. Some buildings have glass-covered solar panels that use solar energy to heat water. They are painted black inside to absorb the heat. Solar energy is a clean fuel that will continue to reach Earth long after all the fossil fuels have been used up. Wind, too, is a source of energy, which can be harnessed by sails or blades. In the past, wind powered sailboats and windmills. Today, modern versions of windmills called turbines are used to generate electricity.

MAKING SOLAR POWER

Solar cells convert light into electricity. The first layer in a solar cell is made from N-type silicone, which has many electrons. The second layer is P-type silicone, which has fewer electrons. Solar energy causes electrons to jump from the first layer to the second, producing an electric current.

INSIDE A SOLAR CELL

Sunlight
Protective coating
N-type silicone
P-type silicone

Rows of solar panels are being installed for solar power stations in dry, sunny places, such as southwestern USA, the Australian desert or parts of Spain and Germany.

HARNESSING THE WIND

Wind turbines, with large sails or
blades, convert wind into energy.
Wind farms, as they are called,
are built in very windy locations.
As the wind turns the blades, the
spinning motion produces electricity.

Gearbox
The gearbox, driven
by the turbine shaft,
controls the speed
of the generator.

Generator
The generator converts
the spinning motion
into electricity.

Turbine shaft
Wind turns the blades,
which then turn the
central turbine shaft.

Blades
The blades are set at an angle
that can be changed to suit
wind speed and direction.

Nacelle
This part contains
the machinery;
it pivots to point
the blades into
the wind.

Tower
The tower holds the blades
at a safe height above the
ground. Cables in the tower
carry electricity to the ground.

Cables
Underground
cables collect
the electricity
produced by
the turbines.

Power from water

Hydroelectric power stations use moving water to generate electricity. These enormous concrete structures are usually found in mountain regions that have high rainfall. Engineers build huge dams across steep-sided valleys. Turbines are placed in the path of the water that gushes forcefully through the dam. The blades of the turbines spin and extract enormous energy from the water. Geothermal energy makes use of heat from Earth's molten core to heat water sent in pipes below the surface. Steam from this heated water travels back to power stations on the surface, where its force spins turbines that produce electric power.

Hydroelectric dams have a major advantage over coal-burning power plants. They use a renewable resource – water – which is constantly being recycled in the environment.

The Svartsengi power plant in southwest Iceland is one of five major geothermal power stations that together generate about one-quarter of Iceland's electricity needs.

Since 1958, hot springs have provided a source of electricity generation at the Wairakei geothermal power station in New Zealand's North Island.

Transmission lines
Electric cables carry electricity away from the power plant.

Spillway
Spillway gates open to release water when the level behind the wall is too high.

Reservoir
The deep lake that forms behind the dam wall is called a reservoir.

Dam walls
Dam walls are curved to withstand the force of water behind them.

Generators
Shafts connect turbines to generators. When the turbines spin, the generators make electricity.

Penstocks
These channel water through the dam to the turbines.

Turbines

Drift tubes
Water leaves the turbines through drift tubes.

Transformers
Transformers boost the electrical force from the generators to more than 200,000 volts.

Control room
The operation of the entire power plant is directed from the control room.

POWER PLANT

The first hydroelectric power plant was built in the USA in 1882. Now huge hydroelectric power plants are used in most parts of the world.

INSIDE A TURBINE

Water makes the turbine spin like a high-speed paddle wheel to generate electricity.

Water enters the turbine.

The force of the water spins the turbine.

It then exits through the centre.

Comparing Earth

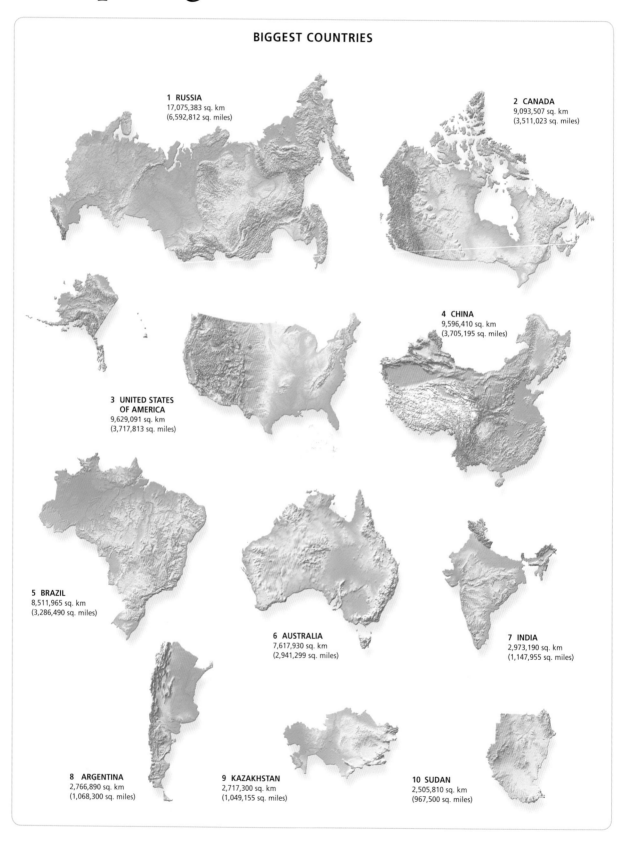

BIGGEST COUNTRIES

1 RUSSIA
17,075,383 sq. km
(6,592,812 sq. miles)

2 CANADA
9,093,507 sq. km
(3,511,023 sq. miles)

4 CHINA
9,596,410 sq. km
(3,705,195 sq. miles)

**3 UNITED STATES
OF AMERICA**
9,629,091 sq. km
(3,717,813 sq. miles)

5 BRAZIL
8,511,965 sq. km
(3,286,490 sq. miles)

6 AUSTRALIA
7,617,930 sq. km
(2,941,299 sq. miles)

7 INDIA
2,973,190 sq. km
(1,147,955 sq. miles)

8 ARGENTINA
2,766,890 sq. km
(1,068,300 sq. miles)

9 KAZAKHSTAN
2,717,300 sq. km
(1,049,155 sq. miles)

10 SUDAN
2,505,810 sq. km
(967,500 sq. miles)

LARGEST LAKES

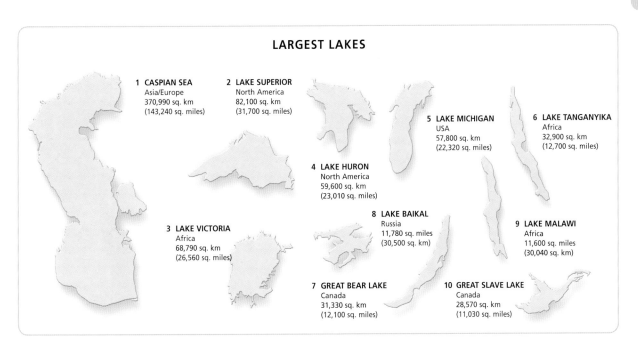

1 CASPIAN SEA
Asia/Europe
370,990 sq. km
(143,240 sq. miles)

2 LAKE SUPERIOR
North America
82,100 sq. km
(31,700 sq. miles)

5 LAKE MICHIGAN
USA
57,800 sq. km
(22,320 sq. miles)

6 LAKE TANGANYIKA
Africa
32,900 sq. km
(12,700 sq. miles)

4 LAKE HURON
North America
59,600 sq. km
(23,010 sq. miles)

8 LAKE BAIKAL
Russia
11,780 sq. miles
(30,500 sq. km)

9 LAKE MALAWI
Africa
11,600 sq. miles
(30,040 sq. km)

3 LAKE VICTORIA
Africa
68,790 sq. km
(26,560 sq. miles)

7 GREAT BEAR LAKE
Canada
31,330 sq. km
(12,100 sq. miles)

10 GREAT SLAVE LAKE
Canada
28,570 sq. km
(11,030 sq. miles)

LONGEST RIVERS

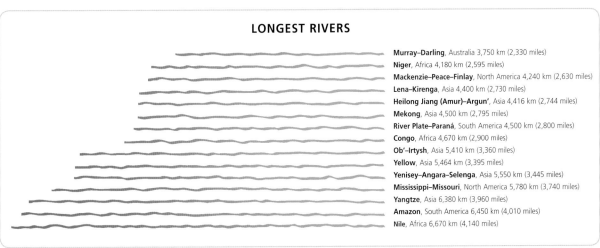

Murray–Darling, Australia 3,750 km (2,330 miles)
Niger, Africa 4,180 km (2,595 miles)
Mackenzie–Peace–Finlay, North America 4,240 km (2,630 miles)
Lena–Kirenga, Asia 4,400 km (2,730 miles)
Heilong Jiang (Amur)–Argun', Asia 4,416 km (2,744 miles)
Mekong, Asia 4,500 km (2,795 miles)
River Plate–Paraná, South America 4,500 km (2,800 miles)
Congo, Africa 4,670 km (2,900 miles)
Ob'–Irtysh, Asia 5,410 km (3,360 miles)
Yellow, Asia 5,464 km (3,395 miles)
Yenisey–Angara–Selenga, Asia 5,550 km (3,445 miles)
Mississippi–Missouri, North America 5,780 km (3,740 miles)
Yangtze, Asia 6,380 km (3,960 miles)
Amazon, South America 6,450 km (4,010 miles)
Nile, Africa 6,670 km (4,140 miles)

HIGHEST MOUNTAINS

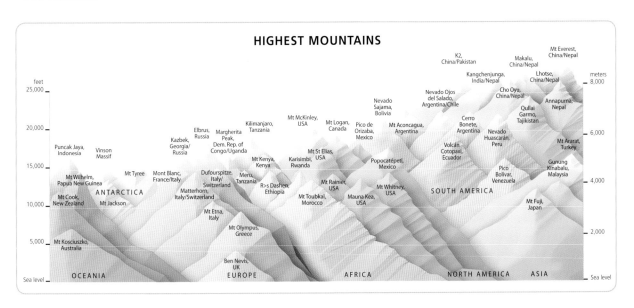

Planet Earth

EARTH THROUGH TIME

Earth's life can be divided into different units of time, called eras, periods and epochs. Different plants and animals lived at different times – for example, the dinosaurs lived only in the Mesozoic era.

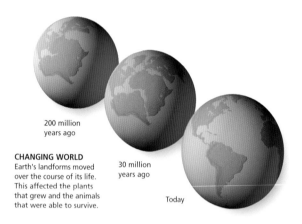

200 million
years ago

CHANGING WORLD
Earth's landforms moved over the course of its life. This affected the plants that grew and the animals that were able to survive.

30 million
years ago

Today

ERAS AND PERIODS

Era	Period	Epoch	Began mya
PHANEROZOIC			
	Pleistogene	Holocene	0.1
		Pleistocene	1.8
Cenozoic	Neogene	Pliocene	5.3
		Miocene	23
	Paleogene	Oligocene	34
		Eocene	55
		Paleocene	65.5
Mesozoic	Cretaceous	Late	100
		Early	146
	Jurassic	Late	161
		Middle	176
		Early	200
	Triassic	Late	228
		Middle	245
		Early	250
Palaeozoic	Permian	Late	260
		Middle	271
		Early	299
	Carboniferous	Pennsylvanian	318
		Mississipian	359
	Devonian	Late	385
		Middle	398
		Early	416
	Silurian	Late	423
		Early	444
	Ordovician	Late	461
		Middle	472
		Early	488
	Cambrian	Late	501
		Middle	513
		Early	542
PROTEROZOIC			2,500
ARCHAEAN			3,800
HADEAN			4,600

WHAT MAKES UP SOIL

Soil consists of broken pieces of bedrock combined with the remains of once-living plants and animals that are decomposing. Living creatures, such as worms, mix up the soil. Rainwater draining through the soil carries minerals with it, which causes older soils to form distinct layers.

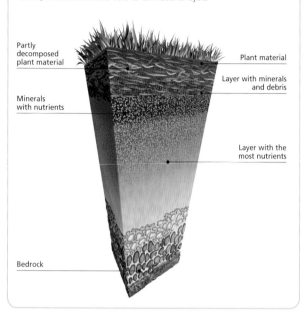

Partly decomposed plant material

Plant material

Layer with minerals and debris

Minerals with nutrients

Layer with the most nutrients

Bedrock

GEMSTONES AND JEWELS

Light bent at large angle

White light

Diamond

Light bent at small angle

White light

Quartz

WHY DIAMONDS SPARKLE

When white light shines through a transparent crystal, it bends and breaks up into its colours, or spectra. Light needs to bend at a larger angle for diamonds than other crystals, which is why they sparkle so brilliantly.

WORLD'S LARGEST DIAMONDS

Ring
1 carat

Blue Hope
45.5 carats

Regent
140.5 carats

Millennium Star
203 carats

Star of Africa
530.2 carats

Volcanoes

DECADE VOLCANOES

There are 16 Decade Volcanoes – volcanoes that are internationally recognised as being important for constant study. They are generally large; have a long history of violent activity; and are located close to towns or cities.

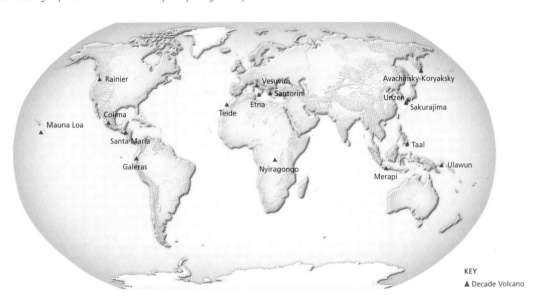

KEY
▲ Decade Volcano

TOP 10 DEADLY ERUPTIONS

Year	Volcano	Location	Fatalities	Cause of deaths
1815	Tambora	Indonesia	92,000	Ash, tsunami, disease, starvation
1883	Krakatau	Indonesia	36,400	Tsunami, ash
1902	Mt. Pelee	Martinique	26,000	Ashflows
1985	Nevado del Ruiz	Colombia	23,000	Mudflows
79	Vesuvius	Italy	16,000	Ash, ashflows
1792	Unzen	Japan	14,500	Volcano collapse, tsunami
1586	Kelut	Indonesia	10,000	Unknown
1783	Laki	Iceland	9,350	Disease, starvation
1919	Kelut	Indonesia	5,000	Mudflows
1631	Vesuvius	Italy	4,000	Mudflows; lava flows

OUT OF THIS WORLD

Volcanoes are not restricted to Earth. They appear on a number of moons in our Solar System. Volcanoes have played a part in shaping the surface of all four inner rocky planets (Mercury, Venus, Earth and Mars) as well as some of the moons of the outer gas giants.

NEPTUNE'S TRITON
Triton's geysers are shown here erupting with freezing plumes of liquid nitrogen. This material rises about 8 km (5 miles) above the surface, before raining down as nitrogen frost.

The Moon
The dark patches on its surface are dried lava lakes.

Venus
Sulphur from Venus's volcanoes formed its thick atmosphere.

Mars
The volcanoes on Mars dwarf those on our planet.

Jupiter's moon Io
This spews fountains of sulphur dioxide from its surface.

Neptune's moon Triton
Not all volcanoes are hot; Triton's geysers are freezing.

Earthquakes

EARTHQUAKE RISK

The chances of being shaken up by an earthquake depend on where on Earth you are. In many places you could live a whole lifetime and never feel the ground move. In other places, tremors are a regular occurrence and the risk of a destructive earthquake is always present.

KEY
- ☐ Low risk
- ☐ Medium risk
- ■ High risk
- ■ Very high risk

EARTHQUAKE THEORIES

As long as people have felt the ground shake, they have sought to explain the frightening phenomenon of earthquakes. But it is only very recently that we have worked out what is happening beneath our feet.

MYTHICAL EXPLANATIONS
According to an ancient Hindu myth, Earth is carried on the back of an elephant, which stands on a turtle that is balanced on a cobra. Whenever one moves, Earth trembles and shakes.

Cross section of Earth's interior from 1665

EARLY MODERN EUROPE
In the 1660s the French philosopher René Descartes suggested that Earth was once as hot as the Sun and that it is still cooling and shrinking. These contractions created the mountains and caused earthquakes.

A Hindu cosmos

MODERN TIMES
Plate tectonic theory had its beginnings in 1915, when German scientist Alfred Wegener suggested that all the continents were once joined together and had subsequently drifted apart. This theory has proved to be a convincing explanation for earthquakes and other geological phenomena.

Seismograph

TOP 10 EARTHQUAKES

Year	Location	Fatalities
1201	Egypt–Syria	1,100,000
1556	Shanxi, China	830,000
1139	Caucasus	300,000
1662	China	300,000
1737	Calcutta, India	300,000
2004	Sumatra–Andaman	283,000
115	Antioch, Turkey	260,000
1976	Tangshan, China	240,000
1139	Aleppo, Syria	230,000
1876	Andaman Islands,	215,000

TOP 5 TSUNAMIS

Year	Location	Fatalities
2004	Sumatra–Andaman	283,000
1755	Lisbon, Portugal	100,000
1908	Italy	70,000
1782	China and Taiwan	40,000
1883	Krakatau, Indonesia	36,000

Extreme Earth

TORNADOES AND HURRICANES

PATH OF DESTRUCTION
A tornado's funnel is like a giant vacuum cleaner that sucks up everything in its path. Buildings and trees in its direct path can be destroyed, but those just either side spared.

FUJITA SCALE

This six -point scale was devised in 1971 to report tornadoes, based on the visible damage they cause.

Scale	Speeds km/h (mph)	Damage
F0	64–117 (40–73)	light
F1	118–180 (74–112)	moderate
F2	181–251 (113–157)	considerable
F3	252330 (158–206)	terrible
F4	331–417 (207–260)	severe
F5	more than 417 (260)	devastating

SAFFIR–SIMPSON SCALE

This scale devised in 1955 by meteorologists at the US Weather Bureau to report the strength of hurricane winds. The five-point scale also takes account of surface pressure and storm surge.

Scale	Pressure hectopascals	Wind speed km/h (mph)	Storm surge m (ft)	Damage
1	more than 980	118–152 (74–95 ()	1.2–1.6 (4–5)	minimal
2	965–980	153–176 (96–110)	1.7–2.5 (6–8)	moderate
3	945–964	177–208 (111–130)	2.6–3.7 (9–12)	extensive
4	920–944	209–248 (131–155)	3.8–5.4 (13–18)	extreme
5	less than 920	more than 248 (155)	more than 5.4 (18)	catastrophic

JOURNEY OF HURRICANE EMILY
Emily developed off the coast of Brazil on July 12. By the 16th, winds were over 125 knots and gusting to 155 knots. After striking land on the 18th, Emily then headed back out to sea on the 19th to regain strength. On the 20th, she came ashore over Mexico as a Category 5 hurricane.

July 12, 2005

July 16, 2005

July 19, 2005

July 20, 2005

EXTREME WEATHER FACTS

WETTEST PLACE
Cherrapunji, India 26,461 mm (1,042 inches) of rain in an average year.

DRIEST PLACE
Arica in Chile's Atacama Desert Annual average rainfall is 0.5 mm (0.02 inch).

LOWEST TEMPERATURE
Vostok Base, Antarctica Recorded a temperature of –89.2°C(–129°F) on July 21, 1983.

HIGHEST NON-TORNADO WIND GUST
Mount Washington, USA Recorded a wind gust of 371 km/h (231 mph) on April 12, 1934.

HEAVIEST RECORDED HAILSTONES
Gopalganj, Bangladesh Recorded hailstones that weighed up to 1 kg (2 pounds 3 ounces) on April 14, 1986, killing 92 people.

RAINIEST PLACE
Mount Waialeale Crater, Kauai, Hawaii 350 days of rain each year.

HIGHEST TEMPERATURE
El Azizia, Libya Recorded a temperature of 57.3°C (136°F) on September 13, 1922.

GREATEST TEMPERATURE RANGE
Verhoyansk, Central Siberia Summer temperatures in this region can reach 98°F (37°C). Winter temperatures can go as low as –68°C (–90°F).

HIGHEST RECORDED TORNADO WIND SPEED
Oklahoma, USA In May 1999, winds gusted to 512 km/h (318 mph).

HOTTEST REGION
Sahara Desert belt Dallol, Ethiopia averaged a daytime temperature of 34°C (94°F) between 1960 and 1966.

Glossary

abyssal plain The smooth, almost level, deep ocean floor, located between the continental slope and the mid-ocean ridge.

acid rain An acidic form of rain that occurs when chemicals produced by the burning of fossil fuels mix with water vapour in the air.

aftershock A tremor that occurs hours, days or weeks after a major earthquake and starts near that quake's hypocentre.

air mass A large body of air, covering most of a continent or ocean, which has approximately the same temperature, humidity, and density at every height.

Antarctic Circle The imaginary line, at 66.5°S, south of which there is at least one day each year when the sun does not rise above the horizon and one day when it does not sink below the horizon.

Arctic Circle The imaginary line, at 66.5°N, north of which there is at least one day each year when the sun does not rise above the horizon and one day when it does not sink below the horizon.

arid A region that is has too little rainfall to be used for agriculture.

ash The mineral residue of a fire. Volcanic ash contains small pieces of rock and lava.

atmosphere A layer of gases surrounding a planet or moon, extending from the surface and held in place by gravity.

atoll A circular reef that encloses a lagoon. It is commonly formed on the crater rim of an extinct underwater volcano.

biodiversity Short for 'biological diversity', it refers to the variety that exists among the living things in the world or in some part of the world.

biome A type of vegetation that covers a large area of the world, determined mainly by climate. Tundra, desert and tropical rain forest are all biomes.

caldera The roughly circular crater at the top of a volcano, formed by the collapse of the roof of a magma chamber.

canyon A deep, steep-sided valley formed by river erosion.

CFCs (chlorofluorocarbons) Industrially produced chemicals used in aerosols, refrigerators and air conditioners.

climate A region's long-term pattern of weather conditions.

cloud A concentration of liquid water droplets or ice crystals in the atmosphere.

condensation The change from a gas to liquid, for example, water vapour changing to liquid water droplets.

continent A large area of continental crust with a surface that is above sea level. There are seven continents: Africa, Antarctica, Asia, Australia, Europe, North America and South America.

continental drift The slow movement of continental plates – the pieces of Earth's crust on which the continents are fixed. This is caused by convection currents circling in the mantle.

continental rise The ocean floor beyond the edge of the continental slope. It is covered with sediment and slopes gently downwards away from the continent.

continental shelf The edge of a continent that lies below the ocean surface.

continental slope The steeply sloping area of ocean floor between the continental shelf and continental rise. Its surface is divided by deep canyons.

convection The upwards movement of an air mass warmed by land or sea. As the warm air rises, condensation may occur, forming clouds.

convection currents (mantle) Movement within the mantle as hot rock rises and cooler rock sinks. This movement most likely causes the movement of Earth's tectonic plates.

coral reef A massive limestone structure built in clear tropical water from the skeletons (corallites) of small soft-bodied animals called polyps.

core The centremost part of Earth, which consists of a solid inner core surrounded by a liquid outer core, both made of iron.

crater A circular depression caused either by volcanic activity (volcanic crater) or by the impact of a meteorite (impact crater).

crust The outer layer of Earth, consisting of solid rock averaging 5 km (3 miles) thick beneath the oceans and up to 64 km (40 miles) beneath mountain ranges.

crystal A solid mineral with a definite geometric shape.

current There are two main kinds of water currents: an ocean current is a stream of water that moves through the water, like a river in the sea, and a surface current is driven by the wind.

cyclone An area of very low pressure, with often gray skies and steady rainfall. Air moves around a cyclone counterclockwise

in the Northern Hemisphere and clockwise in the Southern. (See hurricane)

deciduous A plant or tree that drops its leaves in fall, winter or dry season, and grows new leaves in spring or wet season.

delta The mouth of a slow-moving river, which deposits a layer of sediment that extends beyond the coastline.

desert A region where the amount of rain each year is less than the amount of water that evaporates during the same period.

downdraft a downward-moving air current

earthquake A sudden, violent release of energy in Earth's crust, caused by the rocks cracking deep below the surface as they move to release the strain.

ecosystem A community of living things and the environment in which they live.

El Niño A periodic unusual warming of surface waters off the west coast of South America.

epicentre The point on Earth's surface that is directly above the hypocentre, or starting point, of an earthquake.

equator The imaginary line at 0° that divides Earth into its North and South hemispheres.

era A division of time in Earth's history. Geologists divide eras into periods.

erosion The breaking down and removal of rock and soil by wind, water, ice and mass movements such as landslides.

estuary A partly enclosed area of coastal water that is open to the sea and into which a river flows.

evaporation The change of state from a liquid to a gas.

fault A crack in Earth's crust along which two sections of crust have moved in relation to each other.

fjord A long, narrow, steep-sided coastal inlet at the end of a glacial valley.

floodplain The part of a river valley that is covered with sediment deposited by a river that overflows its banks.

fog Cloud at ground level that reduces visibility to less than 1 km (0.6 miles).

fold A bend in rock layers caused by movement in the crust.

fossil The remains, trace or impression of any living thing preserved in, or as, rock.

fossil fuel Material that comes from the remains of once-living plants or animals, which can be burned to release energy. Peat, coal, oil and gas are fossil fuels.

freezing The change in state of liquid water to solid ice.

front A boundary between two air masses of different temperatures.

geothermal energy Heat that comes from an underground reservoir of rock or water that is much hotter than the surrounding rock. This energy can be used as power.

geyser An opening at Earth's surface, from which a fountain of hot water periodically spouts upwards.

glacier A mass of ice formed by the buildup of compressed snow that moves slowly over the underlying surface.

Gondwana The former southern supercontinent. It contained South America, Africa, Madagascar, India, Sri Lanka, Australia, New Zealand and Antarctica.

greenhouse effect The retention of heat in the atmosphere because it absorbs certain gases, such as water vapour and carbon dioxide.

groundwater Water that moves through the spaces between rocks below ground.

habitat The area where a community of plants and animals lives.

hardness A measure of the ability of one mineral to scratch another.

hemisphere One half of a sphere. Earth is divided into two hemispheres.

hot spot A local area of high volcanic activity, which does not occur at the edges of tectonic plates.

humidity The amount of water vapour present in the air.

hurricane The name for a tropical cyclone that develops in the Atlantic or Caribbean. (See cyclone)

hypocentre The place within Earth's crust where energy in strained rock is suddenly released as earthquake waves.

iceberg A mass of ice that has detached (calved) from a glacier or ice shelf and floats in the sea.

ice sheet The largest form of a glacier, sometimes called an ice cap.

ice shelf An area of floating ice, once part of a glacier, that is still attached to land.

igneous rock A rock that has formed from cooled, hardened magma. Earth's first rocks were igneous rock.

intrusion A body of rock that has formed within pre-existing rocks.

invertebrate An animal, such as a worm, mollusk, trilobite or insect, that does not have a backbone.

jet stream A narrow, strong wind 10–15 km (6–9 miles) above Earth's surface.

lagoon A coastal area of shallow water that is almost completely enclosed, with only a small connection to the sea.

Laurasia The former northern supercontinent. It contained North America, Greenland, Europe and Asia (but not India).

lava Molten rock, or magma, that has erupted onto Earth's surface from a volcano.

lightning An electrical discharge between areas of positive and negative electric charge inside clouds and on the ground.

lithosphere The solid layer of Earth that comprises the crust and the brittle top part of the mantle.

luster The ability of a mineral to absorb or reflect light.

magma Hot liquid rock and crystals found below Earth's surface. When magma erupts onto the surface, it is called lava.

magma chamber A pool of magma in Earth's lithosphere surface where magma is stored until it rises to the surface in a volcanic eruption.

mantle The part of the Earth between the underside of the crust and the outer core. It is semi-solid rock, about the consistency of modeling clay.

margin A boundary between two tectonic plates. These may be moving apart, pushing together or slipping side by side.

marsh A permanently waterlogged area of land, in which grasses grow.

meander The winding course of a river as it flows slowly across almost level ground.

Mercalli scale A scale for measuring the intensity of an earthquake by direct observation of its effect, divided into 12 categories from 'not felt' to 'total devastation'.

mesosphere The layer of the atmosphere above the stratosphere, from about 50 to 80 km (30 to 50 miles) above sea level.

metal A material that is a good conductor of heat and electricity; most metals are solid and shiny at room temperature.

metamorphic rock Rock formed by the transformation of pre-existing rock as a result of extreme heat and/or pressure.

meteor A small extraterrestrial body that burns up as it travels through Earth's atmosphere, producing a 'shooting star'.

meteorite A small extraterrestrial body that has reached Earth's surface.

mid-ocean ridge The range of volcanic mountains that runs along the centre of an ocean floor. They occur where two tectonic plates are moving apart and mantle material is rising to fill the gap and form new oceanic crust.

migration A number of animals moving from one region to another, to breed or to find food during winter or summer.

mineral A naturally occurring substance with a characteristic chemical composition and crystal structure. Rocks are made from minerals.

monsoon A seasonal wind that produces heavy rain in tropical and subtropical zones, especially southeast Asia.

ocean One of five great bodies of seawater: the Pacific, Atlantic, Indian, Arctic and Southern. Together, oceans cover 71 per cent of Earth's surface.

ore A mineral or rock from which it is possible to extract other useful materials such as metal.

ozone A form of oxygen in which the molecule consists of three atoms (O_3) rather than the usual two (O_2).

ozone layer A region of the stratosphere 20–32 km (12–20 miles) above sea level where there is more ozone than anywhere else.

Pangaea The former supercontinent that contained all the present continents. It began to break up about 200 million years ago into Gondwana and Laurasia.

period A standard division of time in Earth's history that is shorter than an era.

photosynthesis The process by which plants produce their own nutrients, in the form of sugars, using daylight, water and carbon dioxide. Plants give off oxygen during photosynthesis.

plate tectonics The theory that Earth's crust consists of a number of rigid sections, called plates. These float on top of the mantle and move in relation to each other.

polar regions The areas around the North and South poles.

precipitation Water that falls from the sky, including fog, mist, drizzle, rain, hail, frost and snow.

pyroclastic flow A mass of ash, rock and gas that flows downhill from an erupting volcano.

rain forest A type of forest that develops in regions with high rainfall or frequent fog throughout the year.

Richter scale An open-ended scale that rates the magnitude of an earthquake based on the amount of energy released. Each number on the scale represents an increase 10 times greater than the number below it.

rift A break between two rocks that were formerly joined. Two or more parallel breaks may allow the section between them to sink, forming a rift valley.

Ring of Fire The region of high volcanic activity that surrounds the Pacific Ocean.

scarp (escarpment) A cliff or steep slope next to level or gently sloping ground.

sedimentary rock Rock formed by extreme compression from pieces of other rocks, often with plant and animal remains included.

seismic waves Energy waves transmitted through Earth that travel away from a seismic source, such as an earthquake.

sheen The reflection of light from structures within a mineral.

soil A mixture of mineral particles and decomposed organic material.

stratosphere The layer of the atmosphere that lies above the troposphere and below the mesosphere. The ozone layer is located in the stratosphere.

streak The mark of powdered mineral left when it is rubbed against unglazed white porcelain (a streak plate).

subduction The sinking of one tectonic plate beneath another. Usually oceanic plates sink below continental.

swamp An area covered by shallow water throughout the year, with plants or trees emerging above the water's surface.

tectonic plates The lithospheric plates that form the Earth's crust. There are two kinds of plates – continental and oceanic plates.

temperate Regions which are neither very hot nor very cold. Temperate areas have four distinct seasons.

Tethys Sea The sea that once separated the supercontinents of Laurasia and Gondwana.

tide The regular rise and fall of the sea due to the gravitational attraction of the Moon and, to a lesser extent, the Sun.

tornado Rapidly rotating air that is spiralling upwards into a large storm cloud.

trade winds The winds that blow towards the equator from the northeast in the Northern Hemisphere and southeast in the Southern Hemisphere.

trench A deep depression in the ocean floor, often thousands of miles long.

tropics The zone between the Tropic of Cancer (23.5°N) and the Tropic of Capricorn (23.5°S) where there is at least one day each year when the noonday sun is directly overhead.

troposphere The lowest layer of the atmosphere. This is the layer in which we live and in which about 99 percent of Earth's weather occurs.

tsunami A Japanese word for a sea-wave that is caused by an earthquake, volcanic eruption or landslide. Tsunamis can reach significant heights in shallow water before crashing onto land.

updraft A rising air current.

vent A pipe inside a volcano through which lava and gas move from the magma chamber to erupt on the surface.

vertebrate An animal that has a backbone. Mammals, birds, reptiles, amphibians and fish, are vertebrates.

volcano A landform formed from the buildup of lava flows and ash. Volcanoes are typically cone-shaped.

wave A disturbance with a regular, repeating form that occurs in a solid, liquid or gas caused by the movement of energy.

weathering The breaking down of rocks and minerals as a result of the freezing and thawing of ice, the action of chemicals in rainwater or the force of extreme pressure and/or heat deep underground.

Index

A

a'a lava 87
abyssal plain 128, 135, 142–3
    formation 129
abyssal zone (underwater) 135
acid rain 197
acidic rainwater 110, 111, 112
Aconcagua 151
adaptation 160, 174, 178, 187, 202
Africa 153
    mountains 178
    savanna 168
aftershock 102, 103
agate 70
agriculture see farming
air currents 206, 214, 216
air pollution 192, 196
air pressure 214, 218
Alaska 154, 170
    Current 131
    earthquake (1964) 102
albatross 127, 195
alexandrite 72
algae 31, 77, 122, 134, 136, 139,
        140, 188
alligator 184
alligator lizard 162
Allosaurus 83
Alps
    European 176
    New Zealand 178
altocumulus clouds 211, 212, 213
altostratus clouds 211, 212, 213
aluminum 75
Alvin 140
Amazon Basin 151, 165
Amazon River 151
amazonite 68, 69, 71
amber 76, 79
amethyst 72, 73
ammonite 79
    pyritised 78
amphibolite 62
anaconda 163
anchovies 140
Andes 151, 176, 178
andesite 58, 59
Andromeda Galaxy 13
Angel Falls 151, 180
anglerfish 141
animals
    adaptation 160, 174, 178,
        187, 202
    Arctic 187
    climate change, effects 228
    desert 174–5
    estuary 182
    fossils see fossils
    grassland 168
    mountain 178
    temperate forest 166–7
    tropical forest 162, 164
    tundra 170–1, 186
    wetland 184–5
Annapurna mountains 154
anole lizard 163
Anomalocaris 31

Antarctic Ocean see Southern Ocean
Antarctic regions 188–9
Antarctica 126, 149, 201
    desert, as 173
    ice sheet 106, 173
    tourism 189
anteater, silky (pygmy) 163
antelope ground-squirrel 175
antelope jackrabbit 202
anthracite coal 63, 236
apatite 69
Apollo spacecraft 23
aquamarine 73
Arabian Sea 122
aragonite 70
Araucaria 37
Archaeocyathid 31
Archaeopteryx 40, 76, 80
Archean era 26
Arctic Ocean 116, 124–5, 149
Arctic regions 186–7
    ice caps, shrinking 229
    research 187
Arctic tern 187
Arctic tundra 170–1, 186
Argentine pampa 168
arid zones 202
armadillo, giant 163
Armstrong, Neil 22
Arsinoitherium 42
arthropods 30, 34
Arthur's Seat 94
asbestos 68
ash, volcanic 86, 91, 92, 96
Asia 154
    desert 173, 174
    mountains 178
asteroids 15, 18
Atacama Desert 151, 172, 202
Atlantic Ocean 53, 116, 117, 120–1
    natural resources 120–1
Atlantic puffin 144
Atlas Mountains 178
atmosphere 17, 204
    water 116, 208
atolls 88, 158–9
    formation 159
auroras 21
Australia 155
    East Australia Current 131
    deserts 172, 173
    grasslands 168
australopithecines 44
autumn 205
avalanches 108
avocets 182, 185
Azores 121
azurite 72

B

bacteria 26
Baffin Island 157
Bagmati River 180
bar-built estuary 183
barite 69

Baryonyx 82–3
basalt 58, 64, 94, 95, 128, 158
bat, lesser long-nosed 175
Bay of Bengal 122
Bay of Fundy 133
beaches 138
Beaufort scale 214
Belemnites 41
Bering Strait 124, 154
beryl 69
Big Bang 12
biodiversity 194–5
biosphere 160
biotite 56
    schist 63
birds
    Antarctic 188
    evolution 40
    wetland 185
birthstones 73
bituminous coal 236
black smokers 142–3
bluefish 182
bogs 184
Bonete 151
bonito 140
Bora Bora 159
boreal forests see coniferous forests
Boreas 166
Borneo 157
brachiopod 78
braided delta 181
brain coral 137
Brazilian tapir 163
breccia 60, 61
breezes 214–15
bright angel shale 65
bromeliad 162, 163
bronze 74
Brünnich's guillemots 125
bubble coral 137
bushmaster snake 163
butterfly, zebra 163
butterflyfish 140
Bwindi Impenetrable Forest 164

C

cactus 173, 174–5, 202
cactus wren 175
Calapoecia 33
calcite 68, 69
calcium carbonate 70, 112
caldera 91, 94, 96
    formation 96
Californian hydrocoral 137
Cambrian period 26, 30–2, 77
    explosion 26, 30
Cameroceras 32, 33
canyons
    formation 61, 64–5, 111, 112–13
Cape Hatteras 130
capybara 163
carbon 237
carbon dioxide 226
    emissions 227

Carboniferous period 28, 36, 77
caribou 187
Carnotaurus 41
Caspian Sea 154
Çatalhüyük 192
cat's-eye chrysoberyl 72
cave art 45
cave formation 112
Cenozoic era 26
cephalopods 32
cereals 190
Ceres 14
Cerro Ojos del Salado 151
CFCs 189, 197
chalcedony hematite 70
Chang see Yangtze River
Chasmosaurus 83
chert 60, 61
Chile
    Valdivia earthquake (1960) 103
Chimborazo 151
China 154
    Tangshan earthquake (1976)
        103
chrysoprase 69
cinder cone 87, 94
cinnabar 70
circumference (Earth) 148
cirrocumulus clouds 211, 212
cirrostratus clouds 212
cirrus clouds 211, 212
cities
    air temperature 214–15
    expansion 192
    lightning strikes 222
Cladoselache 35
clay 66, 110
Clementine 23
Climacograptus 33
climate 200 see also temperature
    timeline 224–5
    zones 202–3
climate change 196–7
    Arctic regions 187
    effects 228–9
    global warming 196–7, 226–9
    ice ages 224–5
clouds 208–11 see also by name
    cloud-to-cloud lightning 222
    cloud-to-ground lightning 222
    colours 210
    formation 210, 218
    freezing 216
    naming 211
    types 211–3
clown anemonefish 123
coal 63, 232, 236–7
    anthracite 63, 236
    bituminous 236
    formation 236
    greenhouse gas emissions 226,
        227, 228
coastlines 138–9
    wind 214
cock-of-the-rock 163
coconino sandstone 65
Cocos Islands 155, 159

Coelophysis 38, 39
coke 237
cold seeps 142
colour
  clouds 210
  sky 223
columns 111, 112–13
Comet Hale Bopp 15
composite volcano 87, 96
Compsognathus 40
conglomerate 56, 60, 181
Congo River 153
coniferous forests 161, 166–7
conifers 28, 29, 166
  life cycle 167
continental drift 52–3
continental shelf 116, 133, 135, 156
continents 150–5
  Africa 153
  Asia 154
  Europe 152
  mapping 148–9
  North America 150
  Oceania 155
  South America 151
convection 210, 214
  currents 49, 50
copper 68, 74, 75
coral 32, 35, 36
  atolls 88, 158–9
  bleaching 228
  cay 159
  reefs 134, 136–7
corallum 136
cordillera 176
core
  Earth 16, 48, 49, 50
  Moon 23
Coriolis effect 207
corundum 69
crabs 123, 142, 182
craters 94, 96
  formation 22
Cretaceous period 27, 29, 40–1, 76
crinoids 32, 37, 77, 79
crocodiles 38
crops 190, 196
crown-of-thorns starfish 137
crust
  continental 51, 128
  Earth 16, 18, 48, 49, 51, 68, 69, 92, 128
  Moon 23
  oceanic 51, 128
crystals 68, 70
Ctenacanthus 35
cumulonimbus clouds 210, 211, 212, 216, 218, 219, 221
cumulus clouds 211, 212, 219
cuprite 71
currents 130–1, 138
  convection 49, 50
  deepwater 131
  surface 131
cycad fossil 76

Cyclonema bilix 33
cyclones 122 *see also* hurricanes
Cynognathus 42
Cyrtoceras 77

D
dams 217
  hydroelectric power 240–1
Danube River 152
Darling River 155
Dead Sea 154
Deccan Plateau 94
deforestation 165, 190, 195, 196
Deinonychus 82
deltas 181
desert roses 70
desertification 172, 196
deserts 17, 160, 168, 172–5, 202
  expansion 172, 196
  temperature 172, 173, 174
Desmatosuchus 38, 39
Devonian period 27, 34–5, 76
diamond 68, 69, 72, 73
Dickinsonia 77
Dimetrodon 42
Dinogorgon rubidgei 36
dinosaurs 38, 40–1, 76, 224
  reconstructing 82–3
Diplodocus 82
disasters (natural)
  earthquakes *see* earthquakes
  floods 217
  hurricanes 200, 214, 221
  mudflows 109
  storms 214, 218–19
  tornadoes 220
  volcanic eruptions 91, 109
diseases 228
Disosauriscus 76
distance
  space 14, 20
Dnieper River 152
dodo 157
doldrums 207
dolphins 120, 140
dove, white-winged 174
downdrafts 218, 219, 222
drizzle 216
drought 172, 228, 229
dry season 207
drydock icebergs 189
ducks 185
Dunkleosteus 34, 35
dwarf planets 14

E
eagle
  golden 178
  harpy 163
Earth 12, 14, 15, 16–17
  climate 205
  formation 18–19, 52–3
  inside 48–9

mapping 148–9
  orbit 204
  rotation 204
earthquakes 50, 98–9
  locations 102–3
  measuring 98
  underwater 100
East African Rift Valley 55
easterlies 207
ecosystems 160–1
  biodiversity 194–5
Ectenocrinus 33
eddies 201
eels, deep-sea 141
El Niño 229
Elasmosaurus 40, 41
Elbe River 152
electrical charge *see* lightning
electricity 226, 228
  solar power 238
elements 68
emerald 72, 73
emerald tree boa 163
emissions 196
  carbon dioxide 227
endangered species 195
  southern bluefin tuna 140
energy
  sources 232–3, 234, 236, 238
  users 232
environments 160–1
  biodiversity 194–5
  global 196–7, 224–7
epicentre 98
epiphytes 162, 163
Eris 14
erosion 17, 50, 56–7, 59, 64, 72, 94, 110–13
  deltas 181
  flooding 217
  soil 197
eruptions
  geysers 105
  volcanic 91, 109
Espelandsfoss 180
Esperanza 127
estuaries 182–3
  types 183
  wetlands 184–5
Eudimorphodon 39
Europe 152
Eusthenopteron 34, 77
evaporation 208
evaporite 61
evolution 26, 30, 32, 34, 36, 38, 40, 42, 44
extinction
  mass 26, 36, 40, 224
eye (storm) 221

F
farming 190–1
  biodiversity, effect on 194
  deserts, expansion of 172

estuaries, damaging 182
  forests, replacing 165, 190
  grasslands, replacing 168
  history 190
  wetlands, replacing 184
faults 54–5
feldspar 56, 110
ferns
  fossils 78
  prehistoric 28
  tropical 164
Ferrel, William 206
Ferrel cells 206
fertilisers 190
fires 228, 229
fish 34, 134, 144
  Antarctic 188
  Arctic 186
  estuaries 182
  sunlight zone 140–1
fisheries
  Atlantic Ocean 120
  Indian Ocean 122
fissure volcano 87
fjord 183
flint 60, 66
  tools 60, 61, 66
floods 216
  prevention 216
fluorite 68, 69, 71
food web
  ocean 144–5
footprints 45, 82–3
forests
  coniferous 161, 166–7
  destruction of 165, 190, 195, 196
  replacing 165, 190
  resource, as 233
  saving 196
  temperate 166–7
  tropical 162–5, 196
fossil fuels 232–3
  coal 63, 226, 227, 228, 232, 236–7
  formation 235
  gas 120, 122, 232
  oil 120, 121, 122, 226, 232, 234–5
  reserves 234
fossils 27, 43, 45, 76–83, 223
  formation 76–7
  reconstructing 82–3
fosterite 72
Fraser Island 155
frontal activity 210, 218
fungi 164

G
gabbro 58, 59
galena 68, 71
gales 214
Galunggung 93
Gambia 153
garnet 62, 6 8, 73

gas, resource 232, 234–5
    formation 235
    limited supply 234
gases 120, 122
    Earth, formation of 18
    solar 20
gases, greenhouse 226, 227, 228
gastropod 78
Geoffroy's spider monkey 163
geothermal regions 104
    power from 232, 240
germination 167
geysers 51, 104–5, 150
ghost nippers 182
giant armadillo 163
Giant's Causeway 95
gila monster 172
gila woodpecker 175
gingko 28, 43
    fossil 79
glacier buttercup 171
glaciers 64, 106–7, 111
    shrinking 170, 228, 229
glass 66, 69
global environment 196–7
    freezing 224–5
    warming 196–7, 226–7
Glyptodon 42
gneiss 63
    banded 56, 62
goat, mountain 178
Gobi Desert 174
gogo fish 34
gold 74, 75
Gondwana 177
Grand Canyon 61, 64–5, 150
Grand Prismatic Spring 104
granite 56, 59, 64, 65, 66, 110
granulite 63
grasshopper 178
grasslands 168–9
    subtropical 160
    temperate 161
gravity 18
    tides and 132
Great Barrier Reef 155
Great Conveyor 131
Great Wall of China 154
greenhouse effect 226
greenhouse gases 226, 227, 228
Greenland 156, 157, 187
grenadiers 141
Grewingkia 33
Guanxi 113
Gulf Stream 130, 131
Gunung Bromo 94
Gunung Semeru 54, 94
gypsum 69, 70

H

habitats see also ecosystems
    coastal 138–9, 182
    deserts 174
    destruction 165, 168, 170, 182,
        184

estuaries 182–3
    mountains 178–9
    ocean 134–5
    rivers 180
    tropical 162–3
    wetlands 184–5
Hadley, George 206
Hadley cell 206
hail 216–17, 218
halite 71
Halkieria 31
Hallucigenia 31
Hare Shetan 96
harpy eagle 163
hatchetfish 141
Hawaii
    tsunamis 103
    volcanoes 89, 90–1, 97
Hawaiian eruption 91
heat
    greenhouse effect 226
    magma 50, 56, 58, 63, 92, 128,
        142, 143, 159
    solar 14, 20, 205, 206, 208, 214
Helicoprion 36, 37
hematite 70, 74
hemispheres 117, 149
hermit shale 65
Hesperornis 41
Himalaya Mountains 51, 55, 112,
        154, 177
    formation 177
Homo erectus 81
Homo habilis 81
Homo sapiens 44, 81
Hong Kong 138
hornfels 63
horsetails 28
hot spots
    global warming 228
    volcanoes 50, 88–9
hot springs 51, 104–5
    geothermal power 104, 232,
        240
housing 192
howler monkey, red 163
Hualalai 90
Huang (Yellow) River 154
Huascarán 151
humanity 44–5
    climate change and 227, 228–9
Huntonia 34, 35
hurricanes 200, 214, 221
    Hurricane Fran (1996) 200
    Hurricane Katrina (2005) 221
    life cycle 221
Hyaeonodon 42
hydroelectric power 233, 240–1
hydrogen 20
hydrothermal vents 142, 144
hypocentre 98

I

ice 116, 189, 201
    Arctic Ocean 124

caps, shrinking 229
    climate change and 187, 228
    creatures frozen in 81
    pack 125
    regions 17, 124–5, 149, 161
    sheets 106–7, 173
    Southern Ocean 126, 189
ice ages 224–5
icebergs 189
    drydock 189
    pinnacle 189
    tabular 189
Iceland
    hot springs 105
    volcanoes 89, 92
igneous rocks 56–7, 58–9
ignimbrite 58
Iguazú Falls 180
Indian Ocean 116, 122–3
    natural resources 122
Indonesia
    volcanoes 93, 94
industrialisation 196
    greenhouse gas emissions
        227
Inostrancevia 37
insects
    Antarctic 188
    desert 174
    fossils 76, 79
    mountain 178
    tropical 162, 164
    wetland 184
interglacials 223
International Hydrographic
        Organization 126
intertidal zone 139
Inuit people 81, 125, 187
invertebrates 78–9
Io
    volcanoes on 97
iron 48, 74, 75
    steel, making 237
ironstone, banded 60
irrigation 191
islands 156–7
    continental 156
    oceanic 156
    volcanic 88, 94, 158–9
isopods, deep-sea 141
Izmit earthquake (1999) 98

J

jackrabbit
    antelope 202
    white-tailed 178
Japan
    earthquakes 99
    hot springs 105
jasper, banded 61
jawless fish 30, 32
jellyfish 140
jet streams 214
Jökulsárlón 228
Jungfrau 152

Jupiter 14, 15
Jurassic period 27, 29, 40, 76,
        81

K

K2 154
kaibab limestone 65
Kanchenjunga 154
kaolinite 68, 71
karst 112–13
Kasaï River 153
Kashima 99
Kashmir earthquake (2005) 103
Kazakhstan
    Aral Sea 229
    steppe 168
Kilauea 90–1, 92
kimberlite 58, 72
king penguins 126
kinkajou 163
Kobe earthquake 99
Kohala 90
Kommunizma 154
Krakatau 93
Kráshnohorská Cave 152
krill 186, 188
Kuiper Belt 14
kyanite 70
Kyoto Protocol (1997) 228

L

La Niña 229
La Paz 151
labradorite 68
laccolith 86, 95
Lachlan River 155
Lagoa dos Patos 151
lakes 184
    Lake Baikal 154
    Lake Superior 150
    Lake Titicaca 151
    Lake Volta 153
    swamps, formation of 184
landmasses 148
    wind from 214, 215
landscapes
    eroded 112–13
    underwater 135
    volcanic 94–5
landslides 108
lanternfish 140, 141
lapis lazuli 70
Lariosaurus 39
lava 48, 51, 57, 58, 86, 87, 90,
        96–7
    tube 87, 89
lemurs 157
Lena River 154
levees 217
    New Orleans 221
life
    Earth 26
    other planets 12

lightning 218, 222
lignite 236
limestone 61, 63, 65, 66, 159
    erosion 112
    steel, making of 237
Linne's two-toed sloth 163
lithosphere 49
Little Ice Age 224–5, 226
llamas 178
lobe-finned fish 34
Local Group 12, 13
logging 165, 196
Loire River 152
'Lucy' 44
Luna spacecraft 23

M

Mackenzie River 150
Madagascar 157
magma 50, 56, 58, 63, 92, 128,
    142, 143, 159
    chamber 86, 87, 88, 91, 96–7,
    104
magnolia 29
malachite 68, 69, 71
Maldives 158
mammals 42–5
Mammoth Caves 150
mammoths 223
mangroves 182
manta rays 141
mantle 48, 49, 88, 128
mapping Earth 148–9
marble 62, 63, 66
    blue 62
    ruby-studded 63
    white 63
Marella 31
Margherita Peak 153
Mariana Trench 17, 50, 116
marlin 140
Maroochy River estuary 182
Mars 12, 14, 15
    volcanoes 17, 97
marshes 184
Matterhorn 152, 176
Mauna Kea 90
Mauna Loa 90, 92, 97, 150
Mawsonites 79
Maxwell Montes 17
meander 131, 180
meandering delta 181
Meganeura 77
Megazastrodon 42
Mekong River 154
Melanesia 155
Menapsis armata 37
Mercalli, Giuseppe 96
Mercalli scale 96
Mercury 14, 15
mesosphere 204
Mesozoic era 26
metals 74–5
    native 75
metamorphic rocks 56–7, 62–3

metamorphism 62, 63
Meteor Crater 18
meteorologists 214
Mexico City earthquake (1985) 102
mica 56, 62, 71, 110
micaceous quartzite 62
Micronesia 155
Mid-Atlantic Ridge 55, 92, 120
mid-ocean ridges 50, 55, 128–9,
    142–3
midnight sun 186, 187
midnight zone (underwater) 135
migration
    human 45
Milky Way 12
Milwaukee Deep 120
minerals 68–71, 142
    ocean reserves 120, 122
    precious and semiprecious 72–3
mining
    coal 236–7
Mir 140
Mississippi River 150
Missouri River 150
Mohs scale of hardness 69
mola mola 141
mollusks 76, 78, 120
monsoon 207
Mont Blanc 152
Monte Rosa 152
Monument Valley 113
Moon 22
    formation 18
    landings 22
    tides and 132
moonstone 69
moraine 107
Mount Ararat 154
Mount Aso 96
Mount Balbi 155
Mount Cook 155
Mount Elbrus 152
Mount Etna 152
Mount Everest 17, 154, 177
Mount Illimani 151
Mount Kenya 153
Mount Kilimanjaro 153, 229
Mount Kosciuszko 155
Mount Logan 150
Mount Marathon 170
Mount McKinley 150
Mount Meru 153
Mount Pelée 92
Mount Pinatubo 93
Mount St Elias 150
Mount Tasman 155
Mount Toubkal 153
Mount Victoria 155
Mount Whitney 150
Mount Wilhelm 155
mountains 17, 44, 161, 176–9
    see also by name
    Africa 153, 178
    Asia 154, 178
    climate 176–9, 202
    Europe 152
    formation 50, 51, 177

North America 150, 178
Oceania 155, 178
South America 151, 178
systems 176
underwater 135, 148
volcanoes see volcanoes
winds 215
mouse opossum 162
muav limestone 65
mud
    boiling 105
    flats 182
    life in 183
mudflows 109
Murray River 155
Murrumbidgee River 155

N

Namazu 99
natural resources see resources
Neandertals 45
neap tides 133
Nemograptus 33
Neogene period 27
Neptune 14, 15
Nevado del Ruiz eruption (1985)
    109
New Guinea 155, 157
New Zealand 155
Niger River 153
Nile River 153, 181
nimbostratus clouds 211, 212
nimbus clouds 211
nodding donkey 234
Nodosaurus 41
North America 150
    desert 173
    mountains 178
    tornadoes 220
Nostoceras 78
nuclear fusion 20
nuclear power 232

O

Ob'-irtysh River 154
obsidian 58
obsidian lava 58
occupations 192
Oceania 155
    desert 172, 173
    mountains 178
oceans 32–3, 116–45, 148, 150,
    160
    basin 128
    coastlines 138–9
    currents 130–1
    food web 144–5
    habitats 134–5
    ice ages, impact of 224
    rising temperatures 187
    spreading 128–9, 228
    temperature 130–1, 134, 137,
    142, 187

tides 132–3
    waves 132–3, 138
    zones 134, 140–3
octopuses 140
oil 120, 121, 122, 232, 234–5
    formation 235
    greenhouse gas emissions 226
    limited supply 234
oil rigs 234–5
olivine 48
Olympus Mons 17, 97
opal 69, 73
Opipeuter 33
orangutan 195
Ordovician period 27, 30, 32–3,
    77
ores 70
Orinoco River 151
Orion Nebula 12
Orizaba 150
Ornithosuchus 39
orthoclase 69
Orthograptus 33
Otzi the Iceman 81
overcrowding 193
overgrazing 197
oxygen 48
ozone layer 189, 197

P

p-waves 99
Pacific Ocean 116–17
pagodas 99
pahoehoe lava 87
Palaeocycas 39
Palaeoniscum 37
Paleogene period 27, 29, 42–3,
    76
pallasite meteorite 59
pampa 161, 168
panda, giant 195
Pangea 38, 53
Pantanal 184
Paracyclotosaurus 38, 39
Paraná River 151
Parasaurolophus 41, 83
pearl 73
peat 236
pegmatite 58, 59, 71
Pele 90
Peléean eruption 91
penguins 126, 188
penumbra 21
peridot 73
permafrost 170, 186
Permian period 27, 28, 36–7, 76
petrified wood 78
phases of the Moon 22–3
Phillipsia 37
phylite 62, 63
phytoplankton 144
pigments 70
Pikaia 31
pikas 178

pinnacles 112–13
    icebergs 189
Pinnacles Desert 173
pisolitic ironstone 60
Piton de la Fournaise 123
Placerias 39
placoderms 34
planets 14–15
    distance from Sun 14, 16, 20
plants 28–9
    adaptation 160, 174, 178, 187,
        202
    climate change, effects 228
    desert 174–5
    endangered 195
    estuary 182
    fossils 78–9
    grassland 168
    mountain 178
    temperate forest 166–7
    tropical forest 162, 164
    tundra 170–1, 186
    wetland 184–5
Plinian eruption 91
Plotosaurus 40, 41
Pluto 14, 15
poaching 169
poison-arrow frog 162, 163, 178
polar bear 124, 170, 186, 187
polar cell 206
polar regions 17, 124–5, 149, 161,
        202
    Antarctic 188–9
    Arctic 170–1, 186–7
    oceans 134
    temperature 170, 186, 188
    tundra 161, 170–1, 186
    winds 207
pollen 167
pollution 194
    city 192
    reducing 196–7
    rubbish 177
    water 180, 190, 197
Polynesia 155
polyps 136–7
Popocatépetl 150
population
    Africa 153, 193
    Asia 154, 193
    Europe 152
    growth 193
    North America 150
    Oceania 155
    overcrowding 193
    South America 151
Postosuchus 38, 39
prairie 161, 168
    farming 190, 191
Precambrian period 77
precipitation 216–17
primates 42
probes *see* space probes
protected areas 197
Proterozoic era 26
Pteranodon 40, 41
pterosaurs 40

Puerto Rico Trench 120
puma 178
pumice 58
pump jack 234
purple hydrocoral 137
Purus River 151
Pyramid of the Magician 67
pyrite 69, 72, 78
pyroclastic flow 86

Q

quartz 56, 69, 70, 73, 110
quartzite 62, 63
Quetzalcoatlus 40, 41
quiver tree 174

R

rain 208–9, 216–7, 218
    acid 197
    climate change 228, 229
    deserts 172, 173, 174
    grasslands 168
    monsoon 207
    records 202–3
    temperate regions 161, 166
    tropical regions 160, 162, 164
    water cycle 208–9
rainbows 223
Ranger spacecraft 23
Ras Dashen 153
rays, deep-sea 141
recycling 192
red howler monkey 163
redwall limestone 65
reefs 32
reforestation 167
reproduction
    conifers 167
reptiles 38
requiem sharks 140
rescue teams 102
resources
    Atlantic Ocean 120–1
    coal 63, 226, 227, 228, 232,
        236–7
    forests 233
    gas 232, 234–5
    geothermal power 104, 232, 240
    hydroelectric power 233, 240–1
    Indian Ocean 122–3
    map 233
    minerals 68–73, 120, 122, 142
    oil 120, 121, 122, 226, 232,
        234–5
    sea power 233
    solar power 233, 238–9
    uranium 232
    wind power 233, 238–9
Rhine River 152
rhodochrosite 68, 70
rhyolite 58
ribbonfish 141
Richter, Charles, 99

Richter scale 98–9
rift valley 129
Ring of Fire 53, 92, 102
Rio Grande River 113, 150
river valley estuary 183
rivers 180–1
    Africa 153
    Asia 154
    Europe 152
    North America 150
    Oceania 155
    pollution 180, 190
    South America 151
    wetlands 184–5
rock hyrax 178
rock pools 139
rocks 56–7, 64–5
    using 66–7
Rocky Mountains 178
roots, shallow 162
rubbish 177
ruby 72, 73
Russia 154
rye 190

S

s-waves 99
saguaro cactus 173, 174–5
Sahara Desert 153, 172
salt
    lakes 71
    rock 71
    sea 131
San Andreas Fault 51, 55
sand erosion 111
sandbar 138, 182
sandpipers 184
sandstone 60, 61, 63, 65, 66, 181
Säo Francisco River 151
sapphire 72, 73
satellites 12
    solar power, capturing 238
    weather 200
Saturn 14, 15
savanna 160, 168, 169
schist 63, 65
    banded 62
    biotite 63
    garnet 63
Scutosaurus 37
sea breezes 214
sea lilies 32, 37, 77, 79
sea power 233
sea stacks 111, 112–13
sea urchin 79
seahorses 134
seals 127, 145, 186, 187, 188
seamounts 88, 135
seasons 204
    changing 205
    tropical regions 162
seaweed 140
sedimentary rocks 56–7, 60–1, 64
seismic waves 99
selenite 69, 70

semiarid zones 203
Sepik River 155
sequoia, giant 195
serpentine 59
Seychelles 153
shale 60, 61, 63, 65, 66, 79, 181
shallow cumulus clouds 213
sharks 34, 36
    requiem 140
shield volcano 87, 91
Shinkai 140
Ship Rock 95
Shispar Peak 108
silicone 48, 238
silky (pygmy) anteater 163
sills 86, 94, 95
siltstone 181
Silurian period 27, 34, 77
silver 75
skarn 62, 63
slate 62, 66
sleet 216
slums 192
snow 216–17
snowflakes 216
snowshoe hare 202
soft coral 137, 141
SOHO observatory 21
solar flares 21
solar power 233, 238–9
Solar System 12, 13, 14–15
Sonoran Desert 173
Sonoran whipsnake 175
South America 151
southern bluefin tuna 140
Southern Ocean 116, 126–7
Sowerbyella 33
space probes 12, 21
spacecraft 23 *see also by name*
spectrum 223
Sphaeragnostus 33
spider monkey, Geoffroy's 163
spinifex 174
Spitsbergen Island 125, 186
splash zone 139
sponges 30, 141, 144
    fossils 78, 79
spoonbills 185
spring 205
spring tides 133
squid 141
stalactites 112
stalagmites 112, 152
Steamboat Geyser 150
steel 66
    making 237
steppe 161, 168
Stethacanthus 34, 35
Stone Age 44
    tools 66
Stonehenge 67
storms 214, 218–19
    cycle 219
    global warming 228
    surge 221
stratocumulus clouds 211, 212, 213
stratosphere 17, 92, 204

stratus clouds 211, 212, 213
strawberry 29
stromatolites 27
Strombolian eruption 91
Styracosaurus 40, 41
subduction 92
submersibles 140
subtidal zone 139
subtropical regions 160, 202
Sudan 153
Suez Canal 154
sulphur 68, 70, 72, 142
summer 205
Sun 12, 14, 18, 20–1
    distance of planets from 14,
        16, 20
    formation 20
    heat and energy 14, 20, 205,
        206, 208, 214
    photosynthesis 144, 208
    solar power 233, 238–9
    weather control 204–5, 206,
        208, 214
sunlight 204–5
sunlight zone (underwater) 135, 140
sunrise 223
sunset 223
sunspots 21
supai group 65
supercontinents 38
surface waves 99
Surveyor spacecraft 23
Svartsengi power plant 240
swamps 184

T
tabular icebergs 189
Taj Mahal 67
talc 69, 71
tapeats sandstone 65
tapir, Brazilian 163
Tarawera 93
tectonic estuary 183
tectonic plates 50
    collisions 53–5, 89, 129
    movement 52–5, 88, 92, 98,
        99, 102, 117, 128–9, 177,
        183
temperate regions 202, 203
    forests 161, 166–7
    grasslands 161
    oceans 134
temperature *see also* climate
    air 216
    biodiversity and 195
    deserts 172, 173, 174
    global warming 196–7, 226–9
    ocean 130–1, 134, 137, 142,
        187
    polar regions 170, 186, 188
    records 153, 202–3
    tropical regions 162, 206
    world's highest recorded 153,
        203
temple butte limestone 65
Tentaculites 33

termites 165, 174
terraced cultivation 191
Tethys Sea 177
Thames River 180
    Little Ice Age 224–5, 226
Thar Desert 172, 173
Theia 18
therapsids 36
thermocline 133
thermosphere 204
thunderclouds 218, 220, 222
thunderstorm, formation 218–19
tidal barrage 233
tides 132–3
    estuaries 182
    neap 133
    rock pools 139
    spring 133
    tidal barriers 217
Tien Shan Mountains 178
tin 74
toco toucan 163
Tokyo 154
tools
    stone 60, 61, 66
topaz 69, 73
tornadoes 220
    formation 220
toroweap sandstone 65
Torres del Paine 54
tortoises 122
tourmaline 73
trackways 82
trade winds 207
Transantarctic Mountains 178
Trans-Siberian Railway 154
tree ferns 28
tree frog 163
tree porcupine 163
trenches 17, 50, 116, 120, 129,
    135
Triassic period 28, 38–9, 42, 76
trilobites 30, 31, 32, 34, 36, 77, 79
tripod fish 141
Triton
    volcanoes on 97
Troodon 40, 41
tropical regions 17, 160, 202, 203
    forests 162–5, 196
    oceans 134
    temperature 162, 206
troposphere 17, 92, 204
tsunamis 100–1
    Indonesian (2004) 100
tufted puffin 138
Tugela Falls 180
tumulites 78
tundra 161, 170–1, 186
turbines
    hydroelectric 240–1
    wind 238, 239
turquoise 68, 73
turtles 38, 121
Twelve Apostles 113
twilight zone (underwater) 135
twister *see* tornado
Tyrannosaurus 40, 41, 76, 81

U
Ubangi-Uele River 153
Uluru 155
umbra 21
Universe 12–13
updrafts 218, 222
Ural Mountains 152, 154
uranium 232
Uranus 14, 15
urban areas 192

V
Valdivia earthquake (1960) 103
valleys
    formation 50, 51, 55, 61, 129
    glacier-formed 107, 111
    winds 215
Vatican City 152
Vauxia 31
veld 161
Venus 14, 15
    volcanoes 97
vertebrates 34, 80–1
vesicular basalt 58
vesuvianite 69
viperfish 141
vishnu schist 65
volcanic columns 95
volcanic tuff 58
volcanoes 16, 50–1, 53, 56, 64,
    86–97, 123
    dikes 59, 86, 94, 95
    eruptions 91, 109
    extraterrestrial 17, 97
    formation 54
    hot-spot 50, 88–9
    landscapes 94–5
    locations 92–3
    plugs 59, 94
    types 87
Volga River 152
Voronya Cave 49
Vulcanian eruption 91

W
Wairakei 240
wall cloud 220
Wallace, Alfred 52
walrus 120, 187
water 16, 116
    cloud formation 210
    cycle 208–9
    erosion 17, 50, 56–7, 59, 64, 72,
        94, 110–13, 181
    hot springs 51, 104–5, 240
    hydroelectric power 233, 240–1
    irrigation 191
    oceans *see* oceans
    pollution 180, 190, 197
    storage (plants) 174
    temperature 130–1, 134, 137, 142
    vapour 18, 226

waterfalls 180
waves
    ocean 132–3, 138
    seismic 99
    tsunamis 100–1
weather 200–1
weathering 110–13
    chemical 110
    physical 110
Weddell Sea 201
Wegener, Alfred 52
westerlies 207
wet season 207
wetlands 184–5
whales 42, 121, 134, 140, 145,
    188
whirlwind *see* tornado
white-tailed jackrabbit 178
white-winged dove 174
wind 200, 201
    cycle 214–15
    hurricanes *see* hurricanes
    patterns 206–7
    power 233, 238–9
    records 202–3
    speed 214
    tornadoes 220
    turbines 238, 239
winter 205
Wiwaxia 31
worms
    estuaries 182, 183
    ocean 142
    tropical 162
wulfenite 70, 71
Würm Ice Age 223

X
Xerocrinus 33

Y
Yangtze River 154, 217
Yarlung Zangbo Canyon 113
Yellowstone National Park 104,
    150
Yenisey-Angara River 154
Yosemite Falls 180
Yukon River 150

Z
Zambezi River 153
zebra butterfly 163
zones
    climate 202–3
    ocean 134, 140–3
zooplankton 141, 144–5
zoroaster granite 65

Credits